Ben's Adventures in
WINEMAKING

The Life, Times & Wines of Ben Hardy

Julia,

Thanks for all the fruit
(not to mention the nettles).

Ben

By Ben Hardy

BEN'S ADVENTURES IN WINEMAKING

Published by The Good Life Press Ltd. 2011

Text copyright © Ben Hardy

ISBN 978-1904871903

A catalogue record for this book is available from the British Library.

Published by
The Good Life Press Ltd.
PO Box 536
Preston
PR2 9ZY

www.goodlifepress.co.uk
www.homefarmer.co.uk

CONTENTS

Dedication

For my mother, who – irritatingly – has been proved right.

PREFACE

Home made wine is addictive. Not necessarily in its taste, as these extracts will certify, but in the whole process of creating it. From deciding on the flavour, through picking the fruit, to bottling and then that first glass, each stage has its own pleasure. And it appeals to the miser in me. My cheapest bottle of wine is about thirty pence, and the most expensive is unlikely to exceed £1.50.

I started brewing wine in 1998, and began slowly with a kit bought from Boots. My first real flavour was elderberry, because I had memories of picking these small, bitter fruits with my father along York City Walls in the 1970s. If that batch of wine had been as nasty as some I have made since, then more than likely I would have given it up as a bad job. However, it was delicious, and I felt clever to have created something that both tasted good and transported me into inebriation. Since then I have not looked back, and I delight in trying new and exciting flavours. At the time of writing a batch of nettle wine is sitting in its demijohn, giving the occasional 'bloop' as it sends up another bubble of carbon dioxide.

The diary was given to me by my mother for Christmas, and I was dubious about making notes as I brewed. But I keep a travel diary, and a journal of walks, so another area of my life to record was worth a go. And, as with making the wine, writing about it is compulsive. This is not specifically (and only barely) a book about how to make the wine – for that buy one or both of the two books I commonly refer to: C. J. J. Berry's 'First Steps in Winemaking' and Brian Leverett's 'Winemaking Month by Month', or have a look at my last chapter – but it is a book about what is happening in my life as I make a flavour, or drink a bottle. Food figures heavily, as do classical music, books, *Doctor Who*, and people I know and love. Stories reveal themselves within, and not always in the correct order: the saga of my wisdom tooth starts halfway in an entry in 'Blackberry, it concludes in 'Elderberry', the beginning appears in 'Elderflower', and other references are dotted all the way through. My life, lived, is linear, but here it is akin to time travel. It is a book to be dipped in and out of, and may encourage the reader to give brewing a go too.

There are a number of names that crop up regularly, and it is right that I provide the reader with a *Dramatis Personae* of the most frequently appearing friends and family:

Family

Claire	*My wife*
Mom and Pop	*My parents*
Chris	*My older brother*
Rachael	*My younger sister*
Keith	*My younger brother*
Jaki	*Keith's wife*
Bob and Judith	*Claire's parents*
Andrew	*Claire's younger brother*
Sooz	*Claire's younger sister*
Stan and Aggie	*Our two cats*

Friends

Julia	*An allotment owner and cellist, without whom many of these wines would not have been possible*
Richard and Linda	*Former neighbours, members of Book Group, and occasional cat feeders*
Catherine	*The instigator of Book Group and also the annual Wine Party*
Gina and Gareth	*Former colleagues of mine and members of Book Group*
Madeleine	*A clarinettist*
Shirley	*A much missed oboist and anarchic old lady*
Rachel and Duncan	*A colleague of Claire's and her partner*

Blogs

http://blog.goodlifepress.co.uk/benhardy
http://bensadventuresinwinemaking.blogspot.com

BANANA

CHRISTMAS DAY 2005

Our traditional Christmas walk this year – I say 'traditional', but this is only the second year we have done it – was up and down Pen-y-Ghent. I remembered this walk as a steep climb and my memory proved correct. This was a heart-beating, leg-aching endeavour. At the top the brown, grey and green of the foreground faded into blues in the distance. A glance at the horizon would not reveal where hills stopped and the sky started. We drank sherry and ate Stilton sandwiches at the summit, and walked down in that blinding sunlight that only appears in midwinter.

Once home, with presents having been opened and the meal eaten, I consulted pages 75-76 of 'Winemaking Month by Month' for the Banana Wine recipe, which calls for 4lb of bananas (unpeeled). I cut up the bananas before boiling them, and used 3 pints of water in the pan. It was late when I mashed up the fruit, and drunkenness had struck by that point, so I left everything in the pan overnight. On Boxing Day I poured this over 2½ lb of sugar into a plastic bucket, and used cold tea rather than grape juice tannin. The recipe recommends 12 drops of tannin, but cold tea is easier. I also added a further 5 pints of (cold) water, 2½ teaspoons of citric acid, one of nutrient, and a sachet of yeast. It is an attractive grey colour, reminiscent of stagnating washing-up water. Claire is particularly excited about this flavour.

I put the liquid into its demijohn on 30th December.

When I transferred this from the first demijohn to the second (known as 'racking'), siphoning it so that the sludge at the bottom remained in the first demijohn, I had to add most of a pint of water with 5oz of sugar dissolved in it. I had a little taste. It didn't taste much of bananas; more of uninteresting white wine. Beautifully clear, though.

Quantity:	1 gallon, which provides six bottles.
Region:	Wherever the bananas came from.

Price:	£2.53 for 4lb of bananas (I think), plus £1.10 for the yeast and whatever for the sugar.
Bought at:	'Oakwood Fruit and Veg' in Roundhay.
Yeast Type:	Bordeaux.
Initial Gravity:	1.095.
End Gravity:	1.000.
Percentage:	13½ %.
Date Racked:	11th March 2006.
Date Bottled:	27th August 2006.

INITIAL TASTE:

It is still beautifully clear. It is quite nice, if ordinary, dry white wine until you get the taste of bananas. This is quite subtle, but also quite nasty. Oh well – perhaps it will improve with age. (This paragraph has been sponsored by the word 'quite'.)

THE DRINKING EXPERIENCE

FIRST BOTTLE: Christmas Day 2006. There is a powerful first taste of banana, which quickly becomes chemical and slightly unpleasant. This has not stopped me from pouring a second glass. It has been drunk as one of many aperitifs to Christmas dinner, so perhaps I am not in the best situation to give an accurate description. Andrew says "Not banana-y and dry. And a bit sour" (thanks). Sooz thinks it would go nicely with cheese (brie or mild cheddar). Claire thinks it starts unpleasantly, then gets better, but it needs a lot of gin to get there.

SECOND BOTTLE: 3rd February 2007. This was a post 'Rite of Spring' pre-curry-with-Sam drink. I took it up to 3 The Alders as evidence that not all wine I make is lovely. I think 'No further questions' would follow if presented in court. Judith and Bob said that they had had worse, which was kind. It was drinkable after the first mouthful, but the day as a whole was fantastic.

THIRD BOTTLE: 10th & 11th May 2007. Claire opened this for a 'something to look forward to on a Thursday evening whilst Ben is out playing wind quintets' drink (quite a pithy description, I think). And we finished it on Friday after seeing 'Nothing but the Truth' at the Playhouse – which I disliked but Claire enjoyed. The wine has improved a little – lots of body, less banana – but far from my best.

FOURTH BOTTLE: 25th-27th June 2007. Opened on a Monday because we wanted something to drink. It was, according to newspaper headlines, the wettest day in 50 years, and Claire walked all the way home, so there is some excuse. We ate asparagus in a home-made hollandaise sauce with the wine. The sauce curdled, but tasted fine, and the wine remains okay. I think it is improving with age, and as I write, there is at least a glass left to go with chilli con carné.

FIFTH BOTTLE: 10th November 2007 – the Wine Party. Despite this wine being one of my least favourites, it actually came joint fifth out of thirteen, with an average score of '3.2' out of '5'. At the party I asked my guests to taste the wines blind (so they did not know which flavour they were getting), and to write down any comments they felt appropriate next to the score. Comments included "a little syrupy" and "smooth". Catherine reckons it would go well with a toffee pudding. Maybe – but I am not a huge fan of dessert wines.

SIXTH BOTTLE: 19th-21st January 2008. A bottle of Christmas Tutti Fruti proved insufficient for a Saturday night, so we drank half of this while watching Cabaret on DVD. It is a brilliant, chilling film. The wine hasn't improved any – it is still vaguely nasty, with an overriding taste of 'essence of banana'. We finished it on Monday night (Sunday was spent playing for Sherburn Sinfionetta in Tadcaster) whilst watching the concluding episode of a Cybermen Doctor Who. What is it with Doctor Who? It made me cry – again.

RHUBARB

JANUARY 2006

I chopped up three pounds of rhubarb on 28th January 2006 and left it overnight, covered by 2lb 12oz of white sugar. This resulted in a fair amount of liquid coming from the rhubarb. On 29th January, about 20 hours later, I followed the process set out by C. J. J. Berry on page 151 – mixing the rhubarb pieces and leached liquid with 7½ pints of cold water, sloshing it around, and then draining the liquid into another plastic bucket with 500ml of white grape juice (yes, I know I'm mixing metric and imperial) and the yeast and nutrient. Though the recipe doesn't say so, I'm going to leave it a few days before putting it into a demijohn. I am highly dubious about the whole thing – the rhubarb pieces (which are now separate from the 'syrup') are still sweet and still taste of rhubarb. The syrup is a light pink.

I should have left the sugar on the rhubarb longer. About a week later, when getting round to throwing out the rhubarb, there was quite a lot of liquid.

Quantity:	1 gallon.
Region:	Apparently it is rhubarb from a farm in Pudsey.
Price:	£4.99 for just over 3lb of rhubarb, plus whatever I paid for the yeast, sugar and grape juice.
Bought at:	The greengrocer's on Street Lane.
Yeast Type:	Gervin Wine Yeast No. 3 (good for sparkling, dry table and dessert wines).
Initial Gravity:	1.074 (which seems rather low).
End Gravity:	0.988.
Percentage:	11%.

Date Racked: 23rd April 2006.

Date Bottled: 2nd September 2006.

INITIAL TASTE:
Of nothing. Dull in the extreme. It will need to be very chilled if I am to serve it to others. Disappointing. I will have to try the other recipe.

THE DRINKING EXPERIENCE

FIRST BOTTLE: 18th October 2006. This opened itself and shed half its contents over the hall floorboards. I think turning the heating on caused it to begin fermenting again. Anyway, it was far better than I had expected, though still not very interesting. It was a dry champagne type, with a slight hint of pink tinge. Claire detected a taste of rhubarb, but I did not.

SECOND BOTTLE: 27th January 2007, after a dire performance of the third movement of Gershwin's piano concerto at Music Club. The wine is sparkling, clear with a beautiful pink tinge. The taste is dry and it is an 'open' taste – there is none of that cloying mustiness you get with home-made wine. The accompanying 'menu' is cheesy snacks from Asda. Yum. We are sitting in bed sipping rhubarb champagne with the electric blanket on because it is COLD.

FOURTH BOTTLE: 15th April 2007. I only had a glass of this bottle, being the designated driver. We ate at Richard and Linda's tonight, so plentiful and delicious food – including some tomato-ey risotto balls, and baked Alaska. Using self-control and learning from past occasions, I came away not having eaten too much. Richard claimed he liked the wine, but he is so polite that he would not even declare the Potato as horrid.

FIFTH BOTTLE: 16th August 2007. This opened itself, but was upright at the time, so no disaster. Suitably, today was the day that Claire got her AS Level result for music; a stunning A, with 100% in her exam module and an overall score of 288/300. So a somewhat fizzy white wine with a glorious hint of pink fits the bill nicely. This is a good wine and will be made again.

SIXTH BOTTLE: 10th November 2007 at the Wine Party. Voted seventh of thirteen, with an average score of '3.14' out of '5'. I overheard someone (I forget who) describing it as "bland", which is fair enough. "Fizzy, tart and tasteless" appears on the comment sheets, as does "slightly bitter aftertaste", but the people who liked it did not comment.

(ALTERNATIVE METHOD)

MAY 2007

On 12th May 2007 Claire supervised me carefully in picking rhubarb from our patch, directing which stalks I was allowed or encouraged to pick. One stalk (and leaf) revealed a lupin, previously starved of light. We decided three stalks was safe for the future of the plant, which resulted in 7¾ oz of rhubarb. Paul at the greengrocer's on Street Lane only had 2lb of (forced) rhubarb – it is at the very end of the season – so Claire picked up a bunch of (unforced) rhubarb from the uncovered part of Leeds Market whilst renewing her bus pass, making the weight of rhubarb up to 3lb. She was on the verge of giving up locating any rhubarb. This is the wrong weekend to do Rhubarb wine.

I am following the recipe on page 72 of 'Winemaking Month by Month', except only approximately. I cut the rhubarb into random chunks, none as long as the two inches Brian Leverett directs. Also, I boiled 8 pints of water, not 6, by mistake. Oh well. This was poured into the bucket which contained the rhubarb. I am going to ignore his suggestion of leaving it in the bucket for two weeks (far too long) as well. Ha!

I put the sugar (3lb), yeast and nutrient in on Sunday morning, 13th May. It is a luminescent pink.

14th May: Oh My God – I have created a monster. It is like something from a 1950s Science Fiction B Movie. I have spent the day beating the foam back with a large wooden spoon. Help!

20th May: I put the wine into the demijohn after rearranging the front room. It is a delightful Barbie, bubblegum pink colour and has stopped fermenting quite so aggressively.

On racking, the colour is far less intense and I suspect it will lose its pink hue. It is entirely clear. The deposit was less than most wines, requiring less than half a pint of water with 2oz of sugar dissolved in it, and the slight taste I had was dull.

By bottling there was no hint of pink. It is a clear, yellow wine.

Quantity:	One gallon.
Region:	Various: 8oz from the back garden, 2lb from Pudsey, and 8oz from somewhere around here, probably.
Yeast Type:	Burgundy.
Initial Gravity:	1.100.
End Gravity:	0.990.
Percentage:	16% – though I suspect it is a little lower.
Date Racked:	4th August 2007.
Date Bottled:	2nd December 2007.

INITIAL TASTE:
The taste was Chardonnay, and neither of us could detect any rhubarb. I would not be upset to buy this at Majestic or Sainsbury's, provided I had not paid more than £3.99 for it. I prefer this one to the last, though Claire thinks the first recipe was better.

THE DRINKING EXPERIENCE

FIRST BOTTLE: 27th & 28th April 2008. As it was so close to May, I suggested we open this. But as it was the night before Claire's A' level practical, we decided not to drink the whole bottle. It was finished with glee today (together with a whole bottle of Gooseberry). The wine has gone fizzy, and tastes very much like champagne. It is dry, and I cannot pick out 'rhubarb' as a flavour, but if I were to buy a bottle of champagne, 'rhubarb' would not be amongst the flavours I would look for. It is very slightly pink, and not entirely clear. But overall I am quite pleased with it.

SECOND BOTTLE: 23rd & 24th May 2008. This bottle was chilled in preparation to celebrate my first week of being a solicitor again. But because my life has immediately become more sedentary – drive to work, sit at desk, drive home again – we went swimming on Friday night, and waited until we got home to open the bottle. It fizzed nicely, but I was so tired that one largish glass was plenty. There is still no hint of rhubarb in the taste, but it is a decent, dry white wine – and at about £1 per bottle you cannot say fairer.

THIRD BOTTLE: 21st June 2008. I am getting used to champagne. This is the third night on the trot that I have had genuine bubbly as a celebration for my degree result. But tonight we also had the rhubarb variety at Heworth Green to mark my parents' return from their round-the-world trip. Both said appreciative things about the wine, and Mom said she could taste a hint of rhubarb, though I am not convinced.

FOURTH BOTTLE: 12th September 2008. I bought a bassoon today. It has been nearly nineteen years since I bought my first bassoon, so it was not an impulse buy. The rhubarb champagne was opened to mark the occasion. We drank this to Friday night leftovers – previously stir-fried vegetables, and reheated Thai chicken curry. Then I branched out of my comfort zone and made apple crumble and custard – though the custard was very carefully supervised (at my request) by Claire.

FIFTH BOTTLE: 18th October 2008 at the Wine Party. This got an average of '3', and was another 'mid-table' wine. It had the smallest range of scores, running between '2' and '4'. Claire noticed it smelled worryingly of cheese, and Catherine detected a 'marmite' aroma. Charlotte agreed with me that it tasted like a dry champagne, and Gareth wondered why it was not red.

SIXTH BOTTLE: 26th & 27th December 2008. Well, this was a surprise. There was no hint of cheese, and it wasn't even slightly fizzy. What we had instead was a non-descript white wine, which was perfectly palatable. The first four glasses poured were crystal clear, but thereafter the murk set in. Boxing Day was spent making a pop-up Dalek, watching the Christmas Doctor Who on i-player, eating chocolate and cake, and generally indulging in idleness. So farewell Rhubarb 2007 – on the whole a 'Hit' – and nearly farewell 2008.

MARCH 2008

I bought 7lb of rhubarb on 1st March 2008 after an overnight at Emmaus. Because it is forced rhubarb, it is both very pink and rather weedy: thin, limp columns. I decided to do a double batch because the demijohns will be free by September – the main winemaking month – and the last batch using this method was good.

Chopping the rhubarb took longer than expected, particularly before I worked out I could chop several sticks at once. I broke off in the middle to do an hour's bassoon practice, and then to eat (and have the first bottle of Tea wine). I was worried that the 7lb of rhubarb would not translate into 6lb of usable vegetable/ fruit (which is it?), but it was fine – though there is less than half a pound left. I am following C. J. J. Berry's recipe, which involves covering the rhubarb with sugar and no water (at this stage).

The next part of the operation was done on Tuesday 4th March, after the first performance of 'The King and I', and took ages. I drained the resulting liquid into a large pan, keeping the rhubarb pieces in my second bucket. I then measured the liquid back into the first bucket (4¾ pints), and poured enough water over the rhubarb pieces retained in the second bucket to cover them and stirred. I then drained the liquid from this second bucket into the first bucket (but measuring it first, so I could tell how much liquid I was using), saving the rhubarb in the pan, and then repeated the exercise (so the rhubarb is now sitting in the second bucket – all very complicated!). I have made up the liquid to 18 pints so far (13¼ pints of water), added yeast, a teaspoon of pectolase, and nutrient.

I put it into the demijohns on 9th March. The rhubarb pieces I had saved carefully to one side have gone white and blue and hairy, so I have refrained from using the resultant liquid. It is all a bubblegum pink, and I could probably have added another pint of water in the initial process.

On racking, one batch was darker than the other, so I racked this into a brown demijohn in the hope it would keep its colour. I added 2¼ oz of sugar and three-eighths of a pint of water to each (the sediment was low). The first taste was bland.

Quantity: 12 bottles.

Yeast Type: Champagne.

Initial Gravity: 1.090.

End Gravity: 0.994.

Percentage: 14%.

Date Racked: 8th June 2008.

Date Bottled: 2nd November 2008.

INITIAL TASTE:

There is no difference in colour between the two batches, and both taste a little cheesy.

THE DRINKING EXPERIENCE

FIRST BOTTLE: 16th & 17th February 2009. I fancied opening a bottle after a hard day's Latin, and decided to explore the Rhubarb. From the taste I got when bottling, I was worried this would be poor. However, the taste was good – Claire thinks it was distinctly rhubarb – and the colour and clarity are wonderful. Just a hint of pink – beautiful.

SECOND BOTTLE: The Ides of March 2009. Slightly more cheesy than the last, but still drinkable. I did my first roast dinner today: lamb, roast potatoes, onion gravy, and a variety of cabbages. All were successful, and I did not get stressed doing it. Hoorah!

FOURTH BOTTLE: 25th-28th March 2009. Most of this bottle was drunk on Saturday, after the last Music Club of the season (which I avoided), and a WYSO concert in Heckmondwike, the highlight of which was 'The Young Person's Guide to the Orchestra'. The bassoons rocked. Despite not liking Britten, I came away exhilarated.

FIFTH BOTTLE: 7th & 8th May 2009. Shirley is in hospital, and Claire opened this after I came back from visiting her. It is traumatic seeing one who previously was so vibrant reduced to a feeble old lady, struggling to make her voice heard, strapped to a blood transfusion machine.

SIXTH BOTTLE: 21st & 22nd June 2009. When we opened this bottle Shirley was still alive. Once it was finished she was dead. That makes both this bottle and Shirley's death sound far more dramatic than in fact they were, but as Shirley figures prominently in this book, and in the most recent decade of my life, I need to record her passing. I shall miss her hugely.

SEVENTH BOTTLE: 29th August 2009. On reflection, this wine tastes more like proper white wine than most of my homebrew. This means that my initial thought that it was a little dull was wrong. The day has been uneventful – most excitingly we travelled to Batley to buy upholstery material for a chaise longue, but returned empty handed.

NINTH BOTTLE: 17th-21st October 2009. Of all bottles at the Wine Party, I think this made the least impression. Two people classed it as 'Good' and one as 'Poor', with the comment "Unfortunate cabbage-y taste", but no-one else had anything to say about it. My father has written that it would make a good Christmas present for "your parents", but did not specify whether he meant mine or Claire's.

TENTH BOTTLE: 20th-24th November 2009. It is blowing an absolute gale outside, but we have escaped Cumbria's deluge. They have had more rain in a week than Kent gets in six months! None of this is related to Rhubarb wine though. Claire began this on Friday whilst I was manfully finishing the nasty Rosehip. And then we drank most of the bottle on Monday while eating a delicious sausage, bean and cider casserole with baked potatoes. I am finishing it as I write, taking alternate slurps with a mug of bush tea.

TWELFTH BOTTLE: 31st January & 1st February 2010. This batch was finished over two nights. Yesterday we had just returned from a marvellous extended Taylor family get-together in Sheffield where we travelled on a Big Wheel and looked at a Mapplethorpe exhibition, as well as drinking far too much. And today our house walls were filled with cavity wall insulation (funded in part by the government), I shaved off my beard, and learnt that Great Aunt Elsa had died – the very last of her generation. We raised a glass to her and ate pork chops and onions in cider.

MARCH 2009

After much internal debate about whether to do Rhubarb or Prune and Parsnip, I opted for the former, which proved to be the more expensive by a considerable margin. Rather than go into town and buy rhubarb at 50p a pound, I bought it in from Paul at four times the price. But factoring in the bus tickets, I only spent about two quid more at Paul's greengrocery, and the day was a busy one, so I saved myself about an hour and a half. But it still goes against the grain to spend quite so much on homebrew. It had better be good.

I spent an hour or so on Saturday afternoon, 14th March 2009, washing and chopping the rhubarb while listening to a Radio 4 play from one of Patricia Highsmith's Ripley novels. I chopped the rhubarb very thinly, and stirred three pounds of sugar over it. It is currently sitting in the bucket, leaching its liquid, ready for the next stage on Monday.

I drained the rhubarb in exactly the same way as last time, which felt like that logic problem where you have a boat, a fox, a chicken, and a sack of grain. There were 2¼ pints of liquid from the rhubarb overall, and I swirled the drained pieces in another 6¾ pints of water. Then on Tuesday I drained a further one-eighth of a pint (maybe more) from the rhubarb and added that to the mix in the big bucket. The yeast, pectolase and nutrient were put in on Monday. I put it all into a dark demijohn on 20th March, in the undoubtedly vain hope that this will preserve its Barbie-pink colour. I have filled the demijohn to the top of the neck and so far (Saturday afternoon) there have been no explosions.

By racking, the wine was perfectly clear and, I'm delighted to report, definitely pink. Pale pink, but pink nonetheless. A darkened demijohn is definitely the way forward. I have wrapped the new demijohn in silver foil. The sediment was minimal, and I added three-eighths of a pint of water with 2oz of sugar. The small taste was bland and dry, which at this stage is a good thing.

Quantity: One gallon.

Region: The Rhubarb Triangle.

Price: Too much! £7.50 for the rhubarb, £1-ish

for the sugar, £1.20 for the yeast.

Bought at: Oakwood Fruit & Veg on Street Lane.

Yeast Type: Sauternes.

Date Racked: 13th June 2009.

Date Bottled: 3rd October 2009.

INITIAL TASTE:

By bottling the taste has improved, and I think it is similar to a commercial white wine. Claire detects rhubarb, though I do not. The colour is a glorious light pink – better than any Rhubarb so far.

THE DRINKING EXPERIENCE

FIRST BOTTLE: 4th March 2010. Julia rang at about 6.30, wondering what we were doing tonight. I told her that I'd put a bottle of Rhubarb in the fridge, and she was welcome to come share it and our meal of stir-fried vegetables in black-bean sauce. I had to stay in, though, to make the house less disgusting in preparation for tomorrow's Book Group meeting ('Lady in the Lake' by Raymond Chandler – excellent). I was a little worried that Julia had been fired, or something equally awful. Instead she arrived clutching an offer letter for a grant of vast sums of money over three years for Pyramid of Arts, so we cracked open the Rhubarb, and added strips of steak which Julia has also brought to the stir-fry. The wine is beautiful – it has a metallic pink edge to its colour, and the clarity is faultless. Its taste is perfectly acceptable, with not even the slightest hint of Swiss cheese.

SECOND BOTTLE: 7th-11th April 2010. The first unchilled glass from this bottle was remarkably and unpleasantly cheesy, which was annoying. However, keeping it in the fridge and allowing it to oxidise a little meant that for the following nights it had lost its hint of Jarlsberg. I have no idea why this worked, but it is worth trying in the future. The last third of the bottle was shared between Claire, Mom and me after a lovely warm spring day, when I spent some of the morning shovelling horse manure into plastic bags, and much of the rest of the day in the garden digging up shrubbery roots. The wine felt earned.

THIRD BOTTLE: 17th-19th June 2010. I was at a Black Tie Dinner on Thursday with work, celebrating Business in the Community. Correctly guessing that Claire might fancy a glass of wine, I bunged this in the fridge on Thursday morning. The Black Tie do was alright – its highlight was the ferret racing, and I quite enjoy getting dressed up. Claire was out on Friday playing in Aïda, so I had a couple of glasses while watching 'Mrs Henderson Presents', a diverting film about wartime Nude Reviews. And I finished the bottle tonight, after a WYSO concert of 'Organ and Orchestra' music, which went better than it should. I put it down to my lucky musical socks. The best thing was that afterwards, the Principal of Leeds College of Music came to tell me that I had a lovely tone. I glowed. And the wine was entirely acceptable.

FOURTH BOTTLE: 19th-24th August 2010. I think Claire hoped I would choose to open something nicer whilst she was out string quartetting, but I noticed we had not had a bottle of Rhubarb for a while. Thursday's glasses were to celebrate handing in my Project on 'Ithamar of Rochester'. At the same time as submitting this, I also gave in my university keys, except I didn't. I returned my house keys by mistake, which I only discovered when I got home. This was irritating. I walked back, collected the house key, returned the correct key, and hobbled the three mile journey back again. I drank most of the wine as part of a cheese festival. That involved Claire eating Smoked Applewood, drinking this, and watching Midsomer Murders, which is as cheesy as it gets. I drank a couple of glasses whilst watching Blade Runner, a film I have not seen before. I was expecting to be more gripped than I was. Perhaps it needed a larger screen.

FIFTH BOTTLE: 15th-20th October 2010. I came home from a busy week at work wanting substantial amounts of wine. The following day was to be the Wine Party, so I chose Rhubarb as a flavour that would not appear – except it did, briefly. I have vague memories of pouring Duncan and someone else (possibly my father) a glass, declaring that they would find it cheesy, but I can't remember their reactions, which suggests there was no projectile vomiting. On the Friday I opened this bottle I mopped the floor for the second time in four days (which is unheard of).

SIXTH BOTTLE: 13th March 2011. Rhubarb has figured prominently today. Maybe that is over-egging it a little. Claire has split her grandmother's rhubarb plant and transplanted three sections into different parts of the garden, and we have drunk a bottle of Rhubarb wine. Other than that, thinking about it, rhubarb has barely figured at all. It has been a day involving a fair amount (ie. some) gardening, though. This morning we went to our local stables and shovelled horse manure into plastic bags in the rain. It was more fun than that suggests. Then I spent much of the rest of the morning digging. I forget that I quite enjoy gardening. It always looks like so much effort, but then when I am out there doing it, I realise that I am having a good time.

POTATO

MARCH 2006

I started this on 4th March 2006, and pretty much followed the recipe on page 44 of 'Winemaking Month by Month'. This requires 4lb of potatoes and 1lb of minced raisins to be covered by 4 pints of boiling water as the first step. Next you are to dissolve 2½ lb of white sugar and ½ lb of demerara sugar in water, but I reduced the (white) sugar by 8oz and added an extra three quarters of a pint of water. I did not dissolve the majority of the sugar in boiling water and now wonder if I should have. This all went into the bucket with the juice of two oranges and one lemon.

Peeling several pounds of potatoes is dull, but was aided by the inaugural meeting of Claire's quartet. I chopped the potatoes to about the size I would if making tortillas. The potatoes weighed 4lb after peeling. I used 1lb of sultanas rather than raisins, as the Co-op had run out of the latter.

When racking, oh dear – the little taste I got was awful. The amount of sediment left over was huge and clumpy, needing an extra pint and a half of water, plus 7½ oz of sugar. And the wine isn't particularly clear. I fear dire things (but it is fermenting after racking – as at 29th May).

Quantity:	6 bottles.
Region:	Not sure – the potatoes are 'Estima' variety.
Price:	99p for the potatoes, 40p for oranges, 18p for the lemon, £1.10 for the yeast, £1-ish for the sugar, and 99p for the sultanas.
Bought at:	The Greengrocers on Street Lane.
Yeast Type:	'High Alcohol and Country Wines' yeast.
Initial Gravity:	1.096.
End Gravity:	0.992.

Percentage: 13½ %.

Date Racked: 10th May 2006.

Date Bottled: 22nd September 2006.

INITIAL TASTE:
Reminiscent of potatoes (and all that implies). A little musty. Drinkable, without being particularly nice.

THE DRINKING EXPERIENCE

FIRST BOTTLE: 3rd March 2007 at Heworth Green. On the plus side, this wine has a nice colour, is beautifully clear, has a hint of fizziness, and a distinctive taste. On the minus side I think this is the most disgusting wine I have ever made or supped. It is bitter and tastes of raw potatoes. The most anyone managed, before grabbing gratefully for a bottle of red, was one glass. I have no idea what will become of bottles two to six. Christmas presents?

SECOND BOTTLE: 11th March 2007. Opened for the benefit of Catherine as a joke. We were to pretend it was excellent, and then laugh as Catherine spat it out. Bizarrely, though, this bottle was far more palatable than the last, without actually being nice. The remaining half bottle has yet to be poured down the sink.

THIRD BOTTLE: 21st April 2007. Our DNA spiral twist shelf thing arrived today at great expense, so we felt that a bottle of something cheap was in order. It is beautiful, though – the furniture, not the wine, which Claire described as "bearable if camping". (Better than the first bottle, then.) We have drunk it to courses of melon and Parma ham, asparagus and lemon butter, and a filo pastry parcel stuffed with brie, fried onions, and courgettes – delicious (the food, not the wine).

FOURTH BOTTLE: 10th November 2007 at the Wine Party. The clear loser. Claire was in the kitchen and witnessed person after person (including me) pour this down the sink. Angie took one sniff and refused to drink it. It scored '1.27' out of '5', with one '-3', and five '1's. Amazingly, someone gave it a '3'! This garnered the best comment of the evening: "A waste of potato".

FIFTH BOTTLE: 16th March 2008. Less nasty than expected. This morning Claire declared she would be cooking a hot Thai chicken curry, and we needed an indelicate white to go with it. I put a bottle of Potato and a bottle of Tea wine in the fridge, as my two most 'pungent' (read 'ghastly') whites. The Tea was a back up in case the Potato was truly undrinkable. But in fact the wine is on the verge of okay, and the food was delicious.

SIXTH BOTTLE: 26th & 27th May 2008. This was another case of choosing a 'sharp' white that would not obscure the food we were eating – the mackerel, onion and olive dish described elsewhere herein. It was a Bank Holiday Monday, which I mostly spent mucking out the bedroom, and which Claire spent revising. I finished the last glass tonight while watching Bleak House – a fabulous adaptation. So it is 'Goodbye Potato' – you will not be sorely missed (or, indeed, repeated).

ORANGE

APRIL 2006

I have decided to make a double batch of Orange wine this year because the first bottle of Orange in 2005 was lovely. It tasted like real white wine, with a touch of orange and none of that musty, cloying aftertaste that homebrew often has.

I did all the peeling of 12 and squeezing of 24 oranges on 1st April 2006, and added the yeast, pectic enzyme, and nutrient on 2nd April. I followed the recipe in C. J. J. Berry's book, except I put in 6lb of sugar rather than the 7 I should have put into a double batch. Also, there was 1 pint less water used (half a pint less to cover the orange peel, half a pint less in the bucket), making 15 pints in all. I did not "avoid the pith like the plague", more like the common cold. Some went in, but I tried to minimise it.

Have you any idea how boring yet tricky peeling twelve oranges thinly is? Today, 2nd April, my right shoulder blade really hurts, and this may be down to the squeezing of 24 oranges. Oww!

When racking, which I did in an effort to keep me awake from jet-lag, I added about three eighths of a pint of water and 2¼ oz of sugar to each demijohn.

Quantity:	2 gallons.
Region:	The oranges are 'Maroc DFM'. Does this mean Morocco?
Price:	£4.75 for 24 oranges, plus £1.20 for the yeast, and £2-ish for the sugar.
Bought at:	The Greengrocers on Street Lane.
Yeast Type:	Champagne.
Initial Gravity:	1.094 (at least).
End Gravity:	0.992.
Percentage:	14%.

25

Date Racked: 7th July 2006.

Date Bottled: 4th October 2006.

INITIAL TASTE:
A medium dry white wine with a strong, orangey taste. Maybe a little intense. Probably not as good as last year's, but not bad.

THE DRINKING EXPERIENCE

FIRST BOTTLE: 6th April 2007, after a bottle of Rhubarb (and a jousting competition), drunk with stuffed aubergine slices à la Nigella. This is slightly disappointing after last year's batch. It has a somewhat bitter taste and Sooz thinks it citrusy. The colour and clarity are good. It is okay – drinkable and dry. I'm hoping it will improve as there are another eleven bottles to get through.

SECOND BOTTLE: 14th April 2007. Much better (I think) than the last bottle – not as bitter. There is a taste of orange peel, rather than oranges per se.

THIRD BOTTLE: 28th April 2007. Drunk after a heavy day's trampolining with Zoe and Owen. We had this to Chinese food, expertly cooked by Amie: steamed fish with spring onion and ginger, and a dish of chicken and oyster mushrooms. David said all the right things about the wine, which was satisfying.

SEVENTH BOTTLE: 17th & 18th October 2007. Opened after a business trip to London by Claire (her business plan needed re-drafting), and finished after an act of mutiny, where she told her boss she didn't need to listen to his ranting.

EIGHTH BOTTLE: 31st October & 1st November 2007. This bottle was labelled 'Very Dreggy'. It was opened and mostly drunk by Claire as she is having a poor time at work at the moment. I had a glass and a bit on Thursday, after going to an Opera North concert in the Town Hall. I fell asleep during the Mozart, but only through tiredness.

NINTH BOTTLE: 10th November 2007 at the Wine Party. Voted eighth out of thirteen, with an average score of '3'. I thought it would come higher. How can Banana come three places above?

Somebody described it as "Feisty", and two people as "Strong". The most damning was "Very sour".

TENTH BOTTLE: 21st December 2007. Taken to Richard and Linda's. I wasn't in the mood for a dinner party, not even a very informal one, as I had only just finished my first draft of a difficult (and badly written) essay. Anyway, the meal was lovely, the company entertaining, and I relaxed into the evening. One glass of Orange wine helped – and I will make this flavour again!

ELEVENTH BOTTLE: 31st January & 1st February 2008. Disaster! Shirley has broken her shoulder and will be unable to play the oboe for six months. For the moment my Thursday evenings are empty. To commiserate, I opened a bottle of Orange, and drank much of it whilst watching Torchwood on BBC i-player. We finished what little was left before Book Group ('Suite Française' by Irene Nemerovsky).

FEBRUARY 2008

It was a toss up between Citrus and Orange this month, but as I did Citrus last year, I decided on Orange. I bought the oranges from the uncovered bit of Leeds Market on 2nd February 2008. I went for the cheapest I could find, but now wonder if that was an error, as the resulting oranges were all somewhat small. The lady serving looked surprised that all I wanted was twenty four oranges, so I explained. Her surprise did not particularly diminish.

I did all the peeling and squeezing on 3rd February. My 'thin peeling' technique has improved; twelve oranges did not seem too bad, and Beryl Bainbridge on Desert Island Discs helped pass the time. I cut my finger though, and Claire had to administer first aid. Remembering my sore shoulder from two years ago, I tried to use the 'juicer' attachment on the food processor for squeezing oranges. On the fourth orange I 'juiced' my finger, and Claire had to put on another plaster. I reverted to the manual method, alternating hands in the hope that my shoulder would be okay.

I have covered the peel with 3½ pints of boiling water, and dissolved 6lb of sugar in 10½ pints of cold water. The yeast and two teaspoons each of nutrient and pectolase all went in on 3rd February. I put it all into two demijohns on 8th February. The amount of water used was damn near perfect.

On racking, the wine had cleared beautifully, and is a pale yellow. There was less than a finger's sediment. The taste I got was a little sweet, and I wonder if the yeast type contributes to this, so I did not add any sugar when topping up. One batch got five eighths of a pint of water, and the other got three quarters.

I bottled this after a heavy day's blackberry picking. This wine is clear and flat, so safe to store on its side.

Quantity:	12 bottles.
Region:	Egypt (via Leeds Market).
Price:	£2.40 for the oranges, £1.20 for yeast and £2-ish for the sugar.
Bought at:	Leeds Market.
Yeast Type:	Hock.
Date Racked:	3rd May 2008.
Date Bottled:	25th August 2008.

INITIAL TASTE:
It is a little sweet, but will make a good dessert wine. It is unmistakably orange, though far from overpowering. A qualified 'Hit'.

THE DRINKING EXPERIENCE

FIRST BOTTLE: 15th November 2008. I was persuaded to open this two and a half months early. Claire fancied a white, but none of those that are currently 'on the go', to accompany pizza. But when she got home from shopping, plans had changed – we were going to have crab stir fry, as there was a fish van outside the greengrocer's. Except it all changed again once Claire had cooked the crab – it smelled funny and she did not want a repeat of her Chinese food poisoning experience, so we just had a vegetable stir fry, and the crab ended up in the bin. The wine was delightful – clear and slightly sweet, but with a burnt bitterness that set off the sweetness in a thoroughly good way.

THIRD BOTTLE: 14th February 2009. We had a rare night in on Valentine's Day. After having tidied the front room (a monumental task), we drank this to pizza and watched 'Monty Python and the Holy Grail', which was not as good as I remembered. The wine and pizza were lovely, though.

FIFTH BOTTLE: 12th-14th March 2009. I was out at Quintet on Thursday, and Book Group on Friday. Claire was at a rehearsal for her Sunday concert on Friday, but got in earlier than me, and needed a medicinal glass. I finally got a glass on Saturday night, after a tedious Proms concert in Selby Abbey for Sherburn Sinfionetta. Playing with them feels like doing penance.

SIXTH BOTTLE: 17th & 18th April 2009. This started life as a Friday night bottle, but, perhaps uniquely, we only drank about half. It was finished at the bassoon quartet dinner party, where Claire did a wonderful banquet of vegetarian dishes: tzatziki, stuffed mushrooms, tortilla, the aubergine and tomato dish, asparagus, a cheese course, and banana splits with chocolate ice cream, toffee sauce, whipped cream and cashews.

SEVENTH BOTTLE: 14th-17th May 2009. I opened this after visiting Shirley in hospital. Earlier I had received an e-mail from Francine saying Shirley had a chest infection and was not expected to survive. I started down the path of grief, but then had another from Claire saying Shirley was much better. At hospital she gave me a huge smile, struggled to raise herself up, and said inaudible words. It looks like she may yet live.

EIGHTH BOTTLE: 28th June 2009. We drank this as our second bottle of the evening, whilst on our Welsh holiday with Bob and Judith. The wine was rather good, but not as wonderful as the Blackberry drunk before it. Though a heatwave is predicted for the coming week (in Wales? I have my doubts), it is currently raining. That's more like it.

NINTH BOTTLE: 19th-21st July 2009. The very best quality of Orange wine is its clarity. Even this 'dregs' bottle (it was the last out of its demijohn) has a shine to it down to the last glass. Usually when I am praising the colour or clarity it is because the taste is somewhere between nondescript and nasty. However, this one tastes good too. We opened it on Sunday and drank over half the bottle to a beef lasagne and salad. As I had a heavy night partying on Saturday, not finishing the wine seemed like a sensible idea. Between us we have finished it over the next two days, and tonight we are both slightly anxious that we have pre-Rydal Swine Flu.

TENTH BOTTLE: 5th September 2009. I got up on Saturday morning to find Claire cleaning behind the fridge, which was unusual. Her fridge-related activities then progressed to defrosting the freezer, thus making room for all my excess fruit. She discovered ancient prawns and pancakes, so our meal involved both ingredients, a wonderful tomato based sauce, with white sauce (parsley infused), and a parmesan covering. Claire chose Orange wine to go with it, and after the meal we polished off the blackcurrant ice-cream.

ELEVENTH BOTTLE: 17th-20th October 2009 at the Wine Party. I cannot understand why Orange is so unpopular. This was the clear loser of the evening, with three out of four of its votes in the 'Worst' category. Comments were "Musty smell, horrible (sorry)", "Different" and "Perfect for stripping engines". Two people wrote that they liked it, and I agree with them, so I will continue to make this wine and ignore the (Un)Popular Vote.

APRIL 2009

I bought the oranges on 6th April 2009, but have only got round to making the first stages of the wine today, 10th April (which is also Good Friday). I had a choice of buying seven oranges for a pound, or eight for a pound. I could not see any obvious difference, so (naturally) went for the cheaper option. These are seedless, and larger than last year's oranges.

Today has been spent gardening (sorting through soil in preparation for our raised vegetable bed, and planting lettuce and beetroot seeds in pots), playing on the computer (I must delete 'Spades'), running through some Latin verbs, and winemaking. It has been a good Friday in every sense.

The thin peeling of twelve oranges was as dull as ever, but I had the Classic FM countdown to listen to and feel sniffy about. There is a considerable amount of pith in the orange peelings, but I doubt it will make much difference. I followed last year's quantities precisely, and also swapped hands between oranges. I'm hoping that I will not be stiff or sore tomorrow.

Hurrah! I'm not. I added the yeast, pectolase and nutrient on the morning of 11th April, and then in the evening I strained in the water covering the peel. It has all gone into its two demijohns, and two bottles for topping-up purposes on 15th April. There is more liquid this year than last – probably at least a pint and a half too much. I think it is because the oranges were larger.

On racking, the wine is clear without much sediment, and the sediment which exists is a sun-kissed yellow. The tiny taste I got was too dry, so I divided a pint of water with 6oz of sugar dissolved between the two.

Quantity:	2 gallons.
Yeast Type:	'High Alcohol and Country Wines'.
Date Racked:	Midsummer's Day 2009.
Date Bottled:	11th October 2009, after a fantastic chamber music concert in Rawdon.

INITIAL TASTE:
I bottled this a few days earlier than I had wanted, but I had an unplanned wine to make – Grape and Raisin – and I wanted to be efficient with my sodium metabisulphite. The taste was rather good, with one batch, the one that got slightly more of the syrup mix on racking, being a little rougher, yet more orangey than the other.

THE DRINKING EXPERIENCE

FIRST BOTTLE: 30th December 2009 and 3rd January 2010. The bottle that spanned a decade. Our original intention was to have a chicken chilli, but while preparing the chicken we had bought the day before, Claire thought it smelled odd, and there were a couple of discoloured patches. On the basis that it is better to be safe than violently ill on New Year's Eve, the plans changed to me cooking a lentil curry. The wine was lovely, but neither of us wanted to finish it – so we shared the last glass on our return from Newcastle.

SECOND BOTTLE: 12th & 13th February 2010. My first glass from this bottle was sitting on the bed, catching up with Claire. I have been a neglectful husband this week: Monday to Thursday spent playing in Oliver! and Friday night at the Haydn Orchestra. So I had a lovely hour just chatting over the week with my wife, drinking a glass of Orange wine.

THIRD BOTTLE: 12th-15th March 2010. I have decided I prefer Orange wine to Citrus – it is less astringent, and I was able to have a direct comparison on Friday night, when one glass of Citrus was not enough. My Saturday glass was a treat after playing Schumann's Rhennish Symphony (tedious with not enough bars' rest) in Skipton with the Settle Orchestra, which is not a bad outfit. We finished the bottle tonight on the day that our hallway has been transformed from bare floorboards (that we lived with for years) to laminate flooring. It looks excellent, but the house is in chaos.

FOURTH BOTTLE: 30th March-1st April 2010. Orange wine and chocolate fingers are not the world's greatest combination. My first glass of this was drunk in bed, munching on the chocolate fingers whilst reading 'A Canticle for Liebowitz' – a science fiction novel from the 1950s which is surprisingly scholarly about medieval history. This makes it sound desperately dull – but it really isn't. And our last glass was finished watching 'Glengarry Glen Ross' on DVD. Superbly acted, particularly by Jack Lemmon and Jonathan Pryce. Cold, and a damning comment on human behaviour under desperate circumstances.

FIFTH BOTTLE: 15th & 16th April 2010. Fried onions, mushrooms, egg and chips with Orange wine is a surprisingly good combination. I came home late from an Emmaus finance meeting, which was all very positive, and was pleased that Claire suggested starting a bottle. So we drank more of it than ideal for a work night with our fry-up, and had the remaining half glass each tonight, as a pre-leftovers aperitif.

SIXTH BOTTLE: 15th & 16th June 2010. We stayed up way past our bedtime finishing this bottle. Nichola, a fellow student from my history undergraduate days – and one of the few who was prepared to have an opinion in seminars – has an interview for Assistant Curator at the Thackray Medical Museum, and needed a bed for the night. This bottle was already open, so we force-fed her a glass and discussed nightmare housemates.

SEVENTH BOTTLE: 7th & 8th July 2010. Today has been an eventful day. I have finished the first draft of my 6,000 word project on St Ithamar and the monks of Rochester (though it needs much work). More excitingly, I used the services of a contract killer. Very efficient he was too – in and out in about ten minutes. And he only charged £50. The wasps' nest below our patio doors should now be wasp free.

NINTH BOTTLE: 20th October 2010. I gave this to my mother. This is what she wrote: Once a month this year I have hosted a poetry-reading gathering celebrating a different colour each time, and tonight it was the turn of orange. Since all food and drink also had to be orange, a bottle of Orange wine by Ben seemed the perfect beverage. We were privileged as he says he practically never gives away a whole bottle. Happily few guests take alcohol, so Simon and I got to drink most of it. I normally don't like white wine, but orangish white wine – lovely!

TENTH BOTTLE: 8th-10th November 2010. Every glass from this bottle served as a nightcap, but what I really want to write about has nothing to do with the wine. I discovered today that Paul is closing his greengrocer's on Christmas Eve. No-one is buying fruit and veg from independent small shops any more. It makes me both cross and sad. I have loved our Saturday morning shopping, chatting to Paul, Glynis and Laura. And now it will be no more. I could weep.

ELEVENTH BOTTLE: 16th-18th January 2011. This bottle was finished after a day of trying on Uncle Gerry's three-piece 1960s suit and taking it to the dry-cleaners. He was a tall, dapper man (there was a comb and hankie in one of the pockets), and I am surprised it fits. The trousers reach my nipples, though.

TWELFTH BOTTLE: 19th-22nd February 2011. I was in the mood for celebrating on Saturday night when we opened this. Madeleine, David, and I had just played Glinka's Trio Pathetique at Music Club, and despite a shaky start we went on to play it brilliantly. Thunderous applause. As always, I only enjoyed it in retrospect. During playing I was concentrating too hard to feel any emotion – unless one counts 'anxiety'. Tonight I shared the remnants of the bottle with Mick Dalton who fitted our new doors last year. On my way out to a committee meeting I couldn't lock the door. I left a pathetic message on his business line and he came round after 8pm and fixed it. What a hero! Said nice things about the wine, too.

BARLEY

MAY 2006

On 29th May, after a bitterly cold, windy and wet visit to Sandal Castle, with the ensuing walk cancelled, and a loss at Pub Cricket to Claire, I started the Barley wine. The recipe is from C. J. J. Berry. I have used 1lb of raisins rather than grape concentrate, and 1lb of pearl barley flakes rather than straight forward barley. Also, I have used 2¾ lb of sugar rather than 3lb. Other than that I have followed the recipe so far (soaking the barley overnight, mincing the raisins and barley, putting the sugar, barley, raisins and water in the bucket), except the barley did not do much in the food processor. I added two teaspoons of citric acid, one of amylase, one of nutrient, and the yeast the following morning.

I put it into the demijohn on 5th June, two days earlier than the recipe dictates. Its appearance is beige with a heavy deposit. I also had to put in quite a lot of water – more than a pint.

On racking, there was a very thick deposit. I had to put in an extra 2 pints of water – one with 6oz of sugar dissolved in it. Also, I added another teaspoon of amylase as it has not totally cleared. I do not hold high hopes for this wine.

On bottling it has cleared nicely, and is a golden colour. It is rather fizzy, so I suspect corks will be self-popping come summer. I'm keeping it upright.

Quantity:	6 bottles' worth.
Region:	It doesn't say on the label, except 'UK'.
Price:	84p for the barley, approx £1 for the raisins and the same again for the sugar, 52p for the lemons and £1.20 for the yeast.
Bought at:	The barley was bought at Beano, the raisins from the Co-Op.
Yeast Type:	Bordeaux.

Initial Gravity: 1.118.

End Gravity: 1.000.

Percentage: Around 15%.

Date Racked: 31st July 2006.

Date Bottled: Boxing Day 2006

INITIAL TASTE:

Taste-wise, this is not too bad at all; a medium wine in dryness, with a slight taste of beer. It will need to be carefully chilled to be entirely satisfactory. Maybe it is a little sweeter than ideal. Possibly one to do again.

THE DRINKING EXPERIENCE

FIRST BOTTLE: 28th May 2007. Another cold May Bank Holiday: apparently it was the coldest Test Match day ever (7.8 degrees in Headingley). It is also the day I go back to solicitoring, which until today I was quite looking forward to. The wine is okay (only). Clear, a good yellow colour, and bubbly, but not actually all that nice. It has a taste of lager to it (that'll be the barley, then). We drank it to a moussaka baked by me, and tzatziki assembled by Claire. Is the hint of retsina pure imagination?

THIRD BOTTLE: 27th July 2007. This had a definite taste of mead, but you had to get past the first swallow, which was face-pullingly nasty. No – that is an exaggeration. Certainly, there were good tastes in there struggling against the bad. It was drunk to celebrate another week of being a solicitor, and to placate Claire for her discovery that I have a Facebook profile and didn't tell her. Ooops.

FOURTH BOTTLE: 24th-26th October 2007. Opened by Claire on a Wednesday evening. This was the 'dregs' bottle and right at the bottom was cloudy with a distinct 'beer' taste. But otherwise this was clear, and a perfectly acceptable taste. On Friday it was drunk as a prelude to bacon and cabbage (a winning combination – really!), mashed potato and fried-up onions, tomatoes and mushrooms – and a bottle of Elderberry. Also the News Quiz tribute to Alan Coren, who died a week ago.

FIFTH BOTTLE: 10th November 2007 at the Wine Party. Tenth out of thirteen, with an average of '2.2' out of '5'. Julia described it as "sledge hammer", and it was the strongest wine of the evening. It got one '1' (with a "sorry" afterwards), but also a '4' (with a "yum" afterwards). Richard wrote "taste unpleasant, bitter", but still awarded it a '2'.

SIXTH BOTTLE: 25th-27th November 2007. We started Sunday drinking with a gin and tonic, so did not fancy a whole bottle. The meal was turkey Thai curry, and possibly one of the nicest things Claire has done with turkey leftovers. Pity about the wine, really. Actually – it is not that awful, and is reminiscent of an extremely strong lager (Carlsberg Special Brew, anyone?). I think after having the six bottles of Barley I probably won't do it again, but it was an interesting experiment.

STRAWBERRY

JULY 2006

The strawberries were picked, washed, and mashed on 8th July. They seemed to be smaller than usual this year. Possibly this was because of the extremely wet May we had. Normally I pick strawberries in hot sunlight and need sun cream and a hat. Today it has been cloudy and chilly for July.

I ended up with over 6lb of fruit, so Claire will experiment with the remaining 2lb. I have followed the recipe in C. J. J. Berry, on page 175, which calls for the mashed fruit to be covered by 4 pints of boiling water, though I also added a handful (small) of our wild strawberries from the garden, and I might have put in 4½ lb of strawberries by mistake.

On 9th July I strained the liquid into a demijohn, keeping the pulp. I then added 2 pints of water to the pulp, stirred thoroughly, and strained again. This filled the demijohn to the neck, so no need to add any more water. I then tipped this all back into the (freshly sterilised) bucket, and added the yeast, nutrient, acid and tannin, rather than fitting an airlock to the demijohn at this stage.

I put it into the demijohn on 14th July, and it didn't explode.

Quantity:	One gallon.
Region:	The 'Pick your Own' farm on Harrogate Road, nearer Harrogate than Leeds.
Price:	£4 for strawberries, £1.20 for the yeast and £1-ish for the sugar.
Yeast Type:	Burgundy.
Initial Gravity:	1.076-ish (though I suspect natural fermentation before I measured it).
End Gravity:	1.000.
Percentage:	10½ %.

Date Racked: 22nd September 2006.

Date Bottled: 23rd January 2007.

INITIAL TASTE:
A little thin really – not very interesting. Bah. [How wrong I was!]

THE DRINKING EXPERIENCE

FIRST BOTTLE: 2nd July 2007. One lump or two? This is the only wine for which I have ever had to use a tea strainer. It is also the only wine I have come across which has made the person pouring it shriek with surprise. It contains a jelly like substance, which (using the strainer) you can eat with a spoon. In fact the taste is good: full of strawberry and a pleasant dryness. Past Strawberries have been a little thin. Thinness is not a quality of which you can accuse this wine. Fatness may be more to the point.

SECOND BOTTLE: 16th September 2007. It wasn't just the first bottle which contained lumps. It is a pity the wine is less (more?) than liquid – the flavour is really good, but the jellified globs are so off-putting. Claire has shaken the bottle, which has had some benefit.

THIRD BOTTLE: 10th November 2007. The winner at our Wine Party, with '3.795' out of '5'. And this is even with the lumps! (However, I don't remember seeing as many lumps as the previous two bottles.) Despite winning it was only awarded one '5'. Julia guessed that this was Pear! Somebody commented that it would be nice on the patio.

FOURTH BOTTLE: 26th December 2007. I think this bottle had all the lumps which were missing from the last. Andrew found it difficult to pour: the globules kept on sticking in the bottle's neck. I distributed the mini-whisks and we were away. Apart from the lumps, this is a particularly good strawberry vintage – colour, taste and clarity are all wonderful. I spent the entire day making a model of the Tardis's interior which was in turns difficult, dull, silly, infuriating and, ultimately, a perfect way to spend Boxing Day.

FIFTH BOTTLE: 25 & 26th March 2008. I find the lumps not only distracting, but somewhat disgusting. Beating your wine with a whisk is all very well, but it really only makes the lumps smaller, and they stick to the side of the glass. I didn't much enjoy this bottle. Even the taste seemed less good than usual. We drank it (both nights) to a 'beanlash' – like a goulash but with beans instead of ghouls – and on Thursday one glass sent me to sleep.

SIXTH BOTTLE: 19 April 2009. It has been over a year since we last had a bottle of this. Unremarkably, it is still lumpy. Today has been spent gardening, mostly, and handing over the Music Club secretaryship to Dawn. Rejoice! Claire's gardening activities have included placing an unlikely broccoli seedling in the cold frame, nearly finishing her raised bed (of which M. C. Escher would be proud), and shovelling horse shit with Julia. Taste-wise this batch has been one of my best strawberries. Texture-wise it will not be missed.

JULY 2007

I picked the strawberries on 2nd July whilst Claire was picking gooseberries. It has been exceptionally wet, but we managed to choose a sunny afternoon. Luck rather than judgment. This is the first year for an age that we are in England at this time, so the strawberries have been picked a week (at least) earlier than usual. They were bigger and riper than in past years; I tried to choose the maroon ones where possible, and to avoid those with feasting slugs. Only about ten strawberries were picked over the 4lb needed, and those have just appeared in a fruit salad of 'Fruit we should have eaten last week'.

After mashing the fruit I poured 4 pints of boiling water over it. Again I added a small handful of berries from our garden. I strained this all on 3rd July after summer orchestra, and it took ages. I had forgotten this was the boring bit of doing Strawberry. Again I followed the method set out last year, putting the pulp into our big pan before mixing it up again with two pints of water. I put it all into the demijohn on 7th July. There may be a large sediment, but I am hoping it will settle.

On racking there was a large sediment, and it was in two layers. I added a pint of water and 6oz of sugar. It is totally clear, and so far with no evidence of slimy lumps.

Still no evidence of slimy lumps on bottling. It is a glorious colour, and for this reason I have put it into clear bottles.

Quantity:	6 bottles.
Yeast Type:	'Yeast for Rosé wines'.
Date Racked:	23rd September 2007.
Date Bottled:	3rd February 2008.

INITIAL TASTE:
The taste is perhaps not as strongly strawberry-flavoured as in previous years, though I had just eaten a sharp Cox's apple before tasting this.

THE DRINKING EXPERIENCE

FIRST BOTTLE: 4th July 2008. "A mix of fruit juice and sherry" is how Roc described this wine, but in a complimentary way. Gina also declared it "lovely", so I told them they could come again. We drank this at July's Book Group here, where we were discussing Graham Greene's 'The Power and the Glory', which split the group, but it was a thoroughly enjoyable evening. The wine, again, is a winner, and distinctly less lumpy than last year's batch.

SECOND BOTTLE: 27th August 2008. We took this over for a meal at Richard and Linda's. It was the evening of the Great Unveiling. Since we got our Spiral Twist we have not been quite sure what to put on it, so we commissioned Linda to make something felty and vaguely cellular. She was nervous about our reaction, but need not have been. It is bizarre, beautiful, and slightly dangerous looking.

THIRD BOTTLE: 18th October 2008 at the Wine Party. As with last year, this was the winner of the evening, but this time by a streak. Its lowest score was a '4', and six people gave it top marks. Just to bask in the glory, the given comments were: "The best, at last worth coming for" (hmmm), "Please give me a bottle to take home", "Lovely. Perfect level of sweetness", "Summer in a glass", "Very drinkable", "Delicious! Quite sweet", "Love it better than the sparkling Strawberry wine from the shops" and "The Tops". I think they liked it. Average score – '4.67'.

FOURTH BOTTLE: 22nd November 2008. Mom chose this bottle with some guidance, and it was put in the fridge in anticipation of either celebration or commiseration after Music Club. I was playing the Hurlstone Trio in G minor for clarinet, bassoon and piano with Madeleine Watson and David Wilks. It went brilliantly, despite my anxiety before the event. Not note perfect, you understand, but it was never going to be. So celebration it was – and with three slices of apple cake to help wash down the wine. A marvellous evening.

FIFTH BOTTLE: 1st February 2009. This was our 'post Mahler and chips' bottle. We spent the day with the New Tyneside Orchestra playing Mahler's Sixth Symphony. Amy and I swapped between first and second bassoon, and though there is not a single hummable tune in the entire piece, despite it lasting well over an hour, it was a splendid day. We recovered at 3 The Alders with roast beef, Yorkshire puddings, and this bottle.

SIXTH BOTTLE: 5th July 2009. We finished this batch of Strawberry on the same day as starting brewing the batch that we shall start drinking in 2010. Marlo has been here, helping with the process, so I thought it appropriate to let her taste the finished product. Her comments are "Pungently sweet" (not sure that is a good thing) and "Assertive character" (ditto). We drank some of this in the garden, marvelling at the triffid-like courgettes, and the amazing expanding rhubarb plant.

JULY 2008

We got up on 6th July 2008 to heavy grey skies, and drizzle set in for the day. I realised I had a choice between staying warm and dry, or having Strawberry wine next year. After consultation with Claire I chose the latter. And even though I offered to go by myself, Claire came with me. I was half expecting the 'Pick Your Own' to be closed, it was such a rotten morning, but it was open and there were even some families in wellies there. The strawberries were less ripe than last year, but some made a satisfying 'pop' as I pulled them off the plant. We only needed 4lb, but between us picked almost 8lb, and this probably only took about twenty minutes. Claire has made jam with the excess, and I predict strawberries and cream for pudding.

I put this all into the demijohn on 11th July, after a fraught week at work.

On 26th September I racked it. It has cleared, and the small taste I had was good. I added most of ¾ of a pint of water, and 4oz of sugar.

Quantity: 6 bottles.

Yeast Type: Burgundy.

Date Racked: 26th September 2008.

Date Bottled: 13th January 2009.

INITIAL TASTE:
I bottled this whilst suffering from some mild flu-ish illness (a lumpy sore throat and shivering). It has its usual clarity and taste – possibly less good than last year's. It is entirely still, so hopefully no explosions.

THE DRINKING EXPERIENCE

FIRST BOTTLE: 1st July 2009. This was our eleventh anniversary bottle. I'm not entirely sure what the correct gift is for wedding anniversary number eleven, but I'm fairly certain it is not 'soft fruit'. The 2008 Strawberry is as good as in previous years. It is clear all the way down the bottle, entirely pink, and tastes of strawberries. There is no fizz, which means I should avoid having to mop it up during hot weather. We drank this on our Welsh holiday in Criccieth. It has been a glorious day full of medieval castles, swimming in the sea, and narrowly avoiding having a latté being tipped into my lap by an inept but entirely charming waitress.

SECOND BOTTLE: 22nd August 2009. This was opened just as the sun was past the yardarm. We are in York, and Chris is here too, so the bottle was shared with my wife, parents and older brother. All said nice things about the wine, which is always pleasing. Pop, Chris and I drank Strawberry wine while watching the world athletics and making vague plans to go to the 2012 Olympics together. Mom showed Chris and me her photos of her 50th High School reunion and an incredibly muddy rodeo. I learnt that Chris has a mud phobia and could not look at the screen. Chris and Pop are currently watching the Ashes highlights (which, unusually, it looks like England are about to win), whilst Mom is cooking trout in the kitchen.

THIRD BOTTLE: 17th & 18th October 2009 at the Wine Party. Gina and Gareth came to the party last night. This was the first time that both have been out together since Lily was born in August. They left her with Gina's parents, who were probably grateful for the opportunity to have a go with the baby. Whilst Gareth asked for a glass of the nastiest wine (I gave him Rosehip), Gina went straight for the Strawberry, remembering it from last year. It was absolutely lovely to see them both. Unusually Strawberry was not this year's winner, though was still popular. Pleasingly someone wrote "Quite possibly the finest desert wine ever". The Sahara is, of course, famed for its strawberries.

FOURTH BOTTLE: 23rd December 2009. I was going to take a bottle of Crab Apple to the Work's Christmas 'Fuddle', but Claire suggested I take something better to ensure that my reputation would be secure. So, even though it is one of my more precious wines, I took Strawberry. Everyone at work had driven, of course, so no-one had much, and some had none at all. Overall people liked it – but irritatingly did not fall upon me with declarations that this was 'Paradise in a Glass'. Matthew declared it "Better than the Orange". The best taste sensation on the table, though, was Pria's samosas. Now they were delicious.

SIXTH BOTTLE: 14th May 2010. This week has been one of sobriety. Claire had her bottom right wisdom tooth out on Monday, and (so far) has made far less fuss about it than I made about mine. And her bruises and swellings are more impressive. Alcohol, therefore, has been pretty much off limits – and I have been out playing the bassoon most nights, which has made it easier. The week's diet has been dominated by either mush or slop because of Claire's mouth. Don't misunderstand me – it has been tasty and nutritious (and much of it assembled by me), but I am looking forward to something with a little texture.

JULY 2009

Marlo returns to America via Berlin next Sunday, and as she had been involved in creating 2008's Christmas Tutti Fruti, I invited her round for a bottling session. Conveniently, the first Sunday in July, the 5th this year (2009), is a traditional time to pick strawberries for wine. So Claire, Marlo and I went off, slathered in sun-cream, with two baskets between us to the 'Pick Your Own' farm. Despite it being the men's Wimbledon final, or perhaps because of it, the place was busier than I have seen it.

Once home I sent Marlo into the garden to pick a handful of wild strawberries. After weighing the fruit, Marlo did almost all the mashing, whilst I stood around boiling four pints of water. The recipe recommends leaving this for 24-36 hours. I left it about 65, which I hope was not a mistake. I strained the fruit out on Wednesday morning, 8th July, after a night of chasing a big white intruder cat round the house and soaking it with water. Consequently I slept badly and was grumpy over my morning cup of tea.

I put it into the demijohn on 12th July.

By racking the wine had cleared, and left 1½ inches of sediment. I have added a pint of water with 5oz of sugar, as the small taste was dry, but not unpleasant.

Quantity: One gallon.

Yeast Type: Burgundy.

Date Racked: 24th September 2009.

Date Bottled: 15th January 2010.

INITIAL TASTE:
My adjective of choice was 'delightful'. Claire's was 'plasticky'. As always, I have put this in clear bottles because it is such an attractive wine.

THE DRINKING EXPERIENCE

FIRST BOTTLE: 3rd July 2010. After spending an afternoon picking strawberries in anticipation of next year's Strawberry wine, this bottle was a natural choice to bring over with us to Heworth Green. Mom has been saying for a couple of weeks that the garden is looking its very best, with strong hints that we should come over. And she is absolutely right: it is a blaze of colour and sweet fragrances. Strawberry wine fitted in perfectly. This is definitely a good batch: the correct level of dryness, its usual wonderful colour, and a strong, deeply flavoured taste. Most of the bottle was finished before our meal, so I moved onto Pop's outstandingly alcoholic rum punch.

SECOND BOTTLE: 15th-18th August 2010. Leslie had expressed an interest in Strawberry wine last time she was over for a meal, and after finishing the Gooseberry I decided we needed more to drink. So I opened this, and Leslie made appreciative noises. I did not drink any on Monday because I had an exceptionally alcoholic lunch with Rodney – we shared two bottles – so just sitting still required some concentration. (Actually, I mowed the lawn.) We finished this tonight, a day on which I have had my final piece of work for the MA bound, in preparation for handing it in tomorrow. So a cool glass of Strawberry wine in a hot bath listening to Stephen Fry discussing gender differences in use of language was a celebration of sorts.

THIRD BOTTLE: 16th October 2010. Strawberry wine traditionally does very well at the Wine Party, and has been the winner on several occasions. This year it only came third (out of ten) with an average of '3.79' out of '5'. The score cards asked the guest to name the wine, and to draw a picture of it. Julia named this "Lolita", and drew a pair of lips holding a strawberry. Her description of it was "Lush crush", and she awarded it a '5'. Mom, who gave it a '3', drew some pins and described it as "prickly". Richard was most effusive, writing "Complex, wonderful, echoes summer". If strawberries were a little cheaper, I would make a double or triple batch of this every year.

FOURTH BOTTLE: 31st December & 1st January 2011. If one does not count the bottle of bubbly, or the various spirits, this was our third New Year's Eve bottle. It was opened mostly because Catherine rejected the Grape and Raisin as nasty. And it would have been impolite not to help her drink the stuff. However, when I woke this morning, I felt more delicate than ideal. Two rounds of washing up, two mugs of tea, two slices of toast (manky old crusts – yum), and a cup of coffee had me feeling human again.

FIFTH BOTTLE: 26th February 2011. Long lost second cousins were a feature of this bottle. Through a series of coincidences Mom managed to make contact with Great Uncle Fred (OBE)'s grandchildren, and three of them – Lisa, Lucy and

Emma – came to York for the weekend. I only have the vaguest of memories of them from my childhood, and I had merged Lisa and Emma. It was a wonderful afternoon and evening, hearing family stories and comparing notes about older generations. When it was time to go, we made promises to stay in touch and, having felt a real connection, I shall make every effort to remain in touch.

SIXTH BOTTLE: 25th-27th March 2011. Even though my last day at Emsley's is not until next week, and I don't officially leave until 15th April, I had my leaving party on Friday night. Whilst I was drinking more beer than was good for me, Claire opened the Strawberry wine. I had a couple of glasses on Saturday night after we had been to a concert given by Leeds Sinfonia. They were playing Elgar's Cello Concerto, Tchaikovsky's Third Symphony – which I do not know at all – and a new piece called 'Metro' by Paul Ayers. Leeds Sinfonia is clearly the best amateur orchestra there is in Leeds. Every section is strong, and they are particularly adept at playing quietly. We finished the bottle tonight, but it was nothing special and, on the whole, this entire batch of Strawberry has been a little disappointing.

BLACKCURRANT

JULY 2006

Julia rang at about five o'clock on Sunday 23rd July, asking if I wanted to pick blackcurrants this evening. As blackcurrant so far has been one of my very best, I did not pass this up. It was a pleasant evening, and we had just come back from a walk around Lindley reservoir.

I picked 4lb 4½ oz, including Julia's contribution, and enjoyed my time doing so. Blackcurrants are a little fiddly to pick, though once picked are far less trouble than elderberries.

I have used the recipe on page 163 of C. J. J. Berry – 3lb of currants (the rest are being frozen – possibly for blackcurrant vodka) and 3lb of sugar. I don't remember boiling the gallon of water with the sugar in it in previous years, but I did this time.

The yeast was put in on Tuesday 25th July, and it was put into the demijohn on 31st July.

On racking there was a heavy deposit, so I made up the space in the new demijohn partly from over a pint of water and 6oz of sugar, and partly from the wine I had saved as 'overflow' in a wine bottle when originally making this wine. If this wine is poor, this will be why.

Quantity:	6 bottles' worth.
Region:	Julia's allotment in Chapel Allerton.
Price:	Essentially free, as I borrowed yeast from Tracey, though the sugar cost about £1.
Yeast Type:	Young's 'super yeast' which is in a plastic pot rather than a sachet.
Initial Gravity:	1.086.
End Gravity:	Unrecorded, though likely to be in the region of 1.000 (most of them are).

Percentage: See above, but I would guess around 12%.

Date Racked: 24th October 2006.

Date Bottled: 2 October 2007.

INITIAL TASTE:

I waited for a very long time to bottle this one, as I thought it would be fizzy and I didn't want exploding wine. In fact it is mostly flat. The taste is not as good as in previous years – thinner, but still drinkable.

THE DRINKING EXPERIENCE

FIRST BOTTLE: 5th October 2007, whilst at Book Group at Gina's discussing 'The Vanishing Act of Esme Lennox' (which got a moderate thumbs up from most). This blackcurrant is okay. If I hadn't made it before, I think I would have been pleased with the result, but as I have, and as it has been splendid before, I was a little disappointed. Roc had a glass, declaring it had a real kick, and I think I finished the rest. Certainly this morning it feels like I did.

SECOND BOTTLE: 10th November 2007 at the Wine Party. This came fifth equal (of 13), tying with Banana. Interestingly, whereas Banana's scores ranged between '2' and '4', this ranged between '1' and '5', with one of each score. It is amazing how people's taste-buds differ. Heather thought I should leave this one a bit longer. Catherine praised the colour and described it as "earthy" and "fizzish", which is not a word. Richard, however, thought it was thin.

THIRD BOTTLE: Given to Julia as she staggered away from the Wine Party.

FOURTH BOTTLE: 14th December 2007. Taken round to Lambert's for an evening of vegetarian Greek food, scrabble, and shivering. The scrabble was slow, and started at 11pm., so we didn't get to bed till past one. Lambert's house was intensely cold, and Claire eventually requested he put the fire on. The wine was somewhat disappointing – not my best batch.

FIFTH BOTTLE: 28th & 29th February 2008. Opened on

the day I properly started writing my dissertation (I started with chapter two: Twelfth Century Miracle Collections in Context), and cooked a rather sloppy fish pie. There was too much sauce – the first dollop of mashed potato sank to the bottom, so I had to balance the rest on a sheet of somewhat random lasagne. Claire poured the first glasses after we had both done about an hour's viola/bassoon practice (mine in anticipation of 'The King and I' all next week). It was a good bottle, and fizzier than all the others.

AUGUST 2007

I picked the blackcurrants on 4th August 2007, a Saturday morning. Julia's allotment has suffered from the deluges of June and July. The blackcurrants are thinner on the ground than last year, and picking 3lb took well over an hour. We were not sure whether I had the full quantity, not having taken a set of scales to the allotment, so picked some white currants to bulk it out. However, I had just picked enough of the black variety, so the white currants will probably contribute to this year's Tutti Fruti. It is not the ideal time to start a wine today as I am meant to be on the road up to Newcastle to pick up Claire, and I should really mow the lawn before I leave – but bugger that!

I mashed the blackcurrants the same day, and poured over 8 pints of boiling water, which was boiled with 3lb of sugar in it. I added the pectolase when we returned from Newcastle on 5th August, and the yeast and nutrient on the morning of the 6th. It is currently (10pm-ish) bubbling nicely.

I put it all into the demijohn on 12th August (which is a day or two later than C. J. Berry suggests, but Gina's leaving do and preparing the house and food for Richard and Linda got in the way), whilst listening to Felix Martin? (I may have that wrong) – (it was actually Felix Dennis – Ed.) – on Desert Island Discs. What an objectionable man. This time I did not stir the mixture whilst it was in the sieve, letting it drain naturally, in the hope this will produce less sediment.

On racking, the sediment was not quite two fingers thick, and as it is so dark I cannot tell about clarity. I added most of a syrup mixture made up of ¾ of a pint of water, and 4½ oz of sugar.

Quantity:	6 bottles.
Yeast Type:	Bordeaux.
Date Racked:	28th October 2007.
Date Bottled:	8th February 2008 (a few days earlier than ideal).

INITIAL TASTE:
Bottling went without noticeable incident. It tasted good – better than last year; thick, sumptuous blackcurrant. There was quite a large sediment for this stage of the process.

THE DRINKING EXPERIENCE

FIRST BOTTLE: 19th & 20th July 2008. This is intense in its 'blackcurrant-ness'. It shouts out its flavour, and is unmistakable. It is far better than last year's attempt. As I am greedy and selfish, and have already given a bottle to Julia when we went to pick gooseberries, this wine will be one of those I choose not to appear at this year's Wine Party. The clarity and colour are excellent, and happily for our floor boards, there is no hint of a fizz.

SECOND BOTTLE: 31st August 2008. What a good bottle of wine. It is frustrating that this year has been poor for blackcurrants so we will be without this wine in 2009. We drank this after a day of Wagner. It is the fourth year of the Northern Wagner Orchestra, and therefore 'Götterdammerung'. Though we were without the singers, it felt like five hours of music without a tune. Lots for the bassoons to do, though. Mostly we drank this bottle before eating, but at 9pm the food was ready, and we ate sausage, mash, strange fractal cauliflower, and fried mushrooms with onion gravy. Delicious and worth the wait.

THIRD BOTTLE: 28th September 2008. I chose a bottle of blackcurrant to take up to Newcastle for Judith's 70th birthday celebration. This was on the basis that blackcurrant is one of my very nicest wines, and I am not sure I have fed it to the Taylors before. Disaster! This was mouth-puckeringly tart. Andrew described it as like mouthwash and lemon, though the others were kinder. We still finished the bottle, though. And Sooz cooked a lovely North African lamb and chickpea dish with couscous – followed by wonderful, wonderful tiramisu done by Claire. All praise St Delia.

FOURTH BOTTLE: 11th January 2009. This bottle was originally going to be Claire's birthday bottle, but Shirley has just given me a bottle of champagne, so we shall have that instead. We raised a toast to being thirty-eight, and drank this bottle to a venison sausage casserole, mashed and spicy sweet potatoes, beet tops, baked potato, and red cabbage with chestnuts. Absolutely lovely. Then we spent the rest of the evening cuddled up watching a Doctor Who DVD and eating Thornton's chocolates. Bliss.

SIXTH BOTTLE: 7th June 2009. We opened this after Claire's concert of the William Tell Overture, the Bruch Concerto for viola and clarinet, a fugue based on 'The Final Countdown', and Beethoven's Fifth. The Rossini and Beethoven were particularly good, with dynamics and everything, but then I'm a nineteenth century kind of guy. As Claire had been playing since ten in the morning she asked me to cook, which I did. But being a man, I feel I need the highest praise and possibly a medal for doing so. Claire tells me that the George Cross is in the post. We had sausages, mash, onion gravy, baked fennel, carrots and swede in butter and horseradish, and spiced, mashed sweet potato. Claire did the last dish, and (in fact) some of the second and fifth – but I did the rest. Mom was here for the concert and the meal, but only had a glass of wine because of the drive back to York. This wine is particularly good, and I hope 2009 will have a bumper crop to make up for 2008.

JULY 2009

After last year's pathetic crop, blackcurrants are back in abundance. When picking gooseberries last week, I also picked about a pound of currants from Julia's bushes. Claire and I returned yesterday, 18th July 2009, to finish the job and picked over 3lb between us. Adding in the 12oz from our blackcurrant bushes, we ended up with 5lb, which is too few for a double batch, but means our freezer is stuffed with blackcurrants – possibly for ice-cream, and certainly for this year's Tutti Fruti.

It was a pleasant late afternoon sitting picking fruit and getting the occasional nettle sting. Claire also picked a punnet of redcurrants and got up early this morning to make jelly. I, however, was feeling delicate after Michael Gaughn's 30th birthday party last night, and did not end up getting dressed until gone noon.

I measured and crushed the fruit today, 19th July – my father's 68th birthday – and I have added 2lb 12oz of sugar boiled up in 6½ pints of water.

The Blackcurrant wine went into a dark demijohn on 24th July, while listening to the second part of Jeanette Winterson celebrating the Moon.

I racked this after a long washing-up session. There was a large sediment, enough to pour a pint and a quarter of water with 6oz of sugar mixed in into the new demijohn. It needed the extra sugar from the sip I got.

Quantity:	One gallon.
Yeast Type:	Burgundy.
Date Racked:	8th October 2009.
Date Bottled:	13th February 2010.

INITIAL TASTE:
When bottled there was a sediment of about a quarter of an inch at the bottom of the demijohn. We only got half a glass to sup, and I let Claire have most of it. As with Redcurrant, I am very pleased with the initial taste – not too dry, and stuffed with fruit (odd, that).

THE DRINKING EXPERIENCE

FIRST TWO BOTTLES: 22nd May 2010. I have never known so many bottles explode in such a short period of time. In the last 48 hours two Redcurrants, one Elderberry, and (most tragically) two Blackcurrants have popped their corks, and a Nettle and another Blackcurrant show every sign of doing so. Upsettingly (and I genuinely mean that), the two Blackcurrants were stored horizontally, so we lost over half a bottle from each, and it drained into our new laminate floorboards, causing their edges to bubble up – which is also depressing. To offset this doom and gloom we have brought these two bottles up to Newcastle, where I shall be 'going ape' tomorrow. It has been a gorgeous, properly hot day, and, as is traditional, we spent much of it in the car. In fact, Claire reckons it is the rapid advancement from a cold spring to a hot early summer that has caused the mass explosion. It was chilly on Monday, and Mediterranean by Thursday. The wine, irritatingly, is delicious – why wasn't it Pumpkin or Plum that exploded? We drank it at Sooz's flat with Sooz, Bob and Judith, and everyone agreed how good it was. Bah!

THIRD BOTTLE: 17th July 2010. This was entirely the correct bottle to open after an hour of picking blackcurrants in the evening sunlight. Sooz is visiting, and Julia came over for our meal of roast belly-pork and summer vegetables – including the first potatoes and runner-beans from the garden (albeit tiny quantities of each). This wine has a definite stab and twist to it; perhaps it needed a touch more sugar, but the blackcurrants are evident, and everyone enjoyed it. It was also a good choice for the pork. The sharpness complemented the richness of the meat, and the bottle disappeared quickly.

FOURTH BOTTLE: 26th September 2010. We drank this bottle in Kenilworth at the beginning of a week's holiday that would take us to Pembrokeshire. Helen and Steve were our hosts: friends that we had not seen for five years, at their wedding. Apparently Steve had really not been looking forward to a bottle of homebrew, but in fact he was entirely complimentary. He admitted he was surprised, but said that it was a picnic bottle of wine, fit for an afternoon at the races, and possibly chilled.

SIXTH BOTTLE: 22nd & 23rd January 2011. Over the two nights on which we drank this bottle, Claire and I both had concerts. On Saturday Claire played three of the Max Bruch Trios for viola, clarinet and piano at Music Club. Halfway through the second there was a tremendous bang as the lid to the music-stand box crashed closed. The entire audience jumped, but Claire calmly continued playing, unruffled. My concert was on Sunday in Saltaire. We played music including Mendelssohn's Scottish Symphony. I have spent the last couple of months practicing the fast second movement of this, which is Very Difficult Indeed (all those semi-quavers). In the morning rehearsal I cracked it. Less so in the afternoon performance, though. Still, the concert as a whole was a good one, and a couple of glasses of fizzy Blackcurrant was the perfect way to celebrate.

BLACKBERRY

AUGUST 2006

Claire and I picked the blackberries on Sunday 27th August 2006 from York Victorian Cemetery. The weather was mostly good, with a (partially realised) threat of rain. To start with, I thought there would not be enough ripe blackberries, but I quickly found several good patches. Around the grave of Watson and Julia Ann Mortimer was particularly lush. It was a pleasant hour, listening to the distant, continual peal of bells. I met an old lady visiting her husband's grave and picking brambles for jam. She said she did not mind if I picked from her grave in future years.

Weighing the blackberries (8lb for a double batch) was dull. I followed the recipe in C. J. J. Berry, which calls for 3lb of sugar per single batch, but added only 14 pints of water rather than 16. I added the yeast on 29th August, and then put it into the demijohns on 2nd September.

By racking, the deposit had shrunk substantially. Each demijohn only required a half pint of water, plus 3oz of sugar. One gallon has been stored in a dark demijohn, and the other in clear glass.

Quantity:	2 gallons, so twelve bottles.
Region:	York Victorian Cemetery.
Price:	£1.10 for the yeast, approximately £2 for the sugar. The blackberries were free, not counting the petrol.
Yeast Type:	Bordeaux.
Initial Gravity:	Impossible to measure.
End Gravity:	See above.
Percentage:	It was not measured, but these things are usually around 13%.

Date Racked: 27th November 2006.

Date Bottled: 24th February 2007 – a little earlier than planned, but I needed a demijohn.

INITIAL TASTE:
As usual, quite good – maybe a little thin. There was virtually no difference between the gallon stored under dark, and that in a clear demijohn. Perhaps the latter has more depth?

THE DRINKING EXPERIENCE

FIRST BOTTLE: Drunk at the Taylors on 4th August 2007 (in every sense). This was the third of three bottles opened during the evening, so my judgment was not all it might have been. But I think it was really rather good – lots of blackberry taste, clear, and it did its job. It accompanied sausages, mostly.

THIRD BOTTLE: 22nd September 2007. I took this to London with me, and Susan, John, Caroline, and Paul were tremendously complimentary, which was very pleasing. We drank it as the first of many bottles with a shin-beef stew, followed by an Araucaria crossword and Zabaglione. I slept extremely well.

FOURTH BOTTLE: 10th November 2007 at the Wine Party. This was the runner up, and the only bottle to be finished at the party, scoring '3.77' out of '5'. It got two '5's, though a couple of '2's, and was my favourite.

FIFTH BOTTLE: 28th & 29th November 2007. Claire is having an absolutely awful time at work, and took Wednesday off because she couldn't face it. I have been out bassooning both nights. Consequently I only got a glass of this one. That was with a turkey, root vegetable and chilli-cheese bake. Nicer than it sounds.

SEVENTH BOTTLE: 13th January 2008. This was a Sunday lunch bottle. Mom and Pop came over before they depart on their world trip. We had a brace of pheasants from the farmers' market, so Claire cooked an amazing pheasant casserole (braised in Madeira, my dear). It was absolutely delicious, and the wine was a suitable accompaniment – Mom was particularly complimentary.

EIGHTH BOTTLE: 10th February 2008. We had this with a lamb and dumpling stew, and finished it off to a Muppets DVD, after a very mixed weekend, which combined being sacked from Bassoon Group (which really hurt), an excellent Music Club, and a dull Music Club committee meeting.

ELEVENTH BOTTLE: 28th June 2008. We took this with us to Chester for a weekend with David, Amie and their children. Amie cooked a marvellous Chinese meal with chicken and mushrooms, and sweet and sour pork. Over the weekend I trampolined, played quartets, played golf, and whacked Owen really hard with a Wii console, causing many tears but no trips to Casualty. Phew!

TWELFTH BOTTLE: 23rd & 24th November 2008. I need to revise my opinion about Blackberry wine being best drunk young. This was delicious – richer than usual. We started it late on Sunday evening after a Nick Meredith concert (Grieg Piano concerto, the last movement of Tchaikovsky's Fifth symphony, and some Hansel and Gretel) whilst watching Doctor Who on DVD, and finished it this evening to a medley of root vegetables.

AUGUST 2007

On 26th August, late morning, Claire, Mom and I went to York Victorian Cemetery armed with receptacles in which to put the blackberries. It has been pleasant weather today, which made the hour-or-so's picking all the more enjoyable. The fruit wasn't as ripe or large as last year (I think), but Claire pointed out we had a summer last year, which may explain things. People whose graves I picked from included William Garvey, solicitor, Lucy Nelson, Harriet Whickham (who must have stepped straight out of Jane Austen), and Melvyn Wilstrop, a one month old with a large and extensive grave. Claire's bodies included Fanny Almond and Edward Chicken – who was apparently (according to his stone) the model for Mr Micawber. Mom picked from William Wilberforce, most likely a descendant of the anti-slavery campaigner.

I picked 4lb 14oz, Claire picked 5lb 8oz, and Mom picked 5lb 1oz. As there is so much fruit (and I am making a triple batch), I have put in less water than may be warranted – 19 pints rather than 24, but I have kept the sugar the same at 9lb. I put in 2 teaspoons of pectolase about 14 hours after putting everything into the bucket.

The next morning (Tuesday) I put in the wine yeast.

I put it into the demijohns on 1st September, in each case leaving plenty of space at the top, and filling four bottles for later topping up. 19 pints proved to be too many. I'm pretty certain 17 would have done.

On racking, one of the demijohns got an extra half pint of water and 3oz of sugar. Another, put into a dark demijohn, got three-quarters of a pint of water and 4oz of sugar. I haven't topped the final one up yet – I tried to filter out the gloop at the end by sieving it into a separate bottle, and I'm waiting for that to clear.

Actually I only gave it 45 minutes and then, on Claire's advice, poured it all in. If it needs to be racked again, so be it. I added nearly a pint of water and 4½ oz of sugar.

Quantity:	3 gallons!
Price:	£2 donation to the cemetery for its upkeep, £1.20 for the yeast, and £3-ish for the sugar.
Bought at:	The sugar was from Sainsbury's, the yeast from Abbey Brew.
Yeast Type:	Burgundy.
Date Racked:	18th November 2007.
Date Bottled:	4th and 9th March 2008.

INITIAL TASTE:
These were pretty much the same as usual. Claire described one as 'medicinal'. I liked it, though. All had a distinct blackberry flavour.

THE DRINKING EXPERIENCE

FIRST BOTTLE: 15th August 2008. Happily, Blackberry is a reliable bottle. Catherine declares it juicy and drinkable – both of which are a Good Thing. We ate beanburgers, tzatziki, courgettes griddled in lemon and dill, a tomato sauce, and delicious nutty new potatoes from Catherine's allotment.

SECOND BOTTLE: 24th August 2008. Drunk to a game of scrabble at Heworth Green, which Mom won, and where I had all vowels three turns in a row. This bottle was delicious – better than the last. And we raised a glass to all the bodies that acted as fertiliser.

THIRD BOTTLE: 29 & 30th August 2008. Claire opened this whilst I was out drinking far too much at Roc's leaving do. Once home and in bed, doing foot point exercises, Claire commented that I had malfunctioning animatronic yeti feet. And today I have been test driving new bassoons, which was great fun. On a juxtaposed, sadder note, we heard that Howard Wyborn died yesterday.

FOURTH BOTTLE: 7th-9th September 2008. After nine and a half hours of playing Wagner, a bottle of Blackberry wine is just the thing. The whole Götterdamerung experience was exhausting, but it was a real achievement to have played the entire Ring Cycle. And I have chosen which bassoon – the Schreiber.

FIFTH BOTTLE: 10th October 2008. I have been feeling sorry for myself today – my wisdom tooth is making a bid for freedom and my face has swollen, meaning I can't close my molars together. The solution? Get drunk, of course. And this bottle did the job. We had sausages (which were a challenge), mash and gravy (which were not).

SIXTH BOTTLE: 15 & 16th October 2008. Claire was made redundant on Tuesday, and was in bed weeping on Wednesday. This bottle helped matters somewhat, and I had a glass after orchestra. Wish I could help.

SEVENTH BOTTLE: 18th October 2008 at the Wine Party. This came third of twelve, and was lower scoring than last year, with an average of '3.64'. It got no '5's, but nothing below '3'. Richard thought it had "curiously little bouquet", but gave it '4½' anyway. I still think it is my favourite.

EIGHTH BOTTLE: 7th November 2008. We drank this for Book Group, discussing 'The Dice Man' by Luke Reinhart – except only Richard could come, so it was an intimate affair. The book was dreadful – an interesting idea poorly executed – but the wine was as good as ever.

TENTH BOTTLE: 21st January 2009. I had a Latin exam today and am now on holiday (until Friday morning). Claire has also taken tomorrow off work for a viola lesson. To celebrate we cracked open a bottle of Blackberry and drank it to a chilli. I'm hoping it will help me sleep – banishing the cough.

ELEVENTH BOTTLE: 19th February 2009. Mostly consumed by Claire. I had half a glass with supper – one of my better beanlashes – and then went to Quintet. Shirley played! Only for half an hour, but it is a leap forward. I came home to a giggling, slurring wife, and a glass of Blackberry wine.

THIRTEENTH BOTTLE: 12th April 2009. I dug a whopping great hole, which was also impressively circular, in the lawn today, in which to plant rhubarb. Claire started building a raised vegetable bed out of bricks and mortar. We drank this rather wonderful bottle to amazingly good lamb koftas, and watched the Easter special Doctor Who.

FIFTEENTH BOTTLE: 9th & 10th June 2009. I was out last night, listening to the Endellion Quartet play Haydn, Bartok 4, and 'Death and the Maiden'. This open bottle awaited my return, so I had a glass. Tonight I returned from orchestra and the Brahms Violin concerto – the soloist resembled a troll – to find Claire baking gingerbread. So I had another glass.

SIXTEENTH BOTTLE: 28th June 2009. Drunk in Wales! This was the first bottle of the evening, and absolutely delicious. We are in a cottage in Criccieth with Bob and Judith, and it has been a glorious day involving swimming in the sea and eating Dragon's Breath ice-cream. This was a pre-meal bottle, with which we ate fried patra and planned which castle to visit.

AUGUST 2008

Claire, Mom and I arrived at York Victorian Cemetery with baskets and plastic bags late in the morning on 25th August 2008. As it has been so wet this summer, and colder than I think is usual – it has been the wettest August for a century – I was worried that the blackberries would be thin on the ground. There have been no available blackcurrants or plums from Julia or my parents this year because of the weather. We needn't have worried – between us we picked about 21lb, many maggots, a couple of woodlice, an ant, and a millipede. Claire picked the most – 8lb 4oz. For future reference, an overfull cardboard basket equates to a double batch of wine.

The weather was kind – a mixture of overcast and sunny, and the blackberries were hanging off their stalks, though there are several weeks of picking left. It was, as always, difficult to stop. I would keep on coming across another abundant patch that cried out for attention.

Amongst those who contributed to the wine were Benjamin Brooke, the Hick Family, Lucy Nelson Champney, John Walker (a butcher) and his wife, Mary, 'Our Dear Mother', and Robert Pottage.

I poured 24 pints of boiling water over the mashed fruit in the bucket (the bucket would not take much more), and I added 2 teaspoons of pectolase on the morning of 26th August. The same night I added the yeast and two teaspoons of nutrient. On 30th August I sieved out the blackberries – putting the juice into 4 demijohns, then poured those demijohns back into the washed and sterilised bucket. To avoid splashes the final two were siphoned. I then poured in the sugar (a 5kg bag, and then an extra pound). Sounds easy? It took over three hours. I'm sure there are 3 or 4 pints too much liquid.

I put the liquid into the demijohns on 3rd September, when I would have preferred to be playing with my new bassoon.

I was going to rack this on 8th November, but it is all still bubbling frequently. Instead I racked it, still bubbling, over two weeks later. Each demijohn got approximately a pint of water and 5oz of sugar. Only one of the demijohns has been brown glass throughout the entire process.

Quantity:	Four gallons!
Price:	Near £5 for the sugar, and £1.20 for the yeast.
Yeast Type:	Burgundy.
Date Racked:	24th November 2008.

Date Bottled: 16th March 2009.

INITIAL TASTE:
Disaster. It is all far too sweet, and I have 24 bottles of the stuff. The base taste is good, as usual, but it needs to be much, much drier.

THE DRINKING EXPERIENCE

FIRST BOTTLE: 11th July 2009 (probably). Quin is organising a 100th birthday party for my long-dead grandfather in Nebraska. Mom is about to fly out, so this bottle is my contribution. Let's hope he enjoys it.

SECOND BOTTLE: 17th July 2009. After second-hand reports via e-mail from Mom about how good this wine was, and because Claire wanted a red, I opened this. It was, as expected, too sweet, but not overpoweringly so. And it was beautifully smooth.

FOURTH BOTTLE: 24th August 2009. A suitable bottle to open after a day of picking and weighing more blackberries than you can possibly imagine. Even though it was Monday, we finished the bottle. Our food was a tomato, aubergine and breadcrumb dish with compulsory courgettes, followed by plum and bramble crumble, after which I continued with 'The Yacoubian Building'.

FIFTH BOTTLE: 13th September 2009. This was our reward (along with a G and T) for a weekend playing Rite of Spring, extracts from Wozzeck (which I found surprisingly pleasant), and five songs by Wagner. It was a fabulous experience. The first half of the Stravinsky was played extraordinarily well, considering the minimal rehearsal.

SIXTH BOTTLE: 18 & 19th September 2009. Our Friday night bottle, opened after a satisfying rehearsal of the Fasch Bassoon Concerto at Laura's. This piece is really coming together, and though musically simple, new aspects keep on revealing themselves. Claire finished this whilst I was playing Beethoven's Fifth and Tchaikovsky's First piano concerto at Ackworth. Excellent.

SEVENTH BOTTLE: 4th-6th October 2009. We drank virtually all of this with roast pork, a fabulous sage and onion stuffing, apple sauce, and lots of vegetables with gravy. A perfect Sunday bottle.

This was the day I venerated a saint's relics, and was blessed by a French Bishop in an effort to recreate an authentic medieval experience. I tried and failed to get to IKEA afterwards.

NINTH BOTTLE: 17th October 2009. This was the only bottle emptied during the Wine Party, and was uniformly enjoyed. I overheard one person say it was a little sweet, but it was at least one person's favourite and someone (though I don't know who) wants to try it mulled.

TENTH BOTTLE: 1st November 2009. We had a feast at Julia's, of which this bottle formed part. Julia cooked lamb and guinea fowl with roast vegetables, and all were delicious. She worried that there was too much, but the five at the table left crumbs and bones. Julia's leftovers will make 'Soup for One'. It was a lovely evening, and this was a good bottle.

TWELFTH BOTTLE: 14th-15th December 2009. We have just returned from our Sainsbury's Christmas shop: £166 on stuff to get us and the cats through to January. It was not as ghastly as it might have been, but the woman on the checkout was bonkers. And now I have to plough on with Christmas cards. Only another 30-plus to do. It is all rather depressing. Bah humbug!

THIRTEENTH BOTTLE: 24th December 2009. The Christmas Eve bottle. I was joint cook, and made beanburgers and boiled up some purple sprouting broccoli. Claire made the tomato sauce and couscous flavoured with salted limes. As it is Christmas and I have nearly two weeks off work, I am re-growing a goatee – entirely for Claire's enjoyment. It will come off on 5th January.

FOURTEENTH BOTTLE: 9th January 2010. I have been a fully paid up member of the Temperance Society for the last six days after the Christmas alcohol bonanza, but as it was a Saturday night, I decided to make an exception.

FIFTEENTH BOTTLE: 19th February 2010. I enjoy a Friday night catch-up with my wife. We shared this bottle over sausages, mash, leftover gravy, and cabbage (prepared by me), and spent a happy couple of hours just chatting. Claire is preparing a paper for publication, but the details escape me. I am contemplating next month's wine. Between us we have decided on 'Exotic Tinned

Fruit'. Claire thinks I should follow the recipe, but I want to double the number of tins involved.

SIXTEENTH BOTTLE: 22nd February 2010. I gave this to our bathroom fitter, Daniel Benn, who made the mistake of sounding interested in the vast number of bottles I have stored around the house. I asked him a couple of days later what he thought and he claimed he had liked it, but in the manner of one who was being polite. And though I have found the whole 'new bathroom' experience stressful (particularly when it was a room of brick, floor boards and dust), he is doing a terrific job.

SEVENTEENTH BOTTLE: 28th March 2010. Claire has just stencilled a beetle onto the back of my neck. Apparently it will wash off. I am feeling very much more positive today (see Elderberry). My mouth hurts less, I haven't had to crash in the afternoon, and I am almost able to chew. The food was still 'general mush' – cottage pie – but really tasty, and the broccoli had a slight crunch. I even tried playing the bassoon today, and it was fine.

EIGHTEENTH BOTTLE: 25th April 2010. I have spent much of the day gardening, and the rest of it half-heartedly preparing a presentation on medieval artistic representations of Death. The gardening was probably more useful, and mostly involved digging. I'm hoping I did not cause too much crocus or tulip fatality. This bottle was drunk to a full chicken roast, including Spanish asparagus. I now need to atone for food miles.

NINETEENTH BOTTLE: 3rd May 2010. Our Bank Holiday treat was a buffalo casserole with four types of exciting mushrooms, including some bright pink ones. We shared this meal with Julia, partly in thanks for her rhubarb supply service. I think buffalo is beef with attitude, but Julia argued it was more gamey. Whichever, it was tremendous, and followed by gooseberry and rhubarb fool.

TWENTIETH BOTTLE: 14 & 15th June 2010. This bottle marked my fortieth birthday. How can I possibly be forty? That is entirely ridiculous. I'm sure I was doing Maths 'A' Level only a few weeks ago. And wasn't it about yesterday that I got married? How does time contract like that? Anyway, we drank this bottle to the Greek lamb dish, and as it was my birthday I insisted it was made with Cheshire cheese, like it was in my youth (ha!) rather than the more authentic feta. We had asparagus, home-grown green salad, and home-made pitta bread to accompany, and rhubarb crumble for pudding. A proper, comforting birthday meal.

TWENTY SECOND BOTTLE: 29th August 2010. We picked blackberries today, and so a bottle of Blackberry 2008 seemed fitting. Bob and Judith are over, so we feasted on lamb tagine with home-made pitta bread and a tomato and pepper salad. It has been an alcoholic, pleasant evening, and I am struggling to keep my eyes open. The candles lighting this page are burning low and I will blow them out shortly. The washing up will have to wait till the morning. G'night.

AUGUST 2009

Claire and I spent the weekend in York because Paul and family were visiting from Canada, and happily this coincided with the traditional weekend for picking blackberries. In fact Claire took Monday off work, so Claire, Mom and I set off for the cemetery on 24th August 2009 at just past eleven. None of us had a watch – mine died on Saturday night – so we agreed to pick until we felt we had enough, and meet at the car.

I went foraging in an area I have not been before – on the rear side of the chapel – and quickly found some small and not particularly ripe berries growing out of the McIntosh's tomb. I wasted some time with these, wondering if we had come too early, and then went exploring. My next stop had some of the largest, ripest blackberries ever encountered, and this was repeated in abundance at the grave after that. Phyllis Helena Hulme and Joseph Edward Hulme, many thanks for your fruit. Gratitude is also due to George Cliff and his niece Annie Elizabeth Allison. Mom picked from the Agar family plot, and Claire's best grave was Thomas Douthwaite.

As ever, stopping picking was difficult, and Mom and I wandered slowly back, finding patches of irresistible brambles as we returned to the car. Claire had been there for at least half an hour, listening to music. Between us we picked 20lb 6oz.

At home I started winemaking around four and finished by eight. Our freezer is now stuffed with fruit, and I haven't done

Elderberry yet. The brewing bucket has 16lb of mashed brambles and 22 pints of boiled water in it. I added the yeast and two teaspoons each of nutrient and pectolase on the morning of 25th August. The blackberries were sieved out and a 5kg bag of sugar (which equates nearly precisely to 11lb) was added on 28th August, a day earlier than planned, but it had stopped fermenting. The kitchen is in chaos, but I shall deal with that tomorrow. Ha! The interjection is Claire's. She rose early and did the clearing up. I put the liquid into four demijohns on the evening of 31st August. 22 pints of water is about right.

On racking, the wine is moderately sweet, so I added a syrup of 2oz of sugar to 1 pint of water. Each demijohn got nearly a pint of syrup.

Quantity:	Four gallons.
Price:	£4.20 for the sugar, and £1.20 for the yeast.
Yeast Type:	Burgundy.
Date Racked:	2nd November 2009.
Date Bottled:	7th March 2010.

INITIAL TASTE:
I am pleased with this wine. It has avoided last year's over-sweetness, and went well with a rabbit and prune casserole.

THE DRINKING EXPERIENCE

FIRST BOTTLE: 6th August 2010. This was the third and final bottle that I took to Rydal this year, and the one that everyone liked the most, even beating the Elderflower. It was sweeter than I remember on bottling, but still delicious. It was the last night of the Rydal holiday, and as is traditional, I drank rather too much. This time, though, I had more excuses than usual. I had volunteered to give the 'Last Night Speech', and I have hardly ever done any public speaking. Wine was needed both before and after, but in fact the whole thing went extremely well. Giving a speech is much like playing music. Once you start you can't stop, but the feeling is exhilarating when it is clear it has gone well.

SECOND BOTTLE: 22nd August 2010. What a marvellous bottle of wine, even if I do say so myself. It bursts with blackberry – which is hardly surprising. I am very pleased, and just a little smug. We drank this to the first roast we have had for a long while: chicken with roast potatoes, runner beans, courgettes, and onion gravy. All the vegetables, including the potatoes, were from our garden. The spuds were particularly good. And then we watched a ridiculous episode of 'Midsomer Murders' with Anna Massey camping it up wielding a carving knife. The DVD comes from the University Library and is stamped 'For Educational Purposes Only'. Presumably for the BA in 'Rubbish Telly'.

FOURTH BOTTLE: 17th-19th September 2010. This is quite possibly the best Blackberry wine I have made. Like a child might imagine red wine to taste. Full of fruit, and slightly sweet. On Saturday night Claire and I each had a glass after playing Rachmaninov's Second piano concerto and Beethoven's Sixth symphony in Ackworth. It was a good concert, and two fabulous pieces of music. More entertaining, though, were our attempts to play pool in the period between the rehearsal and the concert. There was a table and balls, but no cues. My bassoon cleaners were inadequate substitutes, sending the cue ball shooting off in directions that defied the laws of physics.

FIFTH BOTTLE: 23rd & 24th September 2010. Well, I am a girly swot. I got my MA result on Thursday and, as hoped, it was a Distinction. Plus I got the prize, which was pleasing. I now have to write out "I must not be smug" a hundred times. I celebrated by going for lunch with Rodney, and consequently felt tiddly for the rest of the day. Claire opened this after a viola lesson and I managed to force down a glass and a half. This really is a good batch of Blackberry, and we finished it tonight – my glass was after the Harrogate Quintet's final rehearsal before playing for a wedding tomorrow at Goldsborough Hall. It should go well, and it helps that we will be background music. It makes wrong notes less noticeable.

SIXTH BOTTLE: 2nd & 3rd October 2010. We have just had a week's holiday, mostly in Wales, and opened this bottle on our return. Though I had looked forward to being home, I spent all of Saturday late afternoon and evening feeling unreasonably grumpy. The long journey from Warwickshire didn't help, though bassoon practice and an episode of 'QI' did. As did this bottle.

SEVENTH BOTTLE: 16th October 2010. The out and out winner at this year's Wine Party, and achiever of Best Ever Score At Any Wine Party Ever. Out of a possible '45' points, Blackberry scored '44½'. Only my father marked it down by half a point, mostly because he preferred 'Grape and Raisin'. Comments included "More more moreish", "Delicious", "Superb", "Proper nice", and (more opaquely) "All things are relative!"

EIGHTH BOTTLE: 7th November 2010. When anyone asks me if there is anything which I don't eat, I always reply "offal". Claire, though, has a theory that if I don't know I'm eating it then I won't object. Tonight we had steak and kidney stew with dumplings. Irritatingly I thought it was not bad, so I need to reconsider what I refuse to eat. Julia came over to share our meal, and brought sticks of horseradish with her. Claire made some of this into a sauce, which caused all of us, at varying times, to make a 'Fwahahagh' noise as it hit the back of our noses. The Blackberry wine helped wash it all down, and was as good as ever.

NINTH BOTTLE: 1st December 2010. We drank this bottle to mark the earliest and heaviest snowfall that I can remember. There are between eight and ten inches of snow outside. Our caenothus looks as if it has been covered with thick icing, and our front garden is a series of white, undefined mounds. The snow is not undiluted pleasure, however. I was allowed to leave work early at 1.00pm. It took three hours to get home.

TENTH BOTTLE: 12th December 2010. We had my parents and Duncan and Rachel over today for a Mediterranean chicken casserole, courtesy of Delia. Actually, courtesy of Claire – she's the one who got up at 7.30 this morning to cook it. The evening has been one of good food and stimulating conversation – covering everything from Wikileaks, student protests, plans to spend April in Petra, the Black Death, and the social skills of geek millionaires. But now I'm sleepy and must go to bed.

THIRTEENTH BOTTLE: 4 & 5th February 2011. Most of this bottle was drunk at Book Club, accompanying some fantastic homemade pizza and shop-bought Pringles. Gina refused to have any of the wine because of its association with graveyards. Telling her that the majority of bodies contributing to this bottle died in the nineteenth century did not make her more likely to try it.

We had a good evening, though, discussing 'Nice Work' by David Lodge, which is an excellent book. The final glass was drunk to give us courage for Music Club. We needed it: the orchestral rendition of Beethoven's Fidelio Overture was buttock-clenchingly awful.

FOURTEENTH BOTTLE: 23rd February 2011. Hurrah! I have a new job. Jarndyce & Snagsby have agreed to take me on. I found out today whilst at work, and spent much of the afternoon planning which bottle to open as a celebration. It had to be Blackberry. I don't know when I'll start or have final details on salary, but it is a full-time job and could not have come at a better moment. All that worrying I went through. Much to Claire's irritation I drank most of this bottle. She got over a glass and a half, but needed more because of a particularly poor viola lesson. In this instance, though, celebration beat commiseration.

FIFTEENTH BOTTLE: 18th March 2011. Today is Red Nose Day, and we listened to the concert on Radio 3 while drinking Blackberry wine. This came from the Albert Hall, and its main event was a (successful) attempt to break the world record for the largest kazoo orchestra. Hearing nearly 4,000 kazoos playing 'Ride of the Valkyrie' followed by 'The Colonel Bogey March' was very silly indeed. The music sounded like it was scored for orchestra and a swarm of angry wasps. Claire made gingerbread violas throughout in preparation for tomorrow's concert.

SIXTEENTH BOTTLE: 2nd April 2011. Spring is definitely here. We have spent the day wandering around daffodil-strewn lanes and looking at fields full of newborn lambs, all in the bright sunshine. This was all part of a nine mile walk which took in Almscliff Crags, and a dead ash tree covered in slug-like black fungus. We opened and finished this bottle tonight, and it has been remarkably effective.

PLUM

AUGUST 2006

We picked the plums immediately after picking blackberries on 28th August 2006. The extra bucket given by Richard means I can do two wines at once. I do not know what variety the plums are. They are a bright purple/pink colour, but with a good deal of yellow to them, even when ripe. I have made plum wine twice before with only moderate success. First time was bland, but a wonderful colour. Second time was far too sweet.

I am following C. J. J. Berry's recipe, which requires 6lb of plums, but without any wheat or barley – which he says is optional anyway. Also, I only used 3lb of sugar rather than the suggested 3½. Mom suggested putting in ginger, but maybe I'll do that next year. This can be the 'control' year.

After pouring in 4 pints of boiling water I only waited three and a half hours before pouring in the same amount of cold (well, it was late).

I added the yeast on 30th August, forgetting to measure specific gravity (damn!), and put it into the demijohn on 2nd September, using a sieve to filter out the clumps. It is an attractive (honestly) browny/pinky/orange. I did not fill the demijohn to avoid explosion, but have a separate bottle of 'syrup' to use as a top up.

On racking, I added 3oz of sugar and half a pint of water, though it did not all fit. There was a small deposit, but the wine is cloudy. It is an orangey brown, and less attractive than when it was completely opaque.

Quantity:	1 gallon.
Region:	Heworth Green (overhanging my parents' fence).
Price:	£1.20 for the yeast, and about £1 for the sugar.

Bought at: The fruit was free.

Yeast Type: Sauternes.

Date Racked: 5th December 2006.

Date Bottled: 15th March 2007.

INITIAL TASTE:
Still cloudy, though a pleasant pink colour. Tastes alright.

THE DRINKING EXPERIENCE

FIRST BOTTLE: 4th June 2007. Opened partly because it had just started leaking, but mostly to celebrate Claire having done her 'AS' Music, and the house being a Revision Free Zone. The colour and clarity is 'Sunset in smog'; Monet would be proud. You can really taste the plum, and it has a slight fizz. It accompanied that classic Monday dish – fried weekend leftovers. I'm actually really pleased with how this has come out, apart from the cloudiness. It is a dry, fruit filled wine, and one to do again.

SECOND BOTTLE: 10th June 2007. This bottle self-selected itself rather more dramatically than the last. I came back from Sainsbury's to find the hall awash with plum wine. The remainder of the bottle was rescued and put in the fridge, and the other four bottles have been located and stood upright. After drinking this we had a pleasant summer evening's stroll round the extended neighbourhood, nosing in gardens, finding a tenner, and spotting elder trees.

THIRD BOTTLE: 16th June 2007. Drunk at Heworth Green (there's a sentence with two meanings) while playing scrabble and waiting for Doctor Who. Mom thinks I should do this one again. So far Pop's only comment is "fizzy". On pressing he says "It's okay – it's not great. I don't think your mother will like it." I love paternal praise.

FOURTH BOTTLE: 3rd & 4th November 2007. This was started after Music Club. It was an 'orchestral' night: a fairly poor rendition of Mozart's Piano Concerto in G Major (no. 17 or 18?). Good bassoon part, though. The wine was tarter and less plummy

71

than the three previous bottles. While we drank we cleaned, in preparation for Saturday's party.

FIFTH BOTTLE: 10th November 2007 at the Wine Party. A disappointing eleventh out of thirteen, with an average score of '2.1'. I think the fact it had a head made it look intimidating, combined with its failure to clear. I actually quite liked this one, and I thought it had a definite taste of plum. Two people gave it a '1'. Catherine wrote "Not as scary as it looked".

SIXTH BOTTLE: 5th-7th January 2008. This began as our Saturday night bottle, and unusually we did not finish it. This may have had something to do with the rather large whisky-mac I poured myself earlier in the evening. We ate vegetarian Chinese food, with a particularly good noodle dish created by Claire, and then tried watching 'Shrek'. Twenty minutes in we turned it off. On Monday, while Claire was off playing duets with Jonathan, I had the last glass to 'The Lives of Others' – an outstanding film. And so Goodbye Plum 06. It was, it has to be said, tart (though better than the Bulgarian Cabernet Sauvignon I followed it up with tonight). More sugar next time?

AUGUST 2007

I picked the plums on the afternoon of 26th August 2007, risking life and limb doing so. Well, standing a little precariously on the wall and banging my head when Mom asked me to pick a specific fig for her. Unlike the blackberries, the plums are riper this year, and there are not as many of them. Several contained maggots, and after my initial disgust I picked most out. Perhaps the true name of this wine should be 'Plum and Ginger with a Hint of Larvae'. Yum!

To the 6lb of mashed plums covered in 4 pints of boiling water, I have added 1oz of ginger, very thinly sliced, and I have no idea whether this will make any difference to the taste. I added 4 pints of cold water twelve hours later, rather than between four and five, as suggested. It is currently a lovely dark bronze colour.

I added the pectolase at the same time as the water, and strained the mixture about 60 hours later (ie. Wednesday evening). It is no longer a pleasing red brick colour, but is instead a dingy and uninteresting brown. It is also not 'delightfully clear', as promised by the recipe book.

I boiled it up as instructed (there was a scum floating on the top), and then poured it over 3lb of sugar in the freshly cleaned out bucket. I put the yeast and nutrient in the next morning, Thursday 30th August. It was all put into a demijohn on 1st September, though I have left a large space in case of explosion, and kept a separate bottle of liquid for topping up later. I used a sieve to filter out the clumps. I could have put in a pint and a half less water.

By racking it has not come close to clearing, so I added a teaspoon of pectolase. The sediment was small, so I could not quite top it up with half a pint of water and 3oz of sugar. The taste I got was promising, if a little dry.

By 5th January 2008 it has not cleared at all, so I poured in a little of last year's plum wine, as recommended by C. J. J. Berry himself. We shall see.

On 16th April 2008 I nearly bottled the wine, but the specific gravity of 1.010 suggested it might still be fermenting. It was a little fizzy and became fizzier, Vesuvius style, when I added a teaspoon of amylase to clear it.

Quantity:	One gallon.
Region:	The tree at Heworth Green, overhanging my parents' wall (mostly).
Price:	16p(?) for the ginger, £1 for the sugar, and 1.20 for the yeast.
Bought at:	The ginger was bought at Street Lane Greengrocer's.
Yeast Type:	Burgundy.
Initial Gravity:	1.100.
End Gravity:	0.994.
Percentage:	16% approximately.

Date Racked: 3rd November 2007.

Date Bottled: 3rd September 2008.

INITIAL TASTE:
It has not cleared, but is far less fizzy than expected. It has a yeasty taste, the plum is barely detectable, and the ginger not there at all.

THE DRINKING EXPERIENCE

FIRST BOTTLE: 20th September 2008. Not one of my greatest wines. It is cloudy, has little body, and a yeasty taste. Notwithstanding all this, it is still drinkable, and gets better further down the bottle (odd, that). There is no taste of ginger at all, though plum is definitely there. I think I will continue to make single batches of this wine each year free plums are available, but it is no tragedy that 2008 is not one of those years.

SECOND BOTTLE: 18th October 2008 at the Wine Party. This one is difficult to score. It all depends on whether one counts Claire's score of '-7' or not. If not, it comes second from last, with an average score of '2.08'. If so, it is still difficult to score (see 'Pumpkin'), but has an average of '0.79'. This was not a popular wine. Bizarrely Richard gave it a '3' and said it had lots of ginger. Someone else wrote that it was very acidic, and Gareth thought it tasted like medicine. I ended up pouring most of the bottle away.

THIRD BOTTLE: 19th-21st December 2008. Claire was out at the German market eating sausages and drinking beer, as it was one of her colleagues' last day at work, so I took the opportunity to open a bottle of Plum. I don't think this wine is that awful. Half a bottle certainly did its job, and I woke with a headache on Saturday.

FOURTH BOTTLE: 3rd May 2009. Sooz and Andrew are down for the Bank Holiday weekend. Claire has seen this as an opportunity to get rid of a bottle of Plum wine. So, after a day of sauntering round Leeds farmers' market, and Claire buying clothes (one item of which was distinctly Not Blue), and general lying about, I opened this. Claire had one sip before giving the rest of her glass away. Sooz did better, probably having a glass and a half before realising that it reminded her of silage (yum!). That left Andrew and me to finish the bottle, which we did.

SIXTH BOTTLE: 4th December 2010. Today I saw my opportunity to dispose of this bottle. Because of the heavy snow over the last week, the street where I live, which is on a steep hill, has been entirely impassable to traffic. Yesterday Claire and Mary, a neighbour, started shovelling some snow. Other neighbours noticed, so this morning there was a collection of residents armed with spades, hoes and brooms, clearing the road. I have not talked to this many neighbours since moving here 12 years ago. For a brief moment (well, three hours) we were a community, and to celebrate this I mulled my last bottle of nasty Plum wine, and force fed it to those helping. The neighbours were genuinely polite, and before I served it I had a quick taste to make sure I was not poisoning them.

ELDERBERRY

SEPTEMBER 2006

I picked the elderberries on 16th September 2006. The tree in Oakwood where I usually get my elderberries only had a very few, and these were out of reach. It looked like I had come a week too late, so I went exploring round a wood, getting a handful here and there, including some while balancing precariously on a fallen tree. I did wonder whether this was worth a broken leg. I ended up getting most from the trees on the road-side verge (which were not at ideal ripeness), checking with a friendly local whether I was allowed to harvest them.

Stripping 6lb of elderberries is mind-bogglingly dull, and takes about three hours. I did it in two stages because of Music Club. I have poured in 14 pints of boiling water rather than the two gallons in the recipe. I'm going to use 3¼ lb of sugar per gallon, and not the 3½ lb that C. J. J. Berry suggests.

The yeast went in on 17th September, and I put it into the demijohns on 20th September.

On racking, each got half a pint of water with 3¼ oz of sugar. The first (wrapped in tin foil to protect it from the light) got some 'wine' stored in a bottle from the leftover must. The other demijohn, which I have not protected from the light as an experiment to see if it makes any difference, just got the water/sugar mix.

Quantity:	Two gallons.
Region:	Oakwood (second right off the road leading north from the Oakwood clock).
Price:	£1.10 for the yeast, about £1 for the sugar.
Yeast Type:	Burgundy.
Initial Gravity:	1.010.
End Gravity:	0.990.

Percentage: 14%.

Date Racked: 13th December 2006.

Date Bottled: 23rd March 2007.

INITIAL TASTE:

The wine which was kept in the clear demijohns is much the same as in previous years, so it looks like faffing around with dark demijohns and silver foil makes bugger all difference. It was good, if slightly metallic. The wine kept in the dark demijohn was very similar, though perhaps smoother, slightly sweeter, and less metallic.

THE DRINKING EXPERIENCE

FIRST BOTTLE: Opened on 2nd September 2007, following the first 'Siegfried' rehearsal. It is very much the same as previous Elderberries, which is no bad thing. It is clear and dark red. The taste is distinctive – maybe a little too sweet, and maybe a little metallic, but these are minor quibbles. On the whole it is very good.

SECOND BOTTLE: 26th-28th October 2007. This bottle was smoother and better than the first bottle. It was partly drunk as an "It's a Friday – get the corkscrew" bottle, and finished after a marvellous weekend which involved Pop's retirement party, the wind quintet playing, seeing the siblings, many Crowthers, and several people I had not seen for years. I'm very tired now, though.

THIRD BOTTLE: 10th November 2007 at the Wine Party. This came third of thirteen, was awarded more '5's than any other (three), and got an average of '3.583' out of '5'. The worst comment (a '2') was "really metallic", but it also got a "smooth, fruity" and an "Awesome"!

FOURTH BOTTLE: 18th November 2007. Consumed with a lovely lamb neck and bean casserole, with dumplings flavoured with dill. A highly pleasant evening, flirting with Claire while slowly sinking into fuzziness. Woke up with a bit of a hangover, though.

SEVENTH BOTTLE: 3rd February 2008. Claire invented a chestnut and small onion suet pudding, which was delicious, and merited a robust bottle of red, which this was. It did not particularly aid my thought processes in filling out a job application form, but tasted great all the same.

EIGHTH BOTTLE: 21st March 2008. Happy Spring Equinox. Sooz is down for this Easter weekend (the earliest it has been for 95 years, and the earliest it will be for another 220!), so we have had roast duck to celebrate. Absolutely delicious. This weekend it has snowed, and I have turned Sooz's pyjamas blue. Note for future – do not wash blue slippers in light wash.

NINTH BOTTLE: 6th July 2008. This wine has really mellowed out. It was smooth without any trace of metallic bite. Perhaps the answer is to leave it for a year and nine months before drinking. There were lumps at the bottom of this bottle: a worrying development.

TENTH BOTTLE: 23rd August 2008. Slightly chewy, this wine. Claire's final glass, from the bottom of the bottle, contains definite lumps, and she has just swapped glasses with me, so I have first hand experience. Damn her.

TWELFTH BOTTLE: 16th May 2010. It was a double celebration today. I finished my last (ever?) essay – 3,000 words on medieval surgery – and the bedroom got its annual clean, so we needed something special to mark the occasion. The Elderberry has aged well: it is a rounder, more interesting taste than Elderberry 2008, and has lost the metal which the last bottle had. We drank it with sausages, mash, onion gravy, and random veg prepared by me, and rhubarb pies (courtesy of Freda and Shirley, who are much missed), prepared by Claire. Her mouth has recovered from last week's tooth extraction, so we are on proper food again. Hurrah! There were some lumps in this bottle, but they were defeated by a tea-strainer.

SEPTEMBER 2007

On Saturday morning, 15th September 2007, I walked to the far end of Stonegate Fields to investigate the elder trees that Claire and I had spotted in June. There were a couple, but the berries were mostly gone or withered. I picked those I could and then wandered to Stonegate Road. There were more there, but it was still a poor show. My skulking in the woods attracted the attention of a concerned resident. I think I convinced him that my strangeness manifested itself in an entirely harmless activity. Overall I only picked 12oz.

In the afternoon Claire and I went to the usual place in Oakwood. The elder bush which had been most fruitful last year had been cut down, and elsewhere the berries were less than ideal. We had come at least a week too late. We picked what we could and each trod in a pile of dog shit (not the same pile, you understand). Claire was wearing sandals. On a happier note we bumped into (actually, we were hailed by) a friendly resident, who was keen to offload some blackberries. He told a story of his mother's elderberry wine exploding in the pantry, and suggested we might want to try Hetchell Woods near Bardsey. This was a brilliant suggestion. We had a six mile walk there today (Sunday, 16th September) and the elderberries were ripe and plentiful. We picked another 4½ lb, mostly early on in the walk, but could have picked tens of pounds.

Stripping 6lb of berries was not nearly as tedious this year, but I split it between two days, and Claire helped today. I put in 14 pints of boiling water rather than 16. The yeast was added on Monday morning, 17th September. Because of my trip to London, and having very little time, I departed from C. J. J. Berry's method. I added 6lb of sugar on Thursday night, 20th September, and stirred it round the bucket. Then I left it until Sunday 23rd September (giving it a daily but irregular stir), and then put it into demijohns (one dark, one clear), not filling to the top and keeping back two bottles for topping up purposes. I could have put in at least a pint less water.

When I racked this there was very little sediment, so I only needed to add ¾ pint of water and 4½ oz of sugar between them.

> **Quantity:** 2 gallons – 12 bottles.
>
> **Region:** Stonegate, Oakwood, and Hetchell Woods.
>
> **Price:** £2-ish for the sugar, £1.20 for the yeast.

Yeast Type: Burgundy.

Date Racked: 9th December 2007.

Date Bottled: 9th April 2008.

INITIAL TASTE: There is no difference in clarity or colour between the two batches. Taste-wise, that kept in the clear demijohns was very slightly sweeter than that kept in the dark, though both are too dry. I am hoping they will mature.

THE DRINKING EXPERIENCE

FIRST BOTTLE: 3rd-5th September 2008. Opened on the day Claire applied for a new job, and I had three bassoons delivered. I spent half the evening playing with my new toys, and the remainder wanting to. The first taste of this wine was thin and metallic. That makes it sound worse than it was, but it certainly needs time to mature.

THIRD BOTTLE: 18th October 2008 at the Wine Party. Though this came sixth out of twelve, with an average score of '3.13', it was given two '5's, and Will said it was his favourite. It had a couple of '2's, and I think Shirley was to the point when she wrote "Not yet". Food-wise we had a beef chilli (which Gareth awarded a '5'), beanlash for the vegetarians, and more cheese than you can shake a stick at.

SEVENTH BOTTLE: 5th April 2009. We have lived the Good Life today. We walked to the farmers' market and bought wood pigeon and cheese. The remainder of the morning was spent gardening and making bread, and this afternoon consisted of cooking said wood pigeon (x2) and making perhaps the most delicious gravy I have had. I was really quite adventurous with the recipe. The wine was just right, and I think it has matured.

EIGHTH BOTTLE: 3rd May 2009. Drunk to a sumptuous meal of 'Mutton dressed as Raan', which was a leg of lamb marinated in all sorts of spices and yoghurt for three days, together with pitta bread, peshwari rice, pepper and tomato salad, tzatziki, and falafel. Absolutely gorgeous. With rhubarb (from our garden) crumble to finish.

NINTH BOTTLE: 12th July 2009. Claire harvested our first courgettes today. The plants are growing ferociously, and I suspect will try to declare independent statehood shortly. We drank this bottle with those courgettes, griddled and covered in lemon and dill, together with new potatoes, broad beans, spinach, and the world's most expensive lamb chops – over £7 for four. Good job they were tasty. The wine was smooth and suitable.

TENTH BOTTLE: 8th-9th August 2009. Claire's entry – Ben is still in Wales and I fancied something red to go with the steak and kidney stew I've made myself tonight (some people moan about offal!). Hunted through all the damn wine in the house for about five minutes to find a red I thought I'd be allowed to drink. Ben, on returning – We finished it on Sunday after my 8½ hour trip back. I drank most of mine in a much needed bath. This was a delicious bottle, and again proves that Elderberry improves on keeping. Wales was absolutely marvellous.

ELEVENTH BOTTLE: 31st October 2009. I took this over to Ruth and Ross's house for a Saturday night casual get-together. I had spent much of the day researching Bishops' effigies and resurrection motifs in Wells Cathedral, so an evening of chatting and playing games was a welcome break. Ruth introduced us to a board game called 'Blockus' based on tessellating tetrus-type shapes; simple in concept and fiendish to play. The wine was taken over as a Good Bottle, but proved to be too dry and a little disappointing. Perhaps Gooseberry next time.

TWELFTH BOTTLE: 24 & 25th October 2010. It is rare that I save a bottle for three years, and the wait has made this bottle both smoother and drier. Sunday's main activity has been washing the downstairs windows. Whilst this may sound humdrum in the extreme, it was actually a Big Event. I don't think I have done this for half a decade, consequently, the Middle Earth gloom pervading the house has been lifted, and there is no longer a layer of grease coating the kitchen window. The process took several hours and involved much stretching. Elderberry wine was a welcome muscle relaxant.

SEPTEMBER 2008

21st September 2008 was a glorious early autumn day – warmer than the majority of the summer. We went on the same walk as last year, armed with carrier bags for the elderberries and sandwich bags for the sloes. There were virtually no sloes, though; we got fifteen from the bush that was dripping with them last year, and another ten on the remainder of the walk. Elderberries were a different matter. It was towards the end of their season; another week would have been too late; but we were able to pick plenty. We ended up with 9lbs 11oz, and this was two carrier bags, each about three quarters full. Learning from last year, I picked towards the end of the walk, so only had to carry them about two miles.

It took an age to strip the elderberries – about three hours – and this was with Claire and Pop helping. I didn't wash the berries, though I picked most of the creepy crawlies out, and left them overnight in the bucket. (The berries, not the creepy crawlies.)

On the morning of 22nd September I crushed the elderberries and added 19 pints of boiling water. The yeast, nutrient and citric acid (3 teaspoons of each of the last two) went in the same evening, after my first experience of the Yorkshire Wind Orchestra. I strained the elderberries out on 26th September before going for a curry, and whilst my face was swollen because of problems with my bottom right wisdom tooth. I think I shall have to have it pulled, and I'm terrified. Anyway, the liquid was strained into three demijohns and then poured back into the washed and sterilised bucket, with 9½ lb of sugar in it. I put it all into the demijohns again, properly this time, on 28th September. I added exactly the right amount of water, so am pleased with my 'guesstimate'.

I racked these listening to 'The Now Show' and 'The Archers'. The liquid is so dark that it was difficult to see the foot of the tubing, particularly in the brown glass demijohn. I picked up more sediment from each than ideal. All needed topping up with a little less than a pint of water, with 6oz of sugar mixed in. The batch that was in the brown glass is now in a clear glass demijohn, but is being kept in a shadowy corner of our bedroom.

I re-racked one demijohn on 25th April 2009, because it had a larger than ideal sediment. And it is too sweet. I did the same to the other two on 30th April. One demijohn got half a pint of water added, and the other two got a quarter.

Quantity:	3 gallons (18 bottles).
Price:	£3.50-ish for the sugar, £1.20 for the yeast.
Yeast Type:	Burgundy.
Date Racked:	19th December 2008, and then again in late April 2009.
Date Bottled:	26th June 2009.

INITIAL TASTE:

All batches taste the same – somewhat sweet and port-like. There is very little 'metal', which has to be a Good Thing. I was helped in the tasting by Claire and her parents.

THE DRINKING EXPERIENCE

FIRST BOTTLE: 6th-7th September 2009. This is far too sweet. By reducing the water in the recipe I have concentrated the sugar. So, a disappointing first bottle, because otherwise it is good. We drank most of the bottle after a thoroughly satisfying walk up Simon's Seat. I woke up stiff this morning – stiffer than after climbing Snowdon earlier in the summer.

SECOND BOTTLE: 20th & 21st September 2009. As we had spent the afternoon picking elderberries, and I spent the evening stripping them from their stalks (which went on forever), Claire suggested we drink a bottle of last year's Elderberry. On Monday evening, after I had taken my bassoon in for a service and borrowed my old one back, we each had a glass to polish off the bottle, during which time I struggled with 'Tinker, Tailor, Soldier, Spy' – very confusing.

THIRD BOTTLE: 17th October 2009 at the Wine Party. This was my mother's favourite, and at least one other person's too, but Julia hated it. I think the sweetness caused the divide, and my opinion falls between the two extremes. Tracey wrote (curiously in Mom's handwriting) "exceedingly drinkable, slurpable" and Mom wants some for Christmas.

FOURTH BOTTLE: 24th-26th October 2009. We started this on Saturday night after a Halloween themed concert in Morley Town Hall. Mom, Pop, Chris and Kai all came, and Kai claims he enjoyed it. There were far fewer danger points than expected, and I was note perfect for 'In the Hall of the Mountain King'. Our Saturday night meal was leftover curry, and Monday was leftover chicken roast. Both evenings we watched an episode of 'Life on Mars'. Brilliant.

FIFTH BOTTLE: 8th November 2009. I spent much of the time making other wine whilst drinking this: Nettle and Crab Apple. The remainder (apart from the glass in front of me) was drunk whilst eating Delia's meatball goulash and assorted vegetables – including beetroot culled from our garden. I have used the entire day to write much of an essay about burials within Wells Cathedral, which involved plotting a graph of dead Bishops.

SIXTH BOTTLE: 13th-15th November 2009. I appear to have made Elderberry pop. This bottle was fizzy and remarkably drinkable, in the way I imagine alcopops to be. I downed most of the bottle on Friday night after the Emmaus Party at which Terry Waite unexpectedly sang my praises. The drink was welcome. The hangover was not.

SEVENTH BOTTLE: 21st November 2009. This was one of many bottles (well, three – if you don't count the earlier beer or whisky macs) we drank on Saturday at Jo and Ian's after their three children had been put to bed. Without any prompting either Jo or Ian compared it to an alcopop, and both claimed they liked it.

EIGHTH BOTTLE: 31st December 2009. Our New Year's Eve bottle. We spent the celebrations at Sam's, and as he has been a huge fan of Elderberry in the past, I took this. It was a marvellous, fun evening. Hannah brought her Wii, and we played Bowling, Tennis and Boxing. The boxing was exhausting – I floored Claire thrice, and knocked her out once.

TENTH BOTTLE: 26th February 2010. This is another fizzy, light bottle, quite unlike Elderberry wine from previous years. It being a Friday night, there have been plenty of the week's leftovers to polish off. And then, the highlight of the evening, we used our new bath for the first time. It is white rather than mud green, has side taps and spout, allowing two to wallow in comfort, and handy corners on which to perch a glass of wine. Bliss.

ELEVENTH BOTTLE: 26th & 27th March 2010. I am feeling very sorry for myself. I had my bottom right wisdom tooth out on Monday, and not only does my jaw ache as badly as it did on Tuesday, but the rest of my mouth is full of ulcers. I think I am building up a resistance to painkillers, which doesn't help. And I'm getting bored of eating mush that requires no chewing.

TWELFTH BOTTLE: 27th-30th April 2010. Claire came back early from Orchestra on Tuesday night, so we cracked open this bottle and watched an extraordinarily silly episode of 'Torchwood' on DVD (an enormous creature of death wreaking havoc in Cardiff). We finished the wine on Friday to traditional 'The Sick and The Weak', tonight consisting of leftover chicken broth, and an elderly cauliflower bake which contained exploding capsules of tomato-flavoured pain. And, in fact, it was all rather good.

THIRTEENTH BOTTLE: 22nd May 2010. This was the last of the four exploders that we finished tonight. I suppose it was just a matter of time before one of my 'Alcopops' went BANG. Our bedroom floor now has a suspicious purple stain, which suggests a degree of violence. We drank this in Newcastle on a day that has felt like summer.

SEVENTEENTH BOTTLE: 30th & 31st August 2010. I cooked a whole meal for four people, which is possibly the first time I have done this. Admittedly the extra two were only Bob and Judith, and the meal was my standard beanburger and tomato fare, but I am still impressed. One bottle was not enough, so we started this Elderberry. Claire and I finished it after 'Rubbish Orchestra' and 'Outnumbered'.

EIGHTEENTH BOTTLE: 20th February 2011. What a delicious bottle of wine. I detected liquorice undertones, if you can forgive the pretentiousness. It has definitely aged well, and it is a pity this is the final bottle.

SEPTEMBER 2009

Making Elderberry wine makes me unreasonably grumpy. It is the interminable stripping of fruit from its stalks that does it. Even though I had Mom to help this year, I still ended up taking several hours to prepare 10lb 12oz of berries, and it made me cross, and wonder whether Elderberry wine is really worth it. (It is.)

Claire, Mom and I picked the elderberries on Sunday, 20th September 2009, on a glorious walk round Hetchell Woods. We mostly walked at my mother's pace, but a pleasant amble through forest and fields was not a hardship, and the weather could not have been better. It was one of those perfect early autumn days, with sparse clouds floating in a blue sky, the trees turning yellow, and a warm stillness enveloping all. We each filled a plastic bag two thirds full in a remarkably short space of time, and rewarded ourselves with cheese sandwiches as we sat in the sunshine, contemplating the fields and forest laid out before us, discussing medieval leisure time and the Black Death. We spent some time in Pompocali, a series of prehistoric earthworks at which Roman artefacts have been found. It is a strange place with an unfathomable purpose, but wild and beautiful. Then, just as we were getting into the car to drive back, ahead of us an old lady reversed her car calmly and slowly directly into one parked behind her, causing a loud 'crunch'. Luckily (?) the owners of that car were there and she appeared to know them. We drove past with neutral expressions, and made it safely home.

I have put 9lb of elderberries into the bucket, with the remainder in the freezer, and poured 19 pints of boiling water over the fruit. Any spiders I spotted ended up in the compost, and an attractive green leaf-shaped beetle that Claire picked was placed carefully outside. I added the yeast, a teaspoon of pectolase, and two teaspoons each of nutrient and citric acid on 21st September. I strained out the elderberries on 24th September, and the liquid is delightfully dark. This year I have put in less sugar – 8½ lb – learning from last year's batch which is overly sweet. I put it all into demijohns on 26th September. 19 pints of water was a perfect amount. One notable thing about the process this year was Stan's interest in the bags of elderberries. He stuck his head into two of the bags, and when I came back into the kitchen, his front paws were in as well, treading the fruit.

The deposit on racking was relatively small, and I shared two pints of water with 8oz of sugar dissolved in it between the three demijohns.

Quantity: 3 gallons.

Yeast Type: Burgundy.
Date Racked: 5th December 2009.

Date Bottled: 4th July 2010.

INITIAL TASTE:

Strangely, the demijohn that received the least syrup on racking is the sweetest of the three. The wine in another demijohn is slightly fizzy and lighter than the other two. And the remaining demijohn is best of all.

THE DRINKING EXPERIENCE

FIRST BOTTLE: 5th September 2010. I reckon this is going to be an excellent batch of Elderberry. Whilst it is a little sweet and there is a faint taste of metal, these are on the 'barely' side of noticeable. On the whole it has a good flavour, and is both flat and clear. I suspect it will improve on keeping, but it is starting from a high position. We drank this bottle after a day of playing 'Tristan and Isolde' (without the singers) with the Northern Wagner Orchestra. Claire's part is 71 pages, most of it semiquavers. The bassoon parts, though, are playable, if not terribly interesting. The hall we normally rehearse in was not available, so we played in an underground nightclub, complete with glitter ball, which was different.

SECOND BOTTLE: 19th & 20th September 2010. This wine was particularly suitable on Sunday because the afternoon had been dominated by elderberries. Pop and Chris had come over to help pick, even though the weather was dank. They stayed to help strip the berries from their stalks, and so deserved a glass in payment. Chris, though, had to leave before I opened the bottle. Pop stayed for a meal and had one glass before driving home. I left the bottle with Claire whilst I was out playing Spohr's Nonet, and when I returned it was significantly emptier.

THIRD BOTTLE: 29th September 2010. Well, what a good day it has been. Today we have been to a cathedral, bought a painting, sauntered over a golden-sanded beach, and walked along the Pembrokeshire coastal path to St David's Head. And all in glorious sunshine. I don't believe those who say that it always rains in Wales. In the evening Sue cooked us a fabulous beef stew and roast potatoes. We drank this bottle of Elderberry to it, which I thought went perfectly. Sue was as complimentary about this one as she had been about last night's Crab Apple, and we finished the bottle rapidly. Maybe that's why I'm so sleepy.

FIFTH BOTTLE: 27th November 2010. Turkey has featured heavily in our meals over the last few days. It was Thanksgiving on Thursday, and we celebrated with a full feast at Richard and Linda's. Then we had turkey leftovers on Friday. On Saturday we came over to York to meet the new nephew – Ellis, four weeks old and gorgeous – and to visit my father in hospital, who has just had a hip replacement. As Chris and Keith and family were all here, Mom decided to do Thanksgiving, just a couple of days late.

SIXTH BOTTLE: 5th December 2010. I have been in hibernation mode today. Ten hours sleep last night, followed by a day of lethargy involving playing on the computer, writing an article about Dandelion wine for *Home Farmer* magazine, a hot bath, and reading a good chunk of 'C' by Tom McCarthy in preparation for next week's Booker Book Group Party. And all this activity has tired me out. I have only been outside once, and that was for less than three minutes to fix the drainpipe. I blame the weather, of course. Cold with a layer of melting snow on the ground. A day for any self-respecting mammal to curl up and conserve energy. The wine has added to this general feel of befuddlement. We have drunk it to a chestnut, mushroom and cranberry steamed pudding, invented by Claire, with potatoes roasted in goose fat. I can almost hear Christmas approaching.

SEVENTH BOTTLE: 2nd January 2011. I took this bottle to Julia's, where it remains. Julia has spent all Christmas tending to her aged mother down south, and consequently wanted to cook a feast for her Leeds friends. Rather rudely, I accepted her invitation on one condition: that I could listen to the special double-length 60th anniversary episode of 'The Archers' whilst there. This has been trailed for weeks on Radio 4 as 'The episode that will shake

Ambridge to the core'. So, at 7 o'clock, four guests sat in silence in Julia's front room, large glasses of red wine in hand, listening nervously as David and Nigel climbed onto Lower Loxley's roof. It was never going to end happily. Our meal, however, was splendid – a game casserole – and worth giving up a bottle for.

EIGHTH BOTTLE: 12th-14th February 2011. My Valentine's present from Claire this year was two flowers – a daffodil and a tulip-rose hybrid – made from clinical waste-bags and surgical gloves. I was rather more traditional and got her a card, inviting her to be my love cat.

NINTH BOTTLE: 27th February 2011. This afternoon I went to a masterclass about Schubert's Unfinished Symphony, put on for sixth-formers in Wakefield, where WYSO played excerpts to illustrate the points being made by the lecturer. It was fascinating, and consequently I feel much better informed. It is a piece that looked forward to the Romantic Era, but Schubert's prescience was diluted by the fact that the symphony was not performed until 43 years after it was written. All this newfound knowledge required a bottle of Elderberry to aid contemplation. It was a good bottle, and went perfectly with Mexican beef chilli cooked by Claire. The sweet fruitiness of the wine complemented the hot, meaty taste. Yum!

TENTH BOTTLE: 22nd & 23rd March 2011. Claire asked pointedly on Tuesday night after orchestra what bottle I was going to open. I am playing with Leeds College of Music orchestra again - just for this term - and they are doing Sibelius's Second. It is an opportunity for me to defeat my demons (see the last bottle of Crab Apple 2008), but on Tuesday it was also the occasion of my loudest, most vulgar bottom B flat ever. That alone was worth celebrating with a glass of (exceedingly fine) Elderberry wine.

PEAR

SEPTEMBER 2006

I remember my father making pear wine from the tree in the garden of the house that I grew up in. Surprisingly, this is the first year I have followed in his footsteps for this particular flavour. Most of the pears I used were windfalls, as I could not reach the few that were still on the tree. I wonder why I made such a fuss about picking up pears all those years ago.

The recipe I have followed is that on page 191 of C. J. J. Berry. This requires 5lb of pears boiled in a gallon of water for twenty minutes, and the mixture is then strained onto 2½ lb of sugar. Many of the pears used were on the over-ripe side. I cut out the worst of the rot, but that still left plenty of brown patches. I have not put the wine straight into the demijohn after adding the yeast. If I have time I'll do this tomorrow.

As at 23rd September, the wine is cloudy and a light dish-water grey.

On racking, it is still a cloudy and dish-water grey. There was not much deposit. I had a quick taste – really quite nasty with a hint of peardrop. I added 3oz of sugar and half a pint of water. I'm not hopeful.

On bottling (still not particularly clear, but layered in a strange, pink way), I first of all lost the tubing from the end of the sixth bottle, meaning it didn't fill sufficiently. Next (and worse), the tubing, when detaching itself from the bottle, knocked over and emptied my glass of 'first taste' wine – all over the (recently swept) kitchen floor. Then I forgot to measure the specific gravity. Bah! Howard Wyborn rang whilst my swearing was at its most violent.

Quantity:	One gallon.
Region:	Heworth Green, York.
Price:	£1.20 for the yeast and 85p (approximately) for the sugar.

Bought at: My parents would not charge me for windfalls.

Yeast Type: Champagne.

Initial Gravity: Forgot to measure – see above.

End Gravity: No point in measuring – see above.

Percentage: God knows.

Date Racked: 18th December 2006.

Date Bottled: 21st April 2007 (disastrously).

INITIAL TASTE:

What little I got (see above) I thought was okay. Claire thought 'very nasty, very horrid' due to an aftertaste which I could not detect.

THE DRINKING EXPERIENCE

FIRST BOTTLE: 25th August 2007. I have had some damning reviews in my time. "Oily and slightly rancid" is another to add to my collection. This bottle was opened at Heworth Green as a prelude to duck. Mom thinks the wine is okay. Pop hasn't particularly commented, but for Claire it is a resounding miss. It has a strange, somewhat bitter and cloying taste, with a nasty bouquet. The clarity leaves a little to be desired, but is fine. There is a bumper crop of pears on the tree this year, which is a shame, really.

SECOND BOTTLE: 10th November 2007, at the Wine Party. This was not nearly as bad as the first bottle, but still came second to last with an average of '1.792' out of '5', including a zero and three '1's. An amazing number of people (well, two) gave it a '3'. Someone commented "Dead mouse smell", and I suspect a number of glasses were thrown down the sink. Richard wrote "Last one tasted", and from the sprawling handwriting, you can tell. Favourite comment is "Smells foul. Looks bad. Never again".

THIRD TO SIXTH BOTTLES: Given to my father as Really Rubbish Christmas Presents.

CHATEAU HARDY

SEPTEMBER 2006

In August, Mom mentioned that her grapevine was producing a huge number of grapes this year. She was very keen that I make these into wine. I was (am) less keen – you can buy wine made from grapes, and this is bound to be inferior. However Mom has a certain force, and you can find yourself doing something you didn't fully intend to quite easily when she is around. So I visited on 21st September 2006 with the title deeds to Heworth Green, and had grapes thrust at me. Between us we picked 6lb ½ oz, though the recipe in 'Winemaking Month by Month' recommends between ten and fifteen pounds.

These grapes are mostly densely packed on their bunch and small – some no bigger than elderberries. They are a royal purple in colour, except where they are green. It took ages to remove them all from their stalks: over two hours in fact, but Radio 4 provided sufficient entertainment. I put the grapes into my bucket and mashed them. They produced a large amount of liquid, and this comes up to the 'half gallon' mark on my bucket. I did not wash the grapes, so I am taking my chances with bacteria. Watch this space.

I put the yeast in (according to instructions) on 23rd September. On 25th September I added 4 pints of water to bring it past the 'one gallon' mark on the bucket, measured the gravity, added 2lb of sugar, and measured the gravity again. On putting it into the demijohn on 1st October, it is a 'Professor Plum' colour. I have covered the demijohn with silver foil.

On racking it is very clear, and did not have much deposit. It is a bit vinegary, I think.

Quantity:	6 bottles.
Region:	Heworth Green, York.
Price:	£1.10 for the yeast. and 80p-ish for the sugar.
Yeast Type:	Burgundy.

Initial Gravity: 1.026 before the sugar went in, and then 1.090 once it had.

End Gravity: For some reason I did not record this, but it is usually somewhere between 0.990 and 1.000.

Percentage: 13% probably: they usually are around there.

Date Racked: Christmas Eve 2006.

Date Bottled: 12th May 2007.

INITIAL TASTE:
Actually, not bad; a little thin, and perhaps more of a white wine taste. The colour is more rosé than red. Far better than I had expected.

THE DRINKING EXPERIENCE

FIRST BOTTLE: 25th August 2007. Opened at Heworth Green. This is a dark rosé, and was in fact rather good. There was a definite taste of wine, with a hint of bubblegum. It is dry, but not to the extent to cause my mother to pull a face. Strangely, Pop thinks the pear wine was better. Guess what he is getting for Christmas? Mom claims that she is thrilled.

SECOND BOTTLE: 21st October 2007, Heworth Green on the occasion of Keith and Jaki's first Wedding Anniversary. The assembled company agreed that it had wonderful colour with a slight fizz, and was dry but not mouth-puckering – real wine from a very local vineyard! Jaki said, "Strong flavour, no aftertaste". Keith said, "The more you have, the better it gets".

THIRD BOTTLE: 15th December 2007. This was the last bottle of several, so I am not in the best position to judge. We are over at Heworth Green, and Rachael cooked an amazing lamb shank and butter bean casserole, where the lamb fell off the bone. I seem to remember a pink, clear wine which was fairly ordinary – so quite a result really.

FOURTH BOTTLE: 13th & 14th April 2008. To celebrate having my dissertation bound, and Claire finishing her first draft of the comparison of Handel's 'Ode to St Cecelia' with Britten's 'Hymn to St Cecelia', we opened a Chateau Hardy. Even though this was officially the 'dregs' bottle it was entirely clear, even in its last pouring, and a lovely light purple colour. The taste is thin, but adequate.

FIFTH BOTTLE: 7th & 8th December 2008. Because I bottled Parsnip and Prune on Sunday, which provided lots of surplus wine, we only got through half this bottle. It was drunk to a game sausage casserole and mashed root vegetables – both nights – and we watched a fairly poor episode of Doctor Who on DVD (involving Daleks in Manhattan). Earlier in the day we had recycled about two years worth of glass and batteries – so our coal shed is somewhat emptier.

SIXTH BOTTLE: 3rd July 2010. This wine has not aged well. One might argue that it has aged rather badly. Alcoholic cheese comes to mind – but not that tangy, whisky-infused cheddar sold at Christmas. Still, it has an attractive colour. I brought this over to Heworth Green for a 'second bottle of the evening', but I was the only person to have more than a sip. Pop claims he might drink some at some point, so the wine is currently in the fridge. However, I predict that it will be tipped down the sink in the not-too-far-distant future.

The Life, Times & Wines of Ben Hardy

CRAB APPLE

OCTOBER 2006

On 2nd October 2006 I picked 8lb, plus twelve apples, of crab apples from our tree. This, I think, is later than I have started this wine in past years. I tried to pick the reddest, ripest apples. There are still plenty on the tree, and I have little idea of what to do with them. I have already made too much wine. The recipe is on page 118 of 'Winemaking Month by Month', which requires (per single batch) 4lb of crab apples, 3lb of sugar, a gallon of boiling water, and 1lb of minced sultanas, except I have added an extra pint of water.

Chopping eight pounds of crab apples is tedious work. It took well over two hours, with occasional pieces skidding all over the kitchen. I cut each apple into quarters, carefully watching that my fingers did not get in the way.

I put the yeast, nutrient, and pectolase in on 3rd October, and then strained it into the demijohns on 7th October. I have wrapped the first in silver foil, and this has slightly more juice in it than the second. It is a pinky/browny colour and there is more deposit than I remember in past years, but this may just be memory. I am hoping this will compact down. Currently it is splurging up in the manner of an underwater volcano.

I topped both demijohns up with water on 18th October; more than a pint in the first demijohn, and a pint and a half in the second.

When I racked the wine, the first demijohn had a deposit of two fingers width, so I put in 6oz of sugar and a pint of water. The second had a one-and-a-half finger width of sediment, and I added 4½ oz of sugar and about a pint of water. Perhaps I should have added more sugar. The first demijohn may be pinker than the second.

Quantity:	Two gallons.
Region:	Our back garden.
Price:	£1.18 for the sultanas, £1.10 for the yeast,

95

	and approximately £2 for the sugar.
Bought at:	The sultanas and sugar were from Sainsbury's.
Yeast Type:	Champagne.
Date Racked:	The second demijohn was racked on New Years Eve 2006, and the first was racked on 2nd January 2007.
Date Bottled:	28th May 2007.

INITIAL TASTE:

The first demijohn is slightly sweeter than the second, and the second is a little fizzy. Colour-wise they are the same, so the silver foil appears to have made no difference. Both taste really nice, so we will probably start drinking this one early.

THE DRINKING EXPERIENCE

FIRST BOTTLE: 2nd June 2007. From past experience of Crab Apple, it is best to drink it young, before it reaches 'Crap' Apple. Tonight's was actually very nice – Claire says it is the best Crab Apple she has had.

THIRD BOTTLE: 5th August 2007. I heard a 'Pop, glug, glug' while reading on the sofa, and rescued as much as I could. "And the second is a little fizzy" should have given me the clue. I have stood the remaining bottles on their end. The wine has quite a nice taste, reminiscent of champagne. It is not completely clear. And I was only intending to drink one G and T tonight. Foiled.

FIFTH BOTTLE: 1st September 2007. Taken to Richard and Linda's for a meal. I had forgotten that we had served them Crab Apple just three weeks ago. We had this with seafood lasagne and a beetroot, sweet potato and goat's cheese omelette thing (!) – which worked (surprisingly). Despite Claire's earlier promise, I was designated driver.

EIGHTH BOTTLE: 20th & 21st October 2007. I am starting to get precious about my homebrew, and must stop it. I'm concerned, though, that we are drinking it faster than I make it. Opened after Music Club (Madeleine playing a Brahms Clarinet Sonata was the highlight), and finished after meeting Betty Bradbury, a very distant and aged relative.

NINTH BOTTLE: 10th November 2007 at the Wine Party. A disappointing ninth out of thirteen, with an average of '2.884' out of '5'. It split the room though, with someone awarding '1' and someone else giving it a '5'. It is still one of my favourite whites. I don't care what other people think!

TENTH BOTTLE: 24th November 2007. Opened (and finished) with our second night of turkey leftovers; a splendid turkey chilli; after a day reading Helmond of Bosau's twelfth-century 'History of the Slavs' and poring over maps of Germany. I don't know what was in this bottle, but at quarter past nine I had to go to sleep immediately. It is what I imagine being drugged feels like.

TWELFTH BOTTLE: 28th December 2007. We finished 2006's Crab Apple as 2007 slipped away. I cooked a ham, cheese sauce, sweetcorn, fried onion and pasta mix, nearly forgetting to add the sweetcorn, and we watched the 'School Reunion' episode of Doctor Who, which made me cry. Seeing how quickly we got through this double batch, I am pleased I have made a triple for 2007. I may consider a quadruple for 2008.

SEPTEMBER 2007

I picked the crab apples from our tree on the morning of 30th September 2007. The tree is laden this year. 12lb hardly seems to have made a difference. Crab apples are such a pretty fruit; small, round, and near fluorescent in their redness. I tried to pick the ripest, and discovered you can tell these from the colour of their stems. The browner the stem, the readier the apple is to be picked. Some of the apples have tiny white spots, which may be grubs or insects of some kind. Others have scabby hard patches, but mostly the apples look healthy.

Last year I started chopping the apples into quarters; a slow and tedious task. Claire has now introduced me to the wonders of modern technology, and, in particular, the food processor. This speeded up the process no end, and I whizzed through 9lb of crab apples in less than half an hour. It is definitely the way forward!

The liquid was cool enough to add the yeast, 1½ teaspoons of citric acid, 2 teaspoons of yeast nutrient and 3 teaspoons of pectolase the same evening. I strained it all into three demijohns on the morning of 6th October – a few days later than suggested in the recipe – and that took well over an hour. The mixture filled each to about two-thirds full, and I have added some tap water, though only to a safe level as of yet. It looks to be entirely sediment at the moment. One of the demijohns is dark glass, to see if this makes any difference to the colour.

On racking, each had two and a half fingers' width of sediment. I added about a pint and a quarter of water, and about 6½ oz of sugar (combined) to the clear demijohns, and 3oz of sugar and five-eighths of a pint of water to the dark demijohn. I got lots of sediment into one of the clear demijohns, which was an error. There is so little difference in colour that I have decided to rack them all into clear glass.

Quantity:	Three gallons.
Region:	The crab apples are from our back garden, the sultanas from Turkey.
Price:	£1.73 for the sultanas, £3-ish for the sugar, and £1.20 for the yeast.
Yeast Type:	Champagne.
Date Racked:	1st January 2008.
Date Bottled:	13th April 2008.

INITIAL TASTE:
The batch originally in the dark demijohn is the driest and least robust of the three. All are drinkable, and the other two batches are ready now. I currently have 103 bottles in racks around the house!

THE DRINKING EXPERIENCE

FIRST BOTTLE: 18th April 2008. I chose this as 'most likely to explode', and we drank it shockingly quickly on Friday evening listening to 'The Now Show', then eating a variety of stuffed vegetables and one of the best carrot and coriander soups that Claire has made. The wine is the same as it has been in previous years, which is no bad thing.

THIRD BOTTLE: 5th May 2008. Bank Holiday Monday needs a bottle to see it through. We drank this to a tomato, pepper and egg concoction, which was delicious. A toast was made to 'essays' – three have been printed off this evening: Claire's on St Cecelia, and mine on medieval heresy, and on nineteenth century alternative medicine.

FOURTH BOTTLE: 17th & 18th May 2008. Claire opened this whilst I was in Dunfermline visiting Paul and Allie before their emigration to Toronto. What lovely children they have. When I came back we finished the bottle to the first of this season's asparagus, stuffed mushrooms, tzatziki and lemony couscous.

FIFTH BOTTLE: 8th June 2008. Just lost a mouse. It is somewhere in the front room, whereas last night's mouse is somewhere underneath the bath. Let's hope they don't find each other and breed. At least the wine and the chicken chilli were good.

SEVENTH BOTTLE: 9th July 2008. Neither of us fancied swimming, and I am (briefly) on holiday, for my graduation ceremony tomorrow, so we opened this bottle. It was partly a reaction to the miserable July we are having – relentless heavy rain, and sufficient cold to warrant the heating. Drunk with gnocchi, and then in a shared bath.

EIGHTH BOTTLE: 13th July 2008. A Sunday afternoon bottle. All parents were over, and Claire cooked a wonderful vegetarian set of curries. The stuffed aubergines were the highlight. Mom thought this bottle delicious.

NINTH BOTTLE: 7th-9th August 2008. This was the only bottle which self-opened whilst we were on holiday. Thursday was a stressful day, what with being rejected for Arts and Humanities Research Council funding, and coming home to a house full of fleas.

TENTH BOTTLE: 14th August 2008. Another exploder, which Claire caught whilst working at home because of the plumber.

We drank this when Catherine arrived after a monumental drive from Hampshire. There was no food to soak it up, and perhaps it was all the better for it. Somewhat tart. (And I have been chastised for failing to mention Claire got an A in A' level music today.)

ELEVENTH BOTTLE: 6th & 8th September 2008. Opened after a day of rehearsing Götterdammerung with the Northern Wagner Orchestra, and deciding which Adler bassoon I favoured (the more expensive one, natch). After two hefty G and Ts we did not finish the bottle until Monday.

THIRTEENTH BOTTLE: 18th October 2008 at the Wine Party. 'Most Improved Rating' from the 2007 party, going up four places to number five, and increasing its average score from '2.9' to '3.5'. It got one '5', but also a '2' with "nasty". Still okay seven days later.

FOURTEENTH BOTTLE: 6th-8th November 2008. Claire said she fancied opening a bottle while I was at Shirley's. I told her she could either have Plum or Pumpkin, and she asked if I wanted to eat on Friday.

FIFTEENTH BOTTLE: 27th November 2008. This was our Thanksgiving bottle, which we drank at Richard and Linda's. Linda's parents are visiting from Minnesota. We had the full Thanksgiving dinner and I ended up pleasantly full. Claire's pumpkin pie was tremendous, despite the near pumpkin disaster.

SIXTEENTH BOTTLE: 14th December 2008. We left this bottle unopened in Lambert's fridge in part exchange for a bottle of Chateau Neuf de Pape and a marvellous meal, of which the seafood risotto was the highlight, but the baked swordfish was also delicious. In contrast to last year, Lambert's house was hot and I peeled off several layers.

SEVENTEENTH BOTTLE: 29th December 2008. Just watched a fabulous Doctor Who episode – 'The Family of Blood' – which made me cry. And scary scarecrows to boot. We drank this bottle to salmon in pancakes (which was really an excuse to clear the freezer), and I have spent today learning Latin verbs, stripping down my thesis, and taking Stan to the vets.

EIGHTEENTH BOTTLE: 20th February 2009. A Friday night bottle, and the last of the 2007 Crab Apple. It was tart and I think a bottle best drunk young, but still enjoyable. The meal was a chicken chilli and fried tortillas. Claire got her redundancy letter today, and my job is less secure than expected. Hey ho.

OCTOBER 2008

I drew up a list this weekend of jobs I had to do (finish Latin exercises on computer, tidy desk, put on a second load of washing etc.), and jobs I would quite like to do (mop kitchen floor, tidy front room etc.). This fell into the latter, and was only one of two that I got round to. I picked the crab apples on 4th October 2008. Getting 16lb was not difficult, but some of the best clumps of the reddest apples were frustratingly out of reach. Quite often I would pull at one apple, and the one next to it would plummet into the undergrowth, lost forever. I have left this wine later than last year, and there were a number of apples already rotting. But equally, there are many that have yet to ripen.

I whizzed the apples through the food processor on Sunday 5th October, and this took over an hour. The bucket is only just big enough to hold 16lb of crab apples, 4lb of sultanas, 12lb of sugar, and 20 pints of water. Before the water went in I was wondering if it was all going to go disastrously wrong. In fact disaster was avoided, but each day it was in the bucket I had to beat the apples down to stop them escaping, and stirring was a precarious operation.

The yeast and two teaspoons each of nutrient, citric acid, and pectolase were put in on 6th October. I put it into demijohns on 10th October. The wine is browner than I remember from past years, and the demijohns are all only about three quarters full. And, as usual, I cannot imagine that the wine will clear.

It did clear beautifully, but each demijohn had three fingers' worth of deposit. On racking, each demijohn got just over a pint and a half of water with 6oz of sugar.

Quantity: 4 gallons.

Yeast Type: Champagne.

Date Racked: 30th December 2008.

Date Bottled: 10th April 2009.

INITIAL TASTE:
Oh dear. I am really quite drunk. In the demijohns these all looked slightly fizzy, but in the bottles only one batch seems to be. All are good, though one batch (not the fizzy one) is noticeably blander than the others.

THE DRINKING EXPERIENCE

FIRST BOTTLE: 11th April 2009. This evening did not go as planned. Most of the way through the bottle (delicious) and several vegetarian curries (even more so), Shirley phoned. She had fallen and couldn't get up. We dashed over – walking briskly – and made sure nothing was broken, and came back to watch a new Doctor Who, except i-player wasn't really working. Bah!

SECOND BOTTLE: 14th April 2009. I only took a little persuading to open another bottle (the fourth in four days), and we drank it with tortilla and asparagus (the English season is upon us), and then to a sweet, if overlong, documentary about a Norwegian male voice choir called 'Cool and Crazy'. A couple of days of temperance is in order.

THIRD BOTTLE: 26th April 2009. Opened and only half drunk (unlike those drinking it) at the end of a dinner party at Julia's. Earlier we had been to a concert of three Bach cello suites at St Aidan's in Harehills. The instrument sang, and the space responded in kind.

FOURTH BOTTLE: 10th May 2009. Consumed in Newcastle after Claire's day of a string quartet course, and my day of doing very little except for a jaunt to the quayside. We drank this once Sam came round (within twelve seconds of my 'sweepstake' nominated time) with a berry pavlova, and white chocolate ice cream with a hot berry sauce. Lovely.

FIFTH BOTTLE: 16th May 2009. We went over to Richard and Linda's for the usual large feast, and took this bottle along. The food was plentiful and delicious – particularly the pasta with red onion, artichoke and sun-dried tomatoes, and the wonderful cake. There were also prawns surrounded by a crescent-moon mange-tout, all held together with toothpicks resembling 'Lizard on a Stick'.

EIGHTH BOTTLE: 26th June 2009. Claire culled our basil plantation for pesto tonight, and this bottle went nicely with it. Bob and Judith are over because we are all off to Wales tomorrow. The wine fizzed, and carbon dioxide visibly smoked out of the bottle when I opened it. I'm currently thinking about packing, but without acting upon it.

NINTH BOTTLE: 4th-6th July 2009. The only exploder during our unprecedentedly hot and sunny week in Wales. We were both tired after an exhausting week, so ate lettuce and flatbreads, which is more interesting than it sounds. Claire finished what was left on Monday whilst I was gallivanting with three female students at the Barnsley Mystery Plays till very late.

TENTH BOTTLE: 22nd-23rd July 2009. I had the first glass of this after playing a trio for clarinet, bassoon and piano by Charles Harford Lloyd at Madeleine's – a promising piece and easier than the Hurlstone. We finished the bottle with Julia after rehearsing the Fasch concerto. Today, though, has been horrible. I thought at noon that I had made a £90K mistake, though proved not to have (I think and hope), and my mouth has just started swelling in time for Rydal. More wisdom tooth problems. Fabulous.

ELEVENTH BOTTLE: 2nd August 2009. Claire writes: Exploded just as I was starting to cook dinner (courgette surprise). Ben has gone to Wales to play the bassoon in Antony and Cleopatra, so I am in charge of the wine diary. Continued with courgette curry on Monday, summer orchestra on Tuesday, viola practice and stir-fried courgettes in black bean sauce on Thursday. Thus endeth the eleventh bottle. Tasted exactly the same as usual.

TWELFTH BOTTLE: 19th-21st August 2009. I am currently exceedingly cross with Patrick Charters, a land agent and bully of the worst order, for telling a mutual client that my fees are excessive, before the job even starts. And I am also cross with myself for caring so much. Anyway, I have dulled the anger with whisky and Crab Apple wine, drunk with wonderful stuffed marrows.

THIRTEENTH BOTTLE: 31st August-1st September 2009. I favoured a sober night, but Claire twisted my arm, arguing that we were still on holiday, Claire particularly, as she took Tuesday off to go viola shopping in Manchester. We finished the bottle after Tuesday night orchestra, where the clarinets were the epitome of ghastly – playing a tone out all the way through the Elgar.

FOURTEENTH BOTTLE: 11th & 12th September 2009. This self-opened, and was extremely welcome after our first Rite of Spring play through, and even more so after the first Music Club of the season. Actually, Music Club wasn't so bad. Both Rebecca, and Alan and Tony's quartet were better than expected, and the Mitchells were as good as ever.

FIFTEENTH BOTTLE: 3rd-7th October 2009. My mouth hurts again, and it is obvious I need my bottom wisdom tooth out. This terrifies me. We started the Crab Apple on Saturday, when the remnants of Prune and Parsnip were not enough. I had a glass and a half on Monday while finishing 'Tinker, Tailor, Soldier, Spy': well written if massively confusing. And the dregs were had tonight after orchestra.

EIGHTEENTH BOTTLE: 23rd October 2009. We drank this with a Friday night take out – chicken rogan josh, lamb something, sag bhaji and garlic naans, and then we watched an episode of 'Life on Mars' instead of carving a Jack-o-lantern for Saturday's Halloween concert (a week early). I got more drunk than expected and found myself making bush tea when I meant to ask Claire to do this. The phrase I used was "How fond of you are me?" To which the reply was "No more wine for Benjamin".

NINETEENTH BOTTLE: 15th & 16th November 2009. Despite drinking far too much at Sarah and Julian's wedding party in Haworth on Saturday, we opened this bottle on Sunday. I had a glass only – honest – and we watched one of David Tennant's last episodes of Doctor Who, involving scary water creatures on Mars. Somehow we finished the bottle on Monday. Not sure how that happened.

TWENTY FIRST BOTTLE: 13th December 2009. I have spent much of the last month researching and writing a three thousand word essay on how the laity used cathedrals during the Middle

Ages. It has been one of the most difficult and least satisfactory essays I have written. However, I finished my first draft yesterday. Claire read it today and confirmed that it was poorly structured and hard to understand. One rewrite, several home-made pizzas, and a bottle of Crab Apple wine later, it is far better and I will not hang my head in shame when I hand it in.

TWENTY SECOND BOTTLE: 26th December 2009. Our Boxing Day bottle – not counting the Chilean Merlot before, or, indeed, the whisky mac(s) and gin and tonic. It has been a lazy day, and I have not even left the house – though I have done four sessions of washing up, and made bread. Chris dropped by and we did a 500 piece jigsaw puzzle of a Hoffnung orchestra. Tonight's meal was yesterday's leftovers and a steamed ginger pudding, which was truly marvellous. Andrew has spent much of the evening sitting under a blanket looking like a blue ghost, and my head is spinning in an alarming manner. Probably something I ate.

TWENTY THIRD BOTTLE: 10th January 2010. This morning was spent playing bassoon for the first rehearsal of Oliver! at a school in Kippax. It strikes me as an ambitious school production, and I wonder whether kidnap, child grooming, domestic violence, prostitution, and murder are the best subjects for a school play.

TWENTY FOURTH BOTTLE: 23rd January 2010. The last bottle of Crab Apple was taken as medicine to anaesthetise my bruised ego. It was after a WYSO concert where we played Sibelius's 2nd Symphony. This is possibly my favourite piece of music, and was instrumental in my taking up the bassoon in the first place. The second movement has a mournful, desperately beautiful tune for bassoons in octaves, and during the concert, three-quarters of the way through this moment, I turned two pages rather than one... And Did Not Notice! So I came in wrong, and had to stop as the music flowed past, out of my reach. Twenty four hours later I am still glum. How could I have been so clumsy and stupid? So I drank more than half this bottle in somewhat less than an hour to numb the humiliation. It almost worked.

OCTOBER 2009

Crab Apple wine is a difficult one to write up and still make interesting. "I went into the back garden and picked a shed load of apples" hardly makes thrilling reading. This year is doubly difficult, because I have started two wines on the same day, the main ingredient of both being crab apples. One event of note was a massive crack on the head. I had to go shopping at Sainsbury's this afternoon before starting the wine to get sugar and sultanas, but also other non-wine related items. When putting the flour away in the upper cupboard, I forgot that I had only half opened the cupboard door, and standing up quickly resulted in an enormous bang to the top of my head. I scared the cats by shrieking in pain, crouching to rub my head vigorously, and knocking a large stainless steel mixing bowl to the floor. It really hurt. 'Tears to the eyes' pain that I have not experienced for a very long time. It is now about seven hours later and I'm still alive, which is a relief.

I have followed the usual recipe on 3rd October 2009, and put 12lb of fruit, 9lb of sugar, and 3lb of minced sultanas in the bucket with 15 pints of boiling water. The sultanas are from 'Sainsbury's Basics Range', which I hope will not matter. I think they have been classified as 'Basic' (ie. cheap) because of irregular size and shape. Following my method of the last two years, I whizzed the apples through the food processor using the 'slice' attachment, and felt grateful for twentieth century technology. I added the yeast and one teaspoon each of nutrient, pectolase, and citric acid on the morning of 4th October. It all went into the demijohns on the evening of 8th October, a process that took nearly two hours. I had to add a pint and a half of water to each demijohn, and they still have at least a pint's space each to fill when the fermentation dies down. I added about a pint of water to each on 10th October.

On racking, each had a large sediment, so I put more than a pint of water in which I had dissolved 6oz of sugar into two of the demijohns, and about half that in the other.

Quantity:	3 gallons.
Price:	£2.07 for the sultanas, £3-ish for the sugar, and £1.20 for the yeast.
Bought at:	Sugar and sultanas from Sainsbury's, which, for a Saturday afternoon, was not as irritating as it might have been.

Yeast Type:	Champagne.
Date Racked:	31st December 2009.
Date Bottled:	16th April 2010.

INITIAL TASTE:

All three demijohns are very similar to previous years, which is no bad thing. One is possibly sweeter than the other two, and another is slightly fizzy. The majority of the bottles are destined for mid-week drinking.

THE DRINKING EXPERIENCE

FIRST BOTTLE: 17th April 2010. Claire writes: Ben is at Ella's 30th birthday party, and I have got the 'bottle most likely to explode' and a go at the wine diary. This weekend most of Western Europe's airspace is closed because Eyjafjallajokull is spewing out ash. It has been a glorious sunny day and probably one of very few in my life in which the sky does not have a single contrail. I played quartets this afternoon – 3rd movement of Dvorak's 'American' mostly, but a few minutes at the end spent on the beginning of the 1st movement, which is difficult ensemble-wise. And now for the wine: this was from the driest of the three batches when we tested them last night, but still good. This is sharp, clear, and golden. What's not to like?

SECOND BOTTLE: 23rd April 2010 – St George's Day. It is the traditional day to pick dandelions, but I spent most of it in the office instead. And dandelions make an indifferent wine. I drank this bottle rather quickly and consequently am feeling sleepy (though it being past eleven may contribute). We had a Thai takeout tonight, mostly because we are in need of the plastic tupperware boxes it comes in. But the food was a bonus, even though next time I shall go for a 'one chilli' rating, as tonight's 'two chilli' dishes were just that little bit hot. I claimed that this spiciness was the reason for drinking my wine far quicker than Claire drank hers, but I think she saw through this bluff. And now I must go to bed.

THIRD BOTTLE: 6th May 2010. I wanted a bottle to see in the election results, and thought this would go well with baked cauliflower, beanburgers, fried tomatoes, and cous-cous. I had spent the day writing an essay about medieval surgery, with a brief interval for going to vote. The polling station was busier than usual and contained more children than expected (ie. some). I overheard the man in the booth next to me directing his three year old where to put the cross. My plan for the night had been to stay up until the first batch of seats had been declared, but at ten o'clock, with the exit polls having been revealed, Peter Mandelson was on the radio declaring a hung parliament would essentially be a Labour victory. I decided that going to bed was a much more attractive option.

FOURTH BOTTLE: 19th & 20th May 2010. I am so rubbish at keeping New Year's resolutions. This year it should have been remarkably easy: "I will not join another committee, ever". Yet last night I found myself nodding and saying "Oh go on then" when asked to be the woodwind rep for WYSO. Without any sort of fight at all. I was pleased, therefore, to find that Claire had opened this bottle on my return from orchestra, so I sat in bed reading 'A Canticle for Liebowitz' and supping a glass and a half. The remainder of the night was not without its drama. Claire woke me up, tossing and turning and going for frequent mouthwashes. The socket which had until recently held her bottom right wisdom tooth was leaking foul-tasting pus, keeping her awake. I checked that she was satisfied she would not die of blood poisoning and went back to sleep. Happily she is much better this evening, having been to the dentist, and we finished the wine – which was rather good – to a stir fry with chicken, muscular mushrooms, and spring cabbage. And then a bottle of Redcurrant exploded.

FIFTH BOTTLE: 23rd & 24th May 2010. Summer has briefly arrived, and this was the sixth bottle to explode in the space of three days. We came back from Newcastle to find that two thirds of this bottle had spilled over the hall floor. I drank one of the remaining glasses in the bath, hoping to prevent my body from seizing up. I had spent the day climbing rope ladders, walking precariously across cables, swinging into nets, and gliding down zip-wires at Northumberland's Go Ape as an early 40th birthday present, and my 39 year-old body was letting me know. The wine was delicious; this is from the best of the three batches. Inevitable, really.

SIXTH BOTTLE: 8th June 2010. Claire has taken up ginger-beer production. This tastes fabulous and is highly explosive. Corks pop from bottles with joyous frequency. Therefore, when I was woken by a bang on Sunday morning, I assumed it was from the ginger beer and did not investigate. More fool me. It was, in fact, this bottle of Crab Apple, and I came downstairs to half a bottle, causing more destruction to the laminate flooring. All the remaining Crab Apples are now upright. We shared the remainder of the bottle tonight, and I have spent most of that time reading the opening chapters of 'Bad Science' by Ben Goldacre, which is a readable exposé of dodgy scientific claims, particularly in the realms of health.

SEVENTH BOTTLE: 13th June 2010. I have had a marvellous day, which is fitting for the final day of my thirties. We are up in Newcastle, because Claire was playing Shostakovich's 5th Symphony with the Tynedale Orchestra. I spent the day with Chris and had a lovely time. He showed off his swanky new bathroom (which has considerably more swank than ours), and we spent five hours together in solid conversation about everything and nothing. This incorporated a walk along Cresswell beach with ice creams, and climbing over a stone wall to investigate a tiny thirteenth century castle. Anyway, back at the Taylors' (minus Chris) we drank this bottle before eating, and it was one of my better Crab Apples: it fizzed nicely, was full of flavour, and was finished too quickly.

EIGHTH BOTTLE: 30th June 2010. We have a chaise longue. It is the same chaise longue that I grew up with, but now it is in our house rather than my parents'. It is a ridiculous piece of furniture: far too large for our main room. But it is elegant and beautiful too. This, however, has nothing to do with the bottle of Crab Apple wine which exploded some time last night. I think I heard it go – but in that half-asleep way, and as it was stood upright no wine was lost. I reckon this batch of Crab Apple is one of the best I have made, and despite it being Wednesday, somehow we managed to finish the bottle. Damn.

NINTH BOTTLE: 6th & 7th July 2010. It is obviously exploding Crab Apple season. Despite this being upright it still lost over a glass when it popped its cork. Last night I drank a glass of this either during or just after a mammoth winemaking session when I spent hours sieving redcurrants and gooseberries, so a glass of wine was welcome. Tonight's glass was consumed with an asparagus tortilla, tzatziki, and a salad made from Claire's best lettuce ever. But we are trying to eat the lettuces before Courgette Fortnight descends.

TENTH BOTTLE: 12th-16th July 2010. The batch of Crab Apple that I bottled third is definitely the most explosive of the three. Four out of the last five Crab Apples to detonate have been from this batch. This bottle shot its cork out on Saturday, but we didn't start drinking it till Monday. I had a glass after coming back from Summer Orchestra on Tuesday – where we played proper music, albeit badly. On Wednesday I was out at a Medieval Disco which, disappointingly, did not involve lutes or shawms, but it did involve lots of hits from the 1980s that my fellow MA students did not recognise. Sooz and I finished this bottle on Friday, and as we were both rather hungry, it was really quite effective. Rosehip and Elderberry followed.

ELEVENTH BOTTLE: 7th & 8th August 2010. I had intended an alcohol-free week after the excesses of our week at Rydal, but only managed an alcohol-free nineteen hours. To be fair, we did drink this over two nights, which is unusual for a weekend bottle. On Saturday we shared a couple of glasses while watching 'Sherlock', a terrific updating of Arthur Conan Doyle's stories set in modern-day London. On Sunday we finished the bottle to courgettes stuffed with lamb mince, onions, courgette flesh and herbs, baked in a tomato sauce, and couscous flavoured with salted lemons. All delicious, of course, including the wine.

TWELFTH BOTTLE: 4th-7th September 2010. The remnants of one bottle of Citrus wine on a Saturday night were not enough, but one glass of Crab Apple each was sufficient, particularly as the following day was to involve many hours of playing Wagner. Claire had another glass on Monday evening whilst I was in Harrogate playing wind quintets in preparation for a wedding at the end of the month. The remainder was shared between me and Kirsty tonight. She is staying over because of work, and has not been put off by tales of fearsome cats and general clutter. Today's excitement was nearly crashing the car (which was either through mechanical failure or my carelessness – I suspect the latter, but cannot sort the events clearly), and then calling the AA because it did every impression of having died after a tremendous and scary leap forward. It is running again, but needs to be replaced.

THIRTEENTH BOTTLE: 7th & 8th October 2010. Some of Thursday was spent making Crab Apple wine, and the rest involved Mike the plumber trying to locate the pump for our broken central heating system. Also, Claire has just (voluntarily) reduced her work to four days a week, so a bottle of Crab Apple was a suitable choice. We had a glass each on Friday after coming back from 'Light Night' – an annual Leeds event celebrating all things light on a dark autumn night. At Julia's invitation we went to Pyramid's bird-and-sheep installation, which was imaginative and fun. Best, though, was Bach in the Howard Assembly Rooms. I sat in an old leather armchair watching sweat drip from a cellist's forehead as he played the solo cello suites with passion.

FOURTEENTH BOTTLE: 2nd & 3rd November 2010. We raised the first glass from this bottle to toast Keith, Jaki and Ellis. I had just opened an e-mail from Keith which told me that Ellis was born on Monday. What fabulous news, for all kinds of reasons. Tuesday night I turned into a cat-beater. Stan has developed a massively irritating habit of batting the cat-flap endlessly in the dark hours of early morning, and waking me up. It is Very Annoying. I thundered downstairs, Stan ran out and I locked the cat-flap. Twenty minutes later he tried to get back in. Another thundering downstairs. I opened the cat-flap, picked Stan up, and hit him repeatedly to show my displeasure. Cruel and pointless. And of course I feel guilty about it.

FIFTEENTH BOTTLE: 17th-19th November 2010. This was not a particularly happy bottle of wine. I spent my first glass and a half feeling cross with oboists, and a final glass brooding over a client who accused me of ruining his family's Christmas. The latter accusation is, of course, unjustified. He should never have let the tenants in before they had signed their lease. But I don't like to think of a family weeping over their turkey. The oboist story is too dull to recount.

SIXTEENTH BOTTLE: 12th December 2010. I'm feeling really rather woozy. Tomorrow I graduate, which involves dressing up in a long black gown and green hood, sitting in a large hall, and listening to a dull speech from some Leeds University Big Cheese about plans for the University to conquer the world. Consequently my parents are staying over in preparation for the ceremony. This bottle slipped down rather too easily, and now I'm worried I might graduate with a hangover.

SEVENTEENTH BOTTLE: 10th & 11th February 2011. Thursday was an odd sort of day. Rachael was visiting – we went to Carmen on Wednesday night – and her train back to Leicester was not till 7pm, so I spent most the day with her. Slap bang in the middle, though, was my second interview at Jarndyce & Snagsby. Coming out of this stress levels were high, and happiness levels were low, so Rachael and I went and got our feet nibbled by fish for 15 minutes. It was the perfect thing to do – we sat opposite each other and shrieked and laughed as shoals of fish sucked on our toes. The wine was prescribed to me by Claire as medicine to stop me brooding.

EIGHTEENTH BOTTLE: 27th March 2011. Today is 'Census Day'. I'm sure one is meant to complete it when sober. There are probably laws dictating this. Ours, however, was filled in through a haze of Crab Apple wine. We decided to strike a blow for sexual equality and declare Claire as 'Person One', just to skew the statistics studied by future historians. The 'qualifications' question was irritating: it does not have different levels of 'degree', so I could only tick the box once rather than the three times it deserved. Claire made pizza for our meal and, in fact, burned one because she was so enthralled with the form. We decided that getting tomato and grease stains on the census would not be historically useful, so kept food and civic responsibility separate.

NOVEMBER 2009

Late afternoon on 1st November 2009, after spending the day reading about Bishops' effigies in Wells Cathedral and failing to translate a passage of Latin, I braved the weather and ventured into the garden to pick 8lb of crab apples. This wine is partly an experiment to see if leaving a month makes any difference to the flavour. Certainly the apples are riper, and not necessarily in a good way. Initially I was fastidious, avoiding apples giving signs of rotting. However, as it got colder and darker, and as my fingers lost more sensation, I picked what I could reach, and what did not burst into a brown, sticky mess. This means that some of the fruit that has made it into the mix is, shall we say, over-ripe. The remainder of the apples will now stay on the tree until picked off by the birds.

I washed and sliced the apples on 2nd November, and put them in the bucket with 2lb of minced sultanas (Sainsbury's Basics again) and 6lb of sugar. This time I added 13 pints of boiling water, which only just fitted into the stainless steel pan. This is 3 pints more than dictated by the recipe, but a month ago, when I made this wine, I needed to add a lot more water. I added the yeast and one teaspoon each of nutrient, citric acid, and pectolase on the morning of 3rd November. I was going to put it into demijohns on 7th November, but Music Club went on too long, and I was thoroughly cross when we got home, so I had a large glass of whisky and went to bed. Instead, it was put into demijohns on 8th November, after a day of essay writing. Each got half a pint of tap water added on 9th November.

By racking, both had huge sediments about three fingers' width. I sucked up more sediment from one demijohn than I had meant to, but this is a problem with brown glass demijohns. Each got about 1¾ pints of water, with 6oz of sugar dissolved in it.

Quantity: Two gallons.

Yeast Type: Sauternes.

Date Racked: 24th January 2010.

Date Bottled: 14th August 2010.

INITIAL TASTE:
I waited until August to bottle this batch because the airlocks in each demijohn suggested they had gone fizzy. In fact there is little fizz, though not none at all. Both taste good, and perhaps smoother and sweeter than usual. The one which I had kept in a brown demijohn has a hint of bitterness.

THE DRINKING EXPERIENCE

FIRST BOTTLE: 28th August 2010. I opened this bottle at Heworth Green after a trip to the theatre. We had been to see a youth production of 'Coram Boys', which turned out to be a gothic melodrama set in the eighteenth century involving child murder, teenage pregnancy, public executions, and Handel's Messiah. This makes it sound far more jolly than it actually was. When the play began I wondered what we had let ourselves in for. The dialogue was stilted, the acting wooden, and the pacing tedious in the extreme. To its credit it improved, and some of the actors were above competent, but there were some unintentionally 'suppressed giggle' moments. A bottle of Crab Apple wine was a relief when we got back, and both parents said pleasing things about it.

SECOND BOTTLE: 28th September 2010. This was our first bottle (of three) drunk while I was staying with Sue Jones in St Dogmaels. I had such a good time last year playing in Antony and Cleopatra that I wanted to show Claire Pembrokeshire, and introduce her to Sue – who is entirely lovely. Much of the day was spent driving across rural Wales, starting at Rhayader. It was a beautiful drive, though 'Devil's Bridge' was massively (well, a little) disappointing. Rather than being exciting and dangerous, it was an iron bridge draped in plastic, road works, and tea rooms. Once we arrived at Sue's we hardly stopped talking until we went to bed. She really liked this bottle, and assured me she was not only being polite.

THIRD BOTTLE: 22nd October 2010. There is something rank about this bottle. It isn't entirely unpleasant by any means. Possibly just unpleasant enough. The flavour is somehow fuller than other Crab Apples, and I cannot put my finger on what is different. We drank this bottle in front of a fire, which is currently our only source of heat. The plumber comes on Thursday, and I am counting the hours. We did not have the wherewithal tonight for 'the sick and the weak', so had to order a takeout curry instead (damn!). I spent most of this evening reading a gruesome and gripping crime novel – 'One Step Behind' by Henning Mankell.

SIXTH BOTTLE: 17th & 18th February 2011. I have spent the last few evenings playing 'Oliver!' for a school in Pudsey, and this bottle has been my medicinal relief. Actually, I have really enjoyed the play. There was a tremendous amount of enthusiasm amongst the children, and it would be uncharitable of me to say that this exceeded the talent. Many of the leads were excellent – particularly one of the Nancies (Nancys?), who could become a star. Playing in Oliver, though, means I have hardly seen Claire this week. We vaguely remember what each other looks like. Tonight she had hiccups, so I shouted 'Boo!' at her unexpectedly. This resulted in a mouthful of liqueur being spat over the study, but not in the miraculous cure of her ailment. Oh well.

EIGHTH BOTTLE: 17th & 18th March 2011. I came home from work in a miserable mood, worrying myself (needlessly, I hope) about my future employment. I was certainly in no frame of mind to play trios that evening with Theresa and Donald. My mood improved considerably when I checked my diary and found that trios were planned for Thursday next week, and I could have a bottle of wine instead. This bottle was inexplicably better than the last; fizzy, not overly-dry, and refreshing. We drank it to a ham stock stew and dumplings. The dumplings were molten; my cooling system was to put them in my mouth, forgetting how hot they were, and then spit them violently into my bowl. It was an effective method, if unedifying.

CHRISTMAS TUTTI FRUTI

DECEMBER 2006

I started this on Christmas Eve 2006 as a partially successful attempt to clear the freezer of stored fruit. It consists of 5¼ oz of sloes, 1lb 5½ oz of gooseberries, 1lb 2oz of blackcurrants, 1lb 6oz of blackberries, and (in the spirit of Christmas) one satsuma. I think the sloes are entirely from our bushes out front. I have put in 7 pints of boiling water and 3lb of sugar. Andrew, Sooz, Claire and I all had a go at mashing the fruit, each making a wish as we did a minute with the potato masher. Andrew suggested the name of this wine, Claire suggested the satsuma.

I put in a teaspoon of pectic enzyme on Christmas Day, feeling remarkably grumpy due to the neighbour's singing at well past midnight. The yeast and nutrient went in on Boxing Day. I put it in a demijohn on 31st December, leaving a large gap at the top, and putting some liquid in a wine bottle to top it up next week. I think there will be a large deposit. The colour is not quite as dark as most of my reds.

I topped the demijohn up on 2nd January 2007. On racking, the deposit was not huge – about a finger. I added ½ a pint of water with 3oz sugar dissolved in it. The taste was okay, if a little thin.

Quantity:	One gallon.
Region:	All over, particularly the satsuma.
Price:	The satsuma was maybe as much as 14p. About £1 for the sugar, and £1.10 for the yeast.
Bought at:	The satsuma was bought from Oakwood Fruit & Veg.
Yeast Type:	'High Alcohol and Country Wines'.
Initial Gravity:	1.096.

End Gravity: 1.000.

Percentage: 13%.

Date Racked: 10th March 2007.

Date Bottled: 2nd July 2007.

INITIAL TASTE:
This will be fab – clear, red, and tasting primarily of gooseberries. Far better than the Strawberry we have just drunk. I can't remember what my wish was. You can taste the satsuma.

THE DRINKING EXPERIENCE

FIRST BOTTLE: This and the second bottle were drunk on Christmas Day 2007. I have been looking forward to drinking the Tutti Fruti all year, and it was always going to be saved until today. The first bottle was probably opened around five o'clock to accompany present opening (and what a lot we got this year, much of it alcohol related), and the second at about seven, just before our meal. My first reaction was that this wine is virtually identical to Blackberry, but then was hit by a heavy blackcurrant taste. After the initial taste I got on bottling, I am a little disappointed with the end result. It is fine, but little more. I was hoping for a complex red wine equivalent. The Christmas meal was fantastic, though. Amazingly colourful – from bottle-green spinach to dusky pink ham, with sweet potato, mushy peas, cranberry relish, mashed Jerusalem artichoke and spuds for good measure. And still with trifle to come.

THIRD BOTTLE: 19th January 2008. We drank most of this whilst cooking, as the meal took longer than planned. In fact Claire was cooking and I was peeling vegetables. Artichokes are tricky buggers, and it goes against the grain to remove all the nobbles. The wine is dry and sharp, with several flavours trying to fight through. Far superior to the Banana wine started the same evening.

FOURTH BOTTLE: 20th April 2008. What a delicious wine. *How modest!* No, really. It tastes mostly of blackcurrant, and has a slight fizz. This has been the best of the four bottles so far. I am feeling all smug because not only have I made a terrific wine, I also cooked a lovely chilli and salsa, following Delia's recipe from her Winter Collection (and despite it being April, it certainly feels all wintry). *I refer you to my previous comment.* I'm not quite sure what gremlins have got into this pen.

FIFTH BOTTLE: 12th July 2008. Opened for the Taylors. We were going to eat out tonight, but having ulcers on my tongue (it has been a stressful week or so at work) makes eating a bit of an effort, and ungainly in public. So we stayed in and had roast lamb, mashed potatoes, Yorkshire puds and broccoli with a bottle of Tutti Fruti. It was as good as ever, with some disagreement about which fruit was dominant. Bob and I argued for blackberry, Judith thought blackcurrant. The gooseberry added a sharpness, and who knows where the Satsuma and sloes figured.

SIXTH BOTTLE: 2nd November 2008. We earned this bottle after a cold, muddy six and a half mile trek around the Harewood Estate. Claire even made a steamed ginger pudding as an extra reward. The wine was, as ever, delicious, and it is a shame this is the last bottle, though there is next year's to look forward to. We had sausages, mash, onion gravy, and a surfeit of vegetables. Now the cold weather has set in, comfort food is where it is at!

DECEMBER 2007

I measured the fruit on Christmas Eve 2007. It has 3lb of blackberries, 1lb of gooseberries, 1lb 4oz of elderberries, 12oz of blackcurrants, 1lb of sloes, 8oz of damsons, 2½ oz of bilberries, 3oz of mixed currants (half white currants, half black), and 2oz of pink gooseberries from our garden. This has gone a huge way to clearing our freezer. Oh, there is also a satsuma. It is all in the bucket, defrosting. We taste last year's tomorrow. I hope a double batch was the correct decision.

As the fruit had been in the freezer for several months, and for some of the blackberries possibly several years, it took until Christmas Day to defrost. Back from our Whernside walk everyone had a go at mashing and making their Christmas wish. I got in Claire's way by boiling and adding fourteen pints of water to dissolve the 6lb of sugar already added.

The yeast and one teaspoon each of nutrient and pectolase

were added on Boxing Day morning. I put this into two demijohns, and three bottles for topping up purposes, on New Years Day 2008. I have covered one of the demijohns in silver foil. It smells a little vinegary, which is worrying. As always, I fear an enormous sediment. I could have added a pint less water.

On racking, both demijohns had a large deposit. I added a pint and a quarter of water, plus 6oz of sugar to the one in the clear demijohn, and a pint and a half (plus) of water, 6oz of sugar and about ½ a pint of 'juice' saved from the original mix into the other, kept in a darkened demijohn.

Quantity:	12 bottles.
Region:	Mostly the Leeds conurbation, though I'm not sure about the damsons, or the satsuma. And the blackberries are in fact from York.
Price:	20p for the satsuma, not sure about the damsons or gooseberries, £1.20 for the yeast, and £2-ish for the sugar.
Bought at:	Actually raided from the freezer (except the satsuma).
Yeast Type:	Burgundy.
Initial Gravity:	1.102.
End Gravity:	1.000.
Percentage:	16%.
Date Racked:	1st March 2008.
Date Bottled:	5th October 2008.

INITIAL TASTE:

All the signs for this wine are very good indeed. The two batches are subtly different from each other, with one having more elderberry taste than the other. Gooseberry and blackcurrant are prominent, and it is a smooth wine.

THE DRINKING EXPERIENCE

FIRST BOTTLE: Christmas Day 2008. I have been looking forward to the Christmas Tutti Fruti for months. We opened the first bottle at about six o'clock, after opening all the presents but before eating. This was despatched with alarming speed – all the more alarming after totting up how much I have already drunk this afternoon.

SECOND BOTTLE: Christmas Day 2008. The second bottle was opened for our Christmas meal of duck legs, roast potatoes, cranberry sauce, mashed root vegetables, red cabbage and chestnuts, marrow peas, and onion gravy – a colourful display. The wine is fabulous. I think gooseberry dominates, but it is complex. This bottle, unlike the first, is fizzy, and is from the darkened demijohn.

THIRD BOTTLE: 17th & 18th January 2009. 'Pop [pause] glug, glug' was the sound heard from the hall whilst we were tucking into either hot and sour soup or prawn risotto. I leapt from my seat, located the exploded bottle, did some emergency mopping, and poured us each a glass. I currently have the worst sore throat ever experienced by man, so one glass was plenty. We finished it today with a lentil curry with poached egg, and Seville orange ice cream. I think I am on the mend.

FOURTH BOTTLE: 8th March 2009. Claire spent most of the weekend cooking a lamb tagine, and we needed a robust red to go with it. In fact fizzy Tutti Fruti was a relatively poor choice – it is too light and fizzy. It gave a satisfying pop on opening, though.

FIFTH BOTTLE: 24th May 2009. I heard a bang whilst revising for my Latin exam and rushed into the hall. Happily this bottle was upright, and so only about half a glass fizzed over the floorboards. It is a wonderful brew: full of flavour with a distinct sharpness. I spent some of the time talking to Todd whilst drinking this – during which time an Elderflower exploded – and the rest eating bangers and mash on a beautiful spring evening.

SIXTH BOTTLE: 23rd-25th June 2009. As I was putting on my tie for work I heard a small explosion, and it was this bottle. Wine was bubbling out the top and showed little sign of stopping. Despite it being around 8am I poured a little out (a thimble full) and drank it. Claire says I am on the slippery slope. We had a proper glass after the first meeting of the Summer Community Orchestra, where we are tackling Elgar's Cello Concerto – eek.

SEVENTH BOTTLE: 8th-11th July 2009. The last of the exploders. After decorking itself on Monday, Claire started this on Wednesday. I had a glass after Ian's Sextet (when a glass of wine is most welcome) whilst bathing my thumb in a hot saline solution. During washing up I got a piece of pastry lodged underneath a nail, and my thumb is all sorts of exciting colours, including pus-yellow.

NINTH BOTTLE: 10th October 2009. I have just played Fasch's Bassoon Concerto in C major (arranged for string quartet and bassoon) at Leeds Music Club, and we were fabulous. This bottle was opened in celebration, shared with Claire, my parents and Julia, and drunk to a slab of nutmeg cake. I am sure I shall sleep badly tonight because the adrenalin is up, but I don't care. I was close to note perfect, everyone was in tune, and we followed dynamics and phrasing. In these circumstances modesty is overrated. Good wine too.

TENTH BOTTLE: 17th & 18th October 2009. This was a popular bottle at the Wine Party, and rightly so! Of the five votes, one person rated it their favourite, and all said it was "Good", except my father who thought it "Fizzy and OK, but not great". One person thought blackcurrant dominated. This was one of the bottles closest to being finished. Needless to say, Pumpkin is the fullest.

ELEVENTH BOTTLE: 26th-28th November 2009. Sooz and Andrew are over for Thanksgiving, and this was the second bottle of the evening. We did not finish it, and this may have something to do with the massively strong gin and tonics poured by Andrew earlier. For the first time ever I had to re-dilute mine with more tonic water. Anyway, the bottle was as good as ever, and finished by Claire on Saturday whilst Andrew and I were drinking beer with a Turkey Thai curry – a good use of leftovers.

TWELFTH BOTTLE: 25th December 2009. We have started a new tradition. Can one do that? The last bottle of Tutti Fruti shall be drunk with the first bottle of the new batch. Andrew and Sooz preferred this one to that of 2008, but I'm not so sure. Shockingly, though entirely predictably, we finished this before the food was on the table. It has been an excellent Christmas, though – plenty to drink, wonderful food, a lovely morning walk, finishing 'Wolf Hall', and a grand haul of presents. Now I must sleep. G'night.

DECEMBER 2008

Measuring the fruit on Christmas Eve is becoming a tradition. I had an audience this year of Claire, Andrew, Sooz and Marlo – a Texan who is on the Medieval Studies MA and is in Leeds over Christmas. We have just about cleared the freezer of fruit, though there are still sloes from a couple of years ago for more sloe gin.

This year we have 3lb 12¾ oz of blackberries, 1lb 3oz of rosehips, 1lb of gooseberries, 11¼ oz of elderberries, 4½ oz of blackcurrants, 3oz of sloes, 1oz of crab apples (not from the garden), ½ oz of strawberries, ¼ oz of cranberries, and one satsuma. I calculate that to be 7lb 4¼ oz plus the satsuma. It is currently in the bucket defrosting.

Sooz, Andrew and I mashed the fruit on Christmas Day, each making a wish. As last year's wish failed to materialise, I made exactly the same one again. Watch this space. I have added 6lb of sugar and 13 pints of boiling water, which is one less pint than last year. The rosehips have not mashed well at all, and I fished out the two crab apples to chop them up and put them back in. I added the yeast, one teaspoon of pectolase, and one teaspoon of nutrient on Boxing Day morn, after doing most of last night's washing-up. I strained it into two demijohns on 30th December, leaving quite a gap at the top of each, and put the overflow into two bottles for topping-up purposes. I topped it up to the neck over the following week. It is all currently a glorious dark purple colour.

It has not cleared much on racking, though it is a little difficult to tell. I siphoned up quite a lot of sludge from the bottom of one of the demijohns. Both had a large deposit. The small taste I got was dry, and I added not quite a pint plus 6oz of sugar mix into each.

Quantity: 2 gallons.

Region: Mostly Yorkshire, though not the cranberries or satsuma.

Bought at: The cranberries and satsuma were bought from the Street Lane Greengrocer's. The rest of the fruit was scavenged.

Yeast Type: Burgundy.

Date Racked: 14th March 2009.

Date Bottled: 5th July 2009.

INITIAL TASTE:

I bottled this when Marlo was visiting. She describes the wine as sweet but sharp, balanced and lively. I like this woman. She helped with the bottling and put the cork into the fifth bottle from the second demijohn, so we must raise a toast to Marlo when drinking that one. The wine is clear and mostly flat. Both batches taste the same. It is a more complex taste than usual: no one fruit dominates, and it is difficult to detect the ingredients. I think this promising.

THE DRINKING EXPERIENCE

FIRST BOTTLE: 25th December 2009. Christmas Tutti Fruti always seems to be a winner. This year it is packed with fruit, round and full, and far from being too sweet. Despite the rosehips and gooseberries it is very definitely a red wine, and one to be savoured.

SECOND BOTTLE: 25th December 2009. I had not meant to open a second bottle of this vintage, but by the time we were eating it was clear that a wine shortage was upon us. And what a feast. We had the largest roast rib of beef that I have ever encountered, and it will feed us for days, together with roast spuds, Yorkshire puddings, the best horseradish sauce ever tasted, mashed swede and turnip, kale, chestnut stuffing, and onion gravy, with tiramisu and Doctor Who for pudding. The feasting element of Christmas is my favourite aspect of the whole celebration.

THIRD BOTTLE: 24th January 2010. It has been a phenomenally lazy day, with much of it spent in bed. I was meaning to spend a large proportion reading Anna Karenina, but only managed 32 pages. The Latin homework did not happen either.

FOURTH BOTTLE: 21st & 22nd March 2010. I opened this bottle partly in celebration of the first day of spring, and after the long, long winter it really does seem as if spring has arrived. Claire and I gardened this morning – our lawn is further reduced, this time for a potato bed. My parents came over for a beef chilli and argued about who should drive home. I only had a glass and a half because my lower wisdom tooth was to come out under general anaesthetic the following day, and this was potentially my Last Supper (Drama Queen – moi?). Claire finished the last glass on Monday evening while I was feeling somewhat less sorry for myself than I had expected.

FIFTH BOTTLE: 18th April 2010. This bottle was opened to celebrate our successful ascent of Ingleborough – a large hill which had defeated us on four previous occasions. Today we managed it, and though my legs will ache tomorrow morning, it was a marvellous day.

SIXTH BOTTLE: 30th May 2010. If roasting pork, belly pork is the cut to choose. The high fat content means it stays moist (often a failure with roast pork), and there is a huge amount of flavour. We ate this with new potatoes, roast onions, cabbage, onion gravy, and spicy sweet potato with lime. It was a colourful, tasty mix, and the wine went well.

SEVENTH BOTTLE: 15th July 2010. We drank this on St Swithun's Day, and it rained, which I am sure means something significant. I took this to a proper, grown-up dinner party at Barbara's, where the guests were Claire's string quartet plus husbands. We drank this bottle as an aperitif, and everyone was genuinely complimentary. And Barbara's house is full of Stuff, all of it intriguing.

NINTH BOTTLE: 7th & 8th September 2010. We gave a free choice of flavour to Kirsty, and she chose Christmas Tutti Fruti on the basis of its title. It was well selected. My first taste was peppery – which I have not detected before. Kirsty enjoyed the wine (I think), but at the end of the evening had left half a glass. I had three choices – throw it out (impossible!), drink it (but I had drunk too much already for a work night), or pour it back into the bottle. The hygiene police would be appalled. Claire innocently asked why the funnel was on the table. I couldn't think of a convincing lie, so confessed all.

TENTH BOTTLE: 12th November 2010. It was eight minutes before the sun had passed the yardarm when I opened this bottle. But it being a Friday night, and having just had a miserable, wet drive home from work, I decided eight minutes was insignificant. Claire's day off work was spent clearing the fridge of jars of mould and other unwanted life forms, so she deserved a reward too. The wine is excellent: a complex taste with a kick.

ELEVENTH & TWELFTH BOTTLE: 25th December 2010. We finished the final two bottles of Tutti Fruti on a fabulous Christmas day spent in Newcastle with Claire's family. It has been a proper Christmas – sharp, cold weather with an inch of still-white snow covering all but the roads. Claire, Sooz and I had a winter wander through Jesmond Dene where icicles hung from bridges over a frost-bitten stream, before arriving at 3 The Alders. These two bottles were finished before there was any hint of our sit-down meal. Everyone agreed that they were delicious – having a depth and sweetness missing from the 2009 version. This is definitely a wine that benefits from age. Pity it is all gone, really.

CITRUS

JANUARY 2007

I started this on 14th January 2007, the evening before my Tudors exam, and shortly after my first rehearsal for 'The Love of Three Oranges', which is suitable considering the number of oranges in the wine. I have followed the recipe on page 130 of C. J. J. Berry, which directs that you use three oranges, lemons and grapefruits, except (and a large number of exceptions here):

- I put in 3lb of sugar, not 3½
- I put in 7 pints of water, not 8
- I used 1lb of minced sultanas, not ½ a pint of white concentrate
- I added a lime.

Oranges are the easiest citrus fruit to peel, followed by lemons, grapefruit, and lime. In fact I ended up squeezing the lime rather than segmenting and chopping it. I mashed the rest of the fruit a little and added cold water rather than boiling. Thinly peeling ten different citrus fruits is dull.

I added the yeast on 15th January, after my Tudor exam, which I think was okay. I put the liquid into the demijohn on 23rd January. Unfortunately there is a dead fruit fly floating at the top. I tried to get it out but could not. As it is dead I trust the whole thing will not turn into vinegar. It has a nice yellow colour (the wine, not the fly), but I think the deposit will be huge. According to the recipe I should have waited another six days before putting it into the demijohn.

I racked this listening to 'The Now Show'. There was a large sediment, so I added one and a half pints of water and 6oz of sugar. It is not quite clear yet, and the tiny taste I got was of grapefruit juice.

Quantity: One gallon.

Region: Various, I imagine. Some of the sultanas came from Turkey. The oranges are from Egypt.

Price:	Lemons 79p, Lime 29p, Grapefruit £1.47, Oranges 60p, Sultanas less than £1, Sugar about £1, yeast £1.20 – so pricey!
Bought at:	Street Lane.
Yeast Type:	'High Alcohol and Country Wines'.
Initial Gravity:	1.100.
End Gravity:	1.010.
Percentage:	13%.
Date Racked:	23rd March 2007.
Date Bottled:	12th August 2007.

INITIAL TASTE:
The taste is zingy and mostly of grapefruit. It is shockingly early to be drinking a glass of wine – before 1pm – and I am not yet out of pyjamas. I could get used to this.

THE DRINKING EXPERIENCE

FIRST BOTTLE: 4th & 5th December 2007. Claire noticed that one of the Citrus bottles was leaking, and as she came in on Tuesday evening with a painful shoulder, it was suggested that we might as well try this one, albeit a month early. I am really happy with it. It has a powerful citrus punch, and pleasingly not overbearingly of one fruit. Claire thinks Seville oranges, and I think grapefruits are most prominent. It is clear and a pleasant yellow colour, and overall a good wine. I drank most of it watching 'The Spanish Prisoner', which was an intriguing, cleverly plotted thriller, if mostly ridiculous.

SECOND BOTTLE: 23rd December 2007. I chilled this bottle by leaving it outside. Our fridge is too full of Christmas provisions to allow room for a bottle of wine. It was drunk as an aperitif to beanburgers, a tomato sauce, and couscous with tasty bits in it (the couscous assembled by Claire, the rest by me), with Sooz and Andrew as an appreciative audience. Both claimed they tasted lemon first, before being bombarded by grapefruit. I only get grapefruit.

FOURTH BOTTLE: 16th February 2008. This was our accompaniment to chicken chilli. Claire, though, became obsessed by her viola practice as it was going particularly well. About two hours in I interrupted and pointedly asked whether I could be getting on slicing onions and peppers. Claire gave directions, I had marmalade on toast, and eventually the chilli happened. The wine was as good as ever. The speed we are getting through this one makes me regret I did not make a double batch.

FIFTH BOTTLE: 22nd February 2008. As I was writing an essay about medicine and warfare I heard a noise in the hall. Assuming one of the cats had knocked something over I went to investigate. Horrors! This bottle had popped its cork. I saved what I could and mopped up the rest. We drank what was saved to stuffed buckwheat pancakes, which were delicious. This was after I had been on an 'emergency bassoon reed run' to the Grand, where a bassoonist with Northern Ballet had forgotten his reeds. I am hoping for at least a free ticket to their next performance.

SIXTH BOTTLE: 18th October 2008 at the Wine Party. It was a smaller Wine Party than last year, but lasted longer. I flaked out at midnight, but Claire stayed up with the guests until 2.30am. The Citrus wine was by far the most controversial of the evening, with two '5's, three '1's, and a '-1'. Positive comments included "Very Sauvignon Blanc! Excellent" and "Nice". On a more depressing side were "Reminiscent of toilet cleaner", "Strong and industrial", and "Absolutely disgusting". Well you can't please all the people all of the time, and I liked it. I think a double batch for 2009.

JANUARY 2009

I wish either that I was a stronger person less bound by social niceties, or I had read the last entry for 'Citrus' carefully. The recipe calls for one pint of grape concentrate. I wanted to substitute grape juice, but have been unable to find white grape juice anywhere, so, at Abbey Brew I asked about white grape concentrate. It was the scary bad-tempered man serving, and no sooner had I asked for it, he had rung it through the till. I was too embarrassed to say "How much? Remove that from my purchases, Good Man". I see that two years ago I substituted sultanas, and I will remember that in future. So we have an expensive wine. Never mind.

I also seem to have damaged my thumb. I thinly peeled six oranges, six lemons, two limes and three grapefruits (halving the number of grapefruit suggested for a double batch) on 12th January, and it took hours. I had to grip the knife tightly, and by bedtime my right thumb was untouchable because of pins and needles. A day later it is still tingling, and I cut myself underneath my left thumbnail, which is not great when peeling lemons. As all this took so long, I added the sugar only (6lb), and went to bed thoroughly cross.

Today (13th January), feeling shivery and ill, I poured over 13 pints of boiling water and added the concentrate. This wine had better be good, because so far it has not been a happy experience.

I added yeast, a crushed Campden tablet, and two teaspoons of nutrient (but no pectolase) on 14th January. I put it all into demijohns on 19th January, listening to a programme on George W. Bush's legacy. My thumb still tingles when I think about it, and a doctor has confirmed laryngitis. I can barely speak.

When I racked this the deposit was small, but the wine remains cloudy. I dissolved 6oz of sugar and a teaspoon of pectolase into a pint of water, but only got about three-quarters of the resultant mixture into the two demijohns. The taste was too citrusy, bitter, and dry. Oh dear.

Quantity:	2 gallons.
Region:	Spanish oranges, pink grapefruit from Florida, Argentinean lemons and limes.
Price:	60p for the oranges, 37p for the grapefruit, 40p for the limes, £1.20 for the lemons, £7.35 for the concentrate (eek!), £2-ish for the sugar, and £1.20 for the yeast. I daren't add it up.
Bought at:	The fruit was from Leeds open market, the concentrate from Abbey Brew.

Yeast Type: High Alcohol.

Date Racked: 20th March 2009.

Date Bottled: 28th August 2009.

INITIAL TASTE:
This has turned out far better than I had feared. There is still a hint of industrial bleach, and the lemon and grapefruit are dominant, but it is certainly drinkable. Sooz claims she can detect the orange, but I cannot.

THE DRINKING EXPERIENCE

FIRST BOTTLE: 5th November 2009. Remember, remember. Fireworks were exploding throughout Leeds, and Claire asked which bottle she could open. Before I could confess I had been thinking about Citrus two months early, she suggested it. So Citrus it has been, and I would argue that it is a Good Bottle, even though it will prove unpopular at next year's Wine Party. It is a lovely colour, totally clear, and a dry, bitter, citrusy taste.

SECOND BOTTLE: 9th-13th November 2009. I came home from a wind quintet at Harrogate to find Claire had opened another bottle of Citrus, which is definitely against my policy of trying to space bottles evenly. We have drunk this bottle slowly throughout the week, and I finished it off tonight after the 6th birthday party for Emmaus Leeds. At this party, in a delightfully embarrassing way, Terry Waite (yes, that Terry Waite) gave a speech about me, thanking me for being Chair of Trustees for the last four years. It was a complete surprise, and I went post-box red.

THIRD BOTTLE: 1st January 2010. The first bottle of the decade. We are up at 3 The Alders where it is very snowy indeed, and I have not made a single New Year's resolution. 'Drinking less' is obviously not on the cards. The bottle was shared between the six of us before we sat down to the family meal (another rib of beef, again suggested by Andrew). I spent much of the day reading Anna Karenina, our next Book Group book. Its size is daunting.

FOURTH BOTTLE: 21st & 22nd January 2010. Claire opened this whilst I was at Ian's playing sextets. But, happily, she only drank a glass, so we finished it tonight as a reward for surviving the last proper rehearsal before tomorrow's WYSO concert. We are playing Sibelius's 2nd Symphony – one of the reasons I took up the bassoon – conducted by a woman who conducts the music in her head, and it is frightening.

FIFTH BOTTLE: 4th-6th February 2010. The last two glasses in this bottle were shared at home, helping to reduce my adrenalin. Madeleine, David and I performed a clarinet, bassoon, and piano trio by Charles Harford Lloyd as the last item at Music Club. Despite feeling confident during the day, perhaps too much so, as soon as the music started the nerves hit, and I began to shake. It was not until the last note that I realised we had played brilliantly, and I could relax. The citrus wine helped – a sharp, cool wine that, last night, tasted of success.

SIXTH BOTTLE: 11th & 12th March 2010. Thursday was difficult. I spent the afternoon staring at an ecclesiastical statute, trying to translate it from Latin, and making no progress. It was a tear-inducing frustration, and consequently I went home rather than to the Latin class. I was pleased, therefore, when I returned from an Emmaus meeting, to find that Claire had opened this bottle. I was less pleased, however, to find on Friday night when returning from a rehearsal with the Settle Orchestra that Claire was drinking its last glass. I stole the glass off her and she opened a bottle of Orange instead.

SEVENTH BOTTLE: 5th-7th April 2010. We are now in General Election season, which means Radio 4 will be wall-to-wall political coverage. A perfect excuse to drink more than is sensible. In fact we opened this on Bank Holiday Monday before the election was called, and drank it to strange Chinese pork balls and noodles. I dread to think which part of the pig was involved.

EIGHTH BOTTLE: 15th May 2010. I reckon Citrus wine is more alcoholic than most. After half a bottle my head is swimming in a more random fashion than it should. Today has felt like spring again, to the extent that the lawn had its first cut. Much longer and we could probably have grazed cows on it. However, I spent most of the day bashing my medieval surgery essay into shape. Tonight's meal was the debut of Claire's sour-dough bread – she has spent the last month cultivating yeast – and it worked brilliantly. The texture was superb, and we had it with cream of lemon soup, olives, chorizo, artichoke hearts, sundried tomatoes, and the aubergine, tomato and breadcrumb dish. It has been a lovely, gentle Saturday night.

NINTH BOTTLE: 28th May 2010. Between my second and third glass of this bottle, Claire and I went for an evening stroll round the neighbourhood. The sun was in the process of setting and the air was cool, but it was a lovely amble. I wanted to explore the playing field/wooded area for hawthorn blossom, and we discovered an avenue of shrubs, some of which were hawthorn, but most of which were sloe. This is Useful Information. We returned, peering into gardens as we went, and finished the wine. I went to bed quite tiddly.

TWELFTH BOTTLE: 11th-15th October 2010. Citrus was an unpopular wine at the 2008 Wine Party, so we decided to have the final bottle to ourselves. Monday night's glasses were drunk whilst I was enjoying a hot bath, and Claire sat at the side, chatting amiably about nothing in particular. It is rare that neither of us is off doing stuff, and an hour just talking is lovely. I finished the bottle tonight, after a busy few days combining working hard as a solicitor with domestic drudgery. Our house will be spotless for tomorrow night. I have already mopped the kitchen floor twice.

PRUNE & PARSNIP

FEBRUARY 2007

I boiled up the parsnips in two pints of water, and chopped up the (pitted) prunes on 17th February 2007. There are slightly more than 2lb of parsnips, and slightly more than ½ lb of prunes in this batch. I am following the recipe in 'Winemaking Month by Month' on page 54, which requires (in addition to the above) 3lb of sugar, another 3 pints of boiling water, 2 teaspoons of citric acid, 1 teaspoon each of both amylase and pectolase, and enough cold water to make the liquid up to a gallon. This looked like the most interesting February wine, but 'interesting' does not necessarily translate as 'nice'. I think I may have boiled the parsnips for too long – they are extremely soft. I poured the parsnips and water over the prunes in the bucket, then added the sugar and the 3 extra pints of boiling water.

I put the yeast and chemicals in on the morning of 18th February. Though the recipe does not mention it, I also added yeast nutrient. I put this into a demijohn on 24th February, after finishing a run of 'Love for Three Oranges', which was hugely satisfying. The wine is a nasty brown colour, and I fear a large deposit. I had to add ¾ of a pint of water.

On racking, I added another pint and a half of water and 5½ oz of sugar. It is relatively clear, but browny-orange. The sediment was large – about a finger and three-quarter's worth – and clumpy. The little taste I got was sherry like.

Quantity:	One gallon.
Region:	The parsnips are English, the prunes American.
Price:	£4.05 for the prunes, £2 for parsnips, £1 for sugar, £1.10 for the yeast.
Yeast Type:	Sauternes.

Initial Gravity: 1.108.

End Gravity: I didn't record this, though I did record the percentage – which is...

Percentage: 13%.

Date Racked: 14th April 2007.

Date Bottled: 26th August 2007.

INITIAL TASTE:
This tastes really good, which is a surprise. It is my fizziest wine to date (I think), so will have to be stored upright. It is entirely clear, and a golden colour. Even Claire likes it. Quite sweet.

THE DRINKING EXPERIENCE

FIRST BOTTLE: 2nd February 2008. Okay, it tastes of prunes – but in a good way. The clarity is excellent, and it is a dark yellow-amber wine. It is fizzy and tastes a little of sherry, which is a bizarre mix. The parsnip is undetectable (which pleases Claire), but the prune is distinctive. Overall, I am happy with how this has come out.

SECOND BOTTLE: 20th March 2008. Sooz and I shared this whilst Claire was playing string trios in Roundhay. I came home cross and hungry after standing around at Leeds Station for half an hour waiting for Sooz to arrive, and then giving up. Claire prescribed an immediate glass of wine, and we drank it once Sooz had arrived, gossiping about her new boyfriend. The wine tasted less of prunes than the first bottle, but was just as fizzy and really rather nice.

THIRD BOTTLE: 12th April 2008. We drank the whole bottle after the Music Club AGM, which went on too long and involved discussions over whether 'register of members', 'list of members' or 'membership list' was correct (yawn!). I think a bottle of wine was necessary medicine after that. We watched Doctor Who whilst drinking this – an entertaining episode about Pompeii. I think this wine is really good – each bottle (so far) is an improvement on the last, and it may well become one of my regulars.

FOURTH BOTTLE: 19th-21st May 2008. Claire handed me a glass of this as I stepped through the door on Monday evening after my first day at Emsleys and a meeting at Emmaus. I needed the drink – both work and the meeting were fine – good, even – but it had been a long, exhausting day, and a glass of Prune and Parsnip took the edge off it.

FIFTH BOTTLE: 12th July 2008. We needed a second bottle, and Bob, reading through this journal, raised his eyebrows and remarked "Prune and Parsnip?" so the choice was made. Claire remembered that this bottle is actually quite nice, which is a relief – seeing as I have a double batch brewing this year. It has a strange dry-yet-dessert quality, and is remarkably fizzy. Whilst drinking this we learnt that Judith is off to the Grand Canyon in September, so we have shoved many books and maps her way.

SIXTH BOTTLE: 18th October 2008 at the Wine Party. Not a huge success at the party, which makes me wonder if the double batch was such a good idea. There were comments about it tasting like a fizzy sherry. Its lowest score was a '-2', and this glass ended up down the sink. Somebody thought there was too much parsnip, but it got three '4's, and came ninth out of twelve, with an average of '2.4'. Julia took the half-finished bottle home with her, and then rang shortly after to say "Help, the bottle has exploded". I prescribed keeping it in the fridge and drinking it the next day.

MAY 2008

On 3rd May 2008 I counted up my demijohns, planned the rest of this year's wines, and saw that I could do a double batch this month. As I have been so pleased with last year's Prune and Parsnip, I have decided to repeat it this year. Claire has just asked, aghast, "Are you making double quantities?" and wonders whether it is merited. We shall see.

It is a little late in the year for parsnips, but I found a stall selling them at 50p a pound. I put in 4lbs 2oz of parsnips, 1lb ½ oz of prunes, and 13 pints of water, following Brian Leverett's recipe. I put in 3 teaspoons of citric acid, rather than 4 – which sounded a bit much. The bucket into which this has all been poured still smells of cloves, which could add an interesting element to the taste. I added 1 teaspoon each of amalyse, pectolase and nutrient, and also the yeast on 4th May. The temperature was 25 degrees Celsius. It all went into the demijohns on 10th May 2008 and, as last year, I think the deposit will be huge. There is probably at least a pint and a half's space in each demijohn, which I shall fill with tap water when I know it is safe.

I added ¾ pint of water to each demijohn on 11th May, and then a further ½ pint the next day. In both cases the water had been boiled, but cooled to room temperature.

I racked this after swimming in a particularly crowded pool. Each demijohn had about two fingers of sludge at the bottom, though the wine is totally clear. In one demijohn the wine appeared to have stopped fermenting, and I racked this into my smallest demijohn with the narrowest neck. I added about half a pint of 'syrup' (6oz of sugar to a pint of water) to this demijohn, and maybe more than ¾ pint to the other. The small taste I got was very dry, and somewhat unpleasant.

Quantity:	2 gallons.
Region:	No idea.
Price:	£2 for parsnips, £2.50 for prunes, £2-ish for sugar, £1.20 for yeast, equalling £7.70.
Yeast Type:	Bordeaux.
Initial Gravity:	1.112 (which sounds high, but it will be diluted when put into demijohns).
End Gravity:	1.006.
Percentage:	16%.
Date Racked:	23rd July 2008.
Date Bottled:	7th December 2008.

INITIAL TASTE:
By the time of bottling this wine has become rather sweet. Happily, it is also far nicer than it was four months ago, and sherry-like. It

is golden brown and absolutely clear. A double batch was probably not a mistake.

THE DRINKING EXPERIENCE

FIRST BOTTLE: 2nd March 2009. Opened two months early, but I am trying to decide between this and Rhubarb for the March 2009 wine. Also, today has been horrid. Stan has a lump in his bowel and is probably dying, Claire's job prospects are going tits up, and I had a rubbish Latin exam. Aggie's teeth, however, are fine. So downing a bottle on a Monday night seemed like the best solution. It is good – sherry-like – and I am still undecided.

SECOND BOTTLE: 18th & 19th April 2009. A bottle and a half at the bassoon quartet evening was not quite enough, so we mostly finished this bottle too. It is a strange wine: definite tastes of caramelised toffee, and it does not really taste of wine at all. Maybe drinking it with banana splits affected the flavour.

THIRD BOTTLE: 2nd & 3rd May 2009. This was opened after we had returned from the last night of 'Pirates of Penzance', and finished by Claire on Sunday in preference to the Plum! Both the show and the wine were enjoyed by all, with Andrew comparing it (the wine, not the show) to Croft Original. I drank mine while blowing up an air mattress.

FOURTH BOTTLE: 23rd May 2009. Claire cooked Iraqi food tonight from Guardian recipes, and correctly judged Prune and Parsnip to be a suitable accompaniment. The food was flavoured with pomegranate molasses, so a robust, semi-sweet wine went well. It was a wonderful meal: a chicken and walnut stew, and a bulgur wheat mix with tomatoes, spring onions, and chillies. We had some home-grown lettuce, which so far is a novelty, but I suspect the appeal will wane over the next few months.

FIFTH BOTTLE: 12th-14th August 2009. This bottle has been drunk slowly during the week following a fortnight of riotous living in the Lake District, and then Pembrokeshire. Consequently I have spent all three evenings feeling unnaturally sleepy, and was in bed by nine o'clock after the first glass. Courgettes have figured heavily in the meals eaten with this wine, with tonight's dish being sweet and sour courgettes, and an Actively Delicious bean curd.

SEVENTH BOTTLE: 1st-3rd October 2009. Claire opened this while I was at Ian's Rubbish Sextet, and I needed a glass on my return. The sextet was more septic than usual, with Anthony being a semitone flat for much of it. Ghastly. We finished the bottle tonight, while Claire was cooking and I was making Crab Apple wine, and enjoying each other's company.

EIGHTH BOTTLE: 17th October 2009 at the Wine Party. Someone took this bottle away with them at the end of the evening, which counts as a 'success' in my books. Most people liked it I think, despite initial misgivings inspired by the ingredients. One guest wrote "How this works is a complete mystery!" and someone else put "Definitely the best thing to do with prunes. If they were alcoholic, we'd all be regular".

TENTH BOTTLE: 21st November 2009. Jo requested this flavour specially, and so we took it with us on our 'Not Yet 40' jaunt to Birmingham. Ian claims he thought it delicious and reminded him of Benedictine, but I have no idea what that means.

ELEVENTH BOTTLE: 10th & 11th December 2009. Latin had gone badly – I find sentence structure difficult – and my essay was stuttering, so I needed plenty of alcohol to Make Things Better. Also, Chris was visiting – albeit a day later that he had arranged – and we were eating a North African and Greek meal of lamb tagine, couscous, pitta bread, fried haloumi, and salad. Prune and Parsnip seemed the right choice, banishing the Doom and Gloom.

TWELFTH BOTTLE: 27th-29th December 2009. After a liver-damaging Christmas we decided to embrace temperance by splitting this bottle over two nights. The whisky macs and cranberry vodkas on the second of those nights were perhaps not in the spirit of sobriety, though. The first night we had a beef and potato pie, and the second we had tortillas. For both we watched an episode of Life on Mars. And so ends the Prune and Parsnip, but I have just bought parsnips for a single batch in January 2010 – the first of the new decade. Hoorah.

ASSAM TEA

MARCH 2007

I began this on 10th March 2007 after getting very annoyed with my neighbour's incessant piano practice, and then retaliating with a piccolo (and then feeling guilty). The recipe comes from page 57 of 'Winemaking Month by Month', using oranges rather than the citric acid. The instructions are ambiguous. They tell you to add the tea 'prepared in the usual way', but does this mean the leaves go in or not? And how, exactly, do you prepare 4oz of tea (almost a whole packet) 'in the usual way'? You would need a teapot the size of a phone box.

I put the tea directly into the bucket first, poured over 2½ pints of boiling water, and let it brew while mincing 2lb of sultanas. Once I had added the sultanas I added another 2½ pints of boiling water, the 2½ lb of sugar, and then another 3 pints of boiling water. So the tea leaves are still in there. I then had an hour and a half break (for a rehearsal of the Spohr Nonet for Music Club), before adding the juice from 2 oranges. I added yeast and nutrient after Music Club on the same day.

I put the wine into the demijohn very late on Thursday night (15th March), and added ¾ of a pint of cold water. It is the colour of strong tea (with milk, though no milk was added), and (again) a heavy deposit.

When I racked this I had to add nearly a pint and a half of water, with 5oz of sugar and a teaspoon of pectolase, as its clarity is that of a dense, orangey-brown broth. By bottling, however, it had cleared and is orange – a dark colour for white wine.

Quantity:	One gallon.
Region:	The tea is from the Brahmaputra Valley in North-East India, the sultanas are from Turkey.
Price:	£1.80-ish for the tea, 80p for oranges, £1-ish for sultanas, £1 for sugar, and £1.10 for yeast.

Bought at:	Tea from Beano, sultanas from the Co-op and Sainsbury's, and oranges from the greengrocer's on Street Lane.
Yeast Type:	Bordeaux.
Initial Gravity:	1.110.
End Gravity:	1.002.
Percentage:	16%.
Date Racked:	20th May 2007.
Date Bottled:	30th September 2007.

INITIAL TASTE:
I cannot tell whether I like this or not. There is a definite black tea taste, which has a touch of bitterness to it. The taste is 'thicker' than most, and reminiscent of sherry.

THE DRINKING EXPERIENCE

FIRST BOTTLE: 1st March 2008. Not my greatest wine. It has a distinct taste of black tea, and a dark orange colour. It is both bitter and sweet (builders' tea, perhaps), and the clarity deteriorated with every glass (though that could describe my thought process as well). It is not undrinkable, but you would not want to pay good money for it. We drank it to a bulgur wheat salad, roasted broccoli, and grilled lamb chops, though Claire rejected one of hers as funny-tasting, and mine are now sitting heavily in my stomach.

SECOND BOTTLE: 23rd March 2008 – Easter Day. We fancied something to drink, decided to open a bottle of wine but not to finish it, and drank it all anyway. The meal was a duck and noodle stir fry, much to the cats' envy, and we watched 'The History Boys' on DVD, which Claire enjoyed more than me. The wine is still only on the borders of palatable, but that is good enough for current purposes.

THIRD BOTTLE: 6th-9th April 2008. Claire opened this whilst I was in London for a Chairs of Trustees meeting (which was mostly dull, though gave me a chance to see Bridget, and fail to get into both the Hunterian Museum and Westminster Abbey). I had a glass of the Tea wine on Monday evening on my return, with a strange but successful lentil and sweet potato curry. Because this was towards the bottom of the bottle it was brown and sludgy, but otherwise as disappointing as the other two bottles. Claire finished it on Wednesday.

FOURTH BOTTLE: 20th June 2008. Far from my clearest wine – or, indeed, my loveliest. We drank this to traditional Friday night 'the sick and the weak', after I had come home from a second night of supping champagne to celebrate my 'First' in the History Degree, and prize for girliest swot in the entire year. The Tea wine is something of a comedown from those heady heights.

FIFTH BOTTLE: 22nd August 2008. I suggested a bottle of Strawberry, but Claire vetoed that on the grounds that it would not go with Shropshire blue and broccoli soup. So Tea wine it was. The soup was delicious. The wine was effective. It might have improved a little, and is certainly a distinctive taste.

SIXTH BOTTLE: 18th October 2008 at the Wine Party. A most surprising 'Hit', coming fourth with an average of '3.61'. I kept on hearing comments about it being a delightful dessert wine, mostly tasting of sultanas. On tasting it I was pleasantly surprised – this wine was not as bitter as previous bottles. Maybe it was the maturation time, or possibly that the third bottle out of the demijohn (which this was) was the best, or maybe I was pissed. Richard thought it tasted like a Muscadet, and someone declared it their favourite. I suspect I will not do this one again – or at least not for a while. If I do, I will put in less tea. This all shows how the Wine Party is flawed as a market research tool.

DANDELION

APRIL 2007

I have had a complicated relationship with Dandelion wine. The first time I made it, in 1998, it was delicious. Since then it has been poor at best, and abandoned at worst. I have given it a three year rest in the hope that I can recapture the spark of my first encounter with it. Today, the 14th of April 2007, has been glorious weather, and there are worse things to do than spend an hour in a field picking dandelions, occasionally being greeted by enthusiastic dogs. I got lost trying to find my usual field, and once found, had to do a double take as it has been converted into a young, broad-leafed forest. (The wood adjoining this field has an abundance of bilberry bushes – which is worth remembering for August.) Still, I found sufficient dandelions for the C. J. J. Berry recipe on page 149, which requires 6 pints of flowers, though I added an extra pint and a quarter of dandelions. I think this is the first time I have measured by volume rather than weight. I put the flowers in the bucket, and then poured a gallon of boiling water over them. Omens are not particularly good for this wine though: not only did I get lost and then discover the field had been converted, I have just spent fifteen minutes heating up a small pan lid rather than the gallon of water I intended. I turned on the wrong gas ring – what an idiot.

On Tuesday 17th April I added 3lb of sugar and the thinly sliced peel of the two lemons and one orange, trying to avoid the pith, stirred it around, and put it into the big silver pan to boil. I did not check the instructions, so missed the bit about boiling it for ten minutes – it might have got just three. I then added the juice of the fruit. The yeast and tannin went in on the morning of 18th April.

Before putting the liquid into the demijohn on 21st April, I added a litre of white grape juice rather than the half pint of grape concentrate set out in the recipe. It is an attractive yellow, and I feel positive about this.

Less positive on racking, though. It has hardly cleared at all, so I have put in a teaspoon of pectolase (without much hope). I also added half a pint of water and 3oz of sugar.

Quantity:	Six bottles.
Region:	The field near Lawnswood Crags.
Price:	20p for the orange, 33p for the lemon, £1-ish for the sugar, £1.10 for the yeast, and £1-ish for the grape juice.
Yeast Type:	'High Alcohol and Country Wines'.
Initial Gravity:	1.082.
End Gravity:	0.098.
Percentage:	13%.
Date Racked:	5th July 2007.
Date Bottled:	7th November 2007.

INITIAL TASTE:
It has cleared – hurrah! – and is gloriously yellow. I'm not too keen on the taste, however. It is very dry, thin, and has that home-made wine 'nutty-and-a-little-bit-musty' taste. Claire likes it though. Also it has gone fizzy, so another one to store upright.

THE DRINKING EXPERIENCE

FIRST BOTTLE: 29th & 30th March 2008. The clarity and colour of this Dandelion wine are excellent. It has the look of a wine made by the professionals, and the taste is not too bad. It is dry – a dryness that would lead to my mother pulling her 'Chardonnay' face – but not to my pallet (and Claire is an evil, evil woman who has just knowingly given me the spelling for a wooden platform rather than for 'palate'!) undrinkable. There is an unusual taste, which is probably the dandelion. Overall I would prefer a proper bottle of white wine, but at 60p a bottle I can't complain. Surprisingly there is very little fizz. We opened it after a Music Club at which Claire played viola and violin duets marvellously with Laura, and we are finishing it after a gloriously lazy Sunday, some of which was spent gardening.

SECOND BOTTLE: 19th April 2008. Quiches are mostly rather boring. Not this one though – with its spinach, Shropshire blue, and exploding tomatoes. Dandelion wine was a suitable accompaniment – clear, yellow, and dry. This is definitely my second best attempt at Dandelion, in that it is drinkable without being actively delicious.

THIRD BOTTLE: 16th May 2008. I did not much like this wine. There is nothing actively wrong with it, but it has a strange, slightly bitter taste, reminiscent of a wine that has been left to stand too long. Still, it has done its Friday night job (to the extent that I made real tea rather than bush tea by mistake).

FOURTH BOTTLE: 18th July 2008. Feeling drunker than I should on half a bottle. Dandelion wine is just on the correct side of the 'interesting' dividing line, where the wrong side reaches into the realms of nasty. This is a lovely colour, and was clear to the bottom of the bottle, which are its best features. We drank it to first and second declension nouns, and a Friday night 'not a lot left in the fridge' tortilla.

FIFTH BOTTLE: 18th October 2008 at the Wine Party. This was one of the mid-range, non-descript wines served at the Wine Party, and I suspect few will remember it. It came eighth out of twelve, with an average score of '2.83', and scored between '1' and '4'. One memorable aspect of the Wine Party was being in pain from my wisdom teeth. I popped painkillers with gay abandon during the entire weekend, and at least the party gave me something to take my mind off it. The tooth comes out on 15th December!

SIXTH BOTTLE: 22nd-26th January 2009. We both had a day off work/university on Thursday, so had most of a bottle of Dandelion to celebrate. I spent the day at Starbucks for a morning coffee with Claire, followed by a visit to the Leeds City Museum – good in places – and then went to the university anyway, tracking down books about medieval maps. I suspect Claire spent most of the day playing the viola. We watched Sweeney Todd while drinking this bottle – thoroughly nasty (the film rather than the wine, which was only a little nasty). I suspect this flavour will be revisited only intermittently.

ELDERFLOWER

JUNE 2007

I picked the elderflowers from Golden Acre Park on a cloudy Sunday morning, 10th June 2007. There were plenty of trees, and I picked from a selection. It is really only the beginning of the elderflower season. One man passing was interested, but on the whole I was ignored by the families out for a stroll. Of course I picked nearly twice what I needed. For future reference, a three-quarter sized carrier bag full of elderflowers is far too much for one gallon. Maybe I will look into elderflower cordial.

I stripped the flowers whilst listening to Yoko Ono on Desert Island Discs, followed by a repeat of I'm Sorry I Haven't a Clue, and finally the Food Programme. Yup – it took nearly two hours – tedious. I rescued as many insects as I could, and our kitchen window is covered in small flies. I followed Pop's friend's recipe, which calls for a pint of elderflowers and six pints of water, a 12mg vitamin B tablet, yeast nutrient, a heaped teaspoon of grape tannin, 1 litre of white grape juice, 2½ lb of sugar, and a teaspoon of pectolase. I did not wash the elderflowers or boil the water. The yeast went in 29 hours after everything else.

I put this into the demijohn on 16th June. It is a light, unappetizing beige, and has many tiny dead flies (not fruit flies) floating on top – my equivalent of a dead rat in a bucket of fermenting cider. Protein!

On racking it is mostly clear. There was only a small deposit. I made up a 'syrup' of half a pint of water and 3oz of sugar, but only got about two thirds in.

When I brought this down to bottle there were bits in it – mostly elderflowers. It is slightly cloudy, but not enough to matter.

Quantity:	One gallon.
Region:	Golden Acre Park.
Price:	94p for the grape juice, £1.20 for the yeast, approximately 85p for the sugar.

Yeast Type: Champagne.

Initial Gravity: 1.100.

End Gravity: 0.990.

Percentage: 16% (surely not?).

Date Racked: 1st September 2007.

Date Bottled: Christmas Eve 2007.

INITIAL TASTE:

I got a small taste, which was lovely (hurrah!). However, my parents arrived at the critical moment and downed the two glasses saved for general consumption. Oh well.

THE DRINKING EXPERIENCE

FIRST BOTTLE: 31st May 2008. It is a Saturday night and the weather and meal just called for a white, so I opened this. The wine is still, clear, refreshing, and exactly what you want from an Elderflower wine. We drank it with a leafy salad, a Thai chicken curry with stir-fried beet tops and ginger, and an episode of Doctor Who. This after a day in Pickering, tromping around the castle and looking at medieval (or are they Victorian?) wall paintings in the parish church, whilst feeling sorry for myself because of a painful gum/wisdom tooth and a sore throat.

SECOND BOTTLE: 15th June 2008. Richard chose this bottle to go with my birthday meal (postponed a day so we could go to a concert of Bartok's viola concerto and The Sorcerer's Apprentice). It was a sumptuous feast: spinach and coriander pancakes with lime butter, sweet potato burgers, salsa, tzatziki, goat's cheese and olive green salad, elderflower fritters, and Black Forest gateau. We did not go to bed hungry. The wine was a refreshing white with a distinctive taste. Aggie disgraced herself by bringing in a mouse, which Richard caught and released out of the cat-flap.

THIRD BOTTLE: 18th October 2008 at the Wine Party. This came second out of the twelve bottles, with an average of

'3.78'. It only got one '5', but was a resounding 'Hit' overall. Will and Charlotte gave it the '5', declaring they would buy it. Gareth was most damning, declaring it "blandly appealing", and Shirley said it had a "gorgeous bouquet".

FIFTH BOTTLE: 27th February 2009. We drank this at Heworth Green with a beef and mushroom ghoulash (or however you spell it). There is to be a Taylor family bash this weekend, and Andrew is here, staying with my parents. Much fun has been had looking through some rediscovered school books of mine, written when I was ten. Apparently one of the horrors I imagined that could befall the blind was never being able to see one's tall, handsome nephew who had come to visit. Bizarre.

SIXTH BOTTLE: 28th December 2009. This bottle lay hidden and dusty in the wine racks until I did a stock-take and reordering a few weeks ago. We took it over to Julia's in the belief that we would be served fish. Instead we got the most glorious game casserole, the vital ingredient of which was redcurrants, giving it a fruity sharpness. We sat in the front room before a log fire, and had a marvellous evening setting the world to rights. The wine was alright but I don't think it had improved on keeping, and there were many bits floating in it. I had one (large) glass because I was driving – we had too many instruments with us, and the pavements were too icy to walk.

JUNE 2008

After failing to pick elderflowers last weekend, I returned to Golden Acre Park on 15th June 2008 to see if the elderflowers were any further on. They were a little, but nothing like the many trees I see dripping with bunches of creamy white flowers on my bus journeys to work. It took a little while before I spotted a large tree which appeared to have a good crop. Once spotted, I battled my way through the nettles that surrounded it like some medieval castle defence system. Many of these were the height of my face, but with careful treading down and using my gautex raincoat as armour, I only got properly stung once – on my shin – though my left buttock bizarrely feels like one may have got through my jeans.

As last year I picked about double what I needed, I must remember I only need about half a plastic bag full for a single batch. I could not find any white grape juice in Sainsbury's, so I put in a litre of 'white grape and peach juice drink'. That final 'drink' is either redundant or suspicious. We shall see whether this works.

I put it all in the demijohn on 20th June. There are, I think, fewer flies floating on the top than last year, but still more than none. I added three-eighths of a pint of water on 24th June.

When I racked this it was mostly clear, with only a very small sediment. I added just over half a pint of water and 30z of sugar. The small taste was distinctively elderflower, but overly dry.

Quantity:	Six bottles.
Region:	Golden Acre Park.
Yeast Type:	Champagne.
Initial Gravity:	1.098.
End Gravity:	0.994.
Percentage:	15%.
Date Racked:	30th August 2008.
Date Bottled:	Christmas Eve 2008, with Marlo watching.

INITIAL TASTE:
It has turned out rather well – no indication of cheese, and Claire has declared it suitable for drinking now. The 'grape and peach juice drink' has not been a disaster.

THE DRINKING EXPERIENCE

FIRST BOTTLE: 10th April 2009. As with Peach and Banana (see later), this bottle popped its cork and shed half its contents over the floor. I put it in the fridge and we drank it on Good Friday, whilst I was squeezing oranges and listening to the Classic FM Easter Countdown. The wine is as good as ever. It is bone dry, though that is not necessarily a criticism, and unmistakably made from elderflowers. This bottle at least was fizzy (obviously), but that might have something to do with it being the 'dregs' bottle. We have turned off the hall radiator.

SECOND BOTTLE: 25th & 26th May 2009. This was the bottle that popped its cork whilst I was on the phone to Todd, discussing his Raspberry wine. Claire rescued it, but being upright it did not need much rescuing. We started, and very nearly finished, the bottle on Whit Monday, after a long day of struggling with Peter the Venerable, Heloise, and David and Goliath in preparation for Wednesday's Latin exam.

THIRD BOTTLE: 27th & 28th May 2009. Summer must be approaching. This was the fourth bottle in four days to pop its cork, and the second Elderflower in a row. Still, it was a suitable bottle to celebrate the end of my exams (my last ever? who knows). The Latin exam was worryingly straightforward. I finished nearly an hour before the end, so left early. Much of this bottle was drunk in a hot bath. The cold glass and dry, fizzy wine was a delightful contrast.

FOURTH BOTTLE: 3rd & 4th June 2009. Whilst this bottle did not actually explode, it gave every impression of wanting to do so. The cork was inching its way out of the top. I put it in the fridge during the hottest weekend of the year, and Claire opened it on Wednesday whilst I was at orchestra. I had a sip at her bathside when I came back. Most of the bottle, though, was drunk on Thursday (today), whilst Bob and Judith were visiting as a stop off on their way back from what sounds like an idyllic holiday in France. Bob declared the wine 'superb', and for his reward he has just been sent to fix the toilet flush system with a coat hanger.

FIFTH BOTTLE: 15th-17th June 2009. Two things happened simultaneously on Sunday: I heard the familiar Bang of a cork flying, and the phone rang. I high-tailed it downstairs, established that the hall was not being flooded with wine, answered the phone, and told the caller to wait while I found which bottle had exploded. Luckily it was Sooz ringing with birthday wishes, so she knew the score. Claire and I had a (large) glass each on Monday evening whilst eating birthday cake – a nutmeg sponge as solid as birthday cakes should be. 'Pleasingly substantial' rather than 'solid', which can have pejorative connotations in connection with cake.

SIXTH BOTTLE: 17th-22nd October 2009. Despite the cork
half hanging out of the bottle for months, this succeeded in staying
closed until the Wine Party. A few guests liked it; Duncan in
particular, who prefers his wines white and dry. However, someone
voted it their worst, and I assume it was that person who wrote,
"horrid, bitter". Someone else thought it "rather catty", and Julia
said that corrugated asbestos came to mind, but not in a bad way, I
think. The food for the party, as ever, was excellent, though we over-
catered. Only the cheese was finished, and we will be eating second
hand baked potatoes for weeks to come. Claire made stuffed vine
leaves, Boston baked beans, a tomato, sweetcorn and pepper dish,
two types of hummus – one with beetroot and walnut, which was
a fabulous colour, bread (including Dwarf Bread), and she cooked
sausages. I was in charge of tidying.

JUNE 2009

Today, 13th June 2009, summer has returned. It has been sunny
and warm, to the extent that I am sitting in shorts and a T-shirt at
approaching 9pm, and only feeling slightly chilly. I have decided to
do a double batch of Elderflower this year because (and here, I am
undoubtedly about to curse this wine) it is consistently good. So,
after a lazy morning and a late start, Claire and I went out, plastic
bags in hand, to pick elderflowers. We went to a place just outside
Harewood that I had spotted when picking rosehips in November.
It being mid-June, the field footpath looked as if no-one had
been along it since we were last there: the grass was at shoulder
height, and hawthorn and sloe bushes jutted out into the path.
However, it appeared that the elder trees had been sufficiently
pruned to prevent them flowering. We got a couple of flower heads,
but too few for wine. Instead we trespassed into a field across the
road which had several elder trees in the hedgerow. There was no
evidence of irate farmers, so we helped ourselves. It was quick work
– particularly as I remembered we only needed half a bag each for
the double batch. Despite this I still found it difficult to tear myself
away, and we have ended up with too many.

Once home it took me over three hours to strip the
flowers, and I had to remind myself several times that it was worth
it. Thank God for Radio 4 – even the weekly business show 'The
Bottom Line'. I had forgotten that stripping elderflowers turns my
thumbnail black.

I have followed last year's method, but doubling the water to 12 pints and the sugar to 5lb. The juice is, again, one litre of 'white grape and peach juice drink', though I have bunged in the remainder of the concentrate I bought for Citrus (about half a pint, I suspect). I put in the yeast and nutrient the following evening (my birthday), after an emergency dash to buy peanut butter. It went into the demijohns on 18th June. I could have put in at least another pint and a half of water in the initial mix. I got my thumb stuck temporarily in the demijohn handle when carrying one upstairs, but a bit of wiggling and pulling got it out without too much damage.

When I racked this there was very little sediment, and each demijohn got about three-eighths of a pint of water and 2oz of sugar. Both are mostly clear, and the initial taste was promising.

Quantity:	2 gallons.
Region:	The Harewood Estate.
Price:	£1.20 for the yeast, 82p for the juice, £2.50-ish for the sugar, and the grape concentrate is carried over from Citrus.
Yeast Type:	Champagne.
Date Racked:	24th August 2009.
Date Bottled:	24th December 2009.

INITIAL TASTE:
This isn't crystal clear, but it is near enough, and it is entirely flat, unlike last year's. Both demijohns are good, with the second being 'sharper' according to Sooz, and 'rounder' according to Andrew. It doesn't taste hugely alcoholic.

THE DRINKING EXPERIENCE

FIRST BOTTLE: 11th-13th April 2010. I opened this bottle to placate my mother. She took against July's Gooseberry, but thought this far better – even if it was unchilled. It has been a good bottle; crisp, without being overly dry, and strongly flavoured with elderflower. Sunday night was made more exciting because it is now Hunting Season. Stan brought in a mouse, and he and I chased it round the hallway and through the wine racks, until I caught it by netting it with a tea towel. I'm sure gladiators used a similar method. Ben 1, Stan 0.

SECOND BOTTLE: 29th May 2010. I have to say that this is an exceptionally good Elderflower wine. It is clear, perfumed and refreshing, with exactly the correct level of dryness. We took it over to Richard and Linda's, where they fed us royally. We ate carrot and spring onion fritters, tomatoes stuffed with garlic, breadcrumbs and cheese, salmon and brie risotto, asparagus, and a strawberry and rhubarb cobbler for pudding. After a grey, cold day on which I read the Guardian and did nothing else, this was a tremendous tonic.

THIRD BOTTLE: 5th & 6th June 2010. I chose this as something appropriately English for our summer Book Group Party, which had a Jeeves and Wooster theme. Nobody drank it but me. We had a lovely evening, and decided that whilst Wodehouse books had a peerless style – witty, engaging, effortless – they were style over substance, and the Mapp and Lucia books were better. Many people dressed up, mostly as Aunts. Richard's effort was particularly noteworthy, though his dress was too short and legs too hairy to be entirely convincing.

FOURTH BOTTLE: 20th June 2010. It seems that most of my waking hours today have been spent stripping elderflowers from their stalks. Hence a bottle of Elderflower 2009 proved just the thing. It has actually been a really good day, helped by the glorious weather; we even had lunch in the garden with a whole bottle of homemade ginger beer.

FIFTH BOTTLE: 3rd August 2010. This was my second bottle opened at Rydal Hall, and shared around the orchestra. Today has been a lazy day, partly on account of the weather, but mostly because my knee still hurts from the Fairfield Horseshoe. In tonight's rehearsal I brought Tchaikovsky's Fourth Symphony to a crashing halt single-handedly, of which I am quite proud. People liked this wine, declaring it "summery", "German" and "nicer than Spiced Beetroot".

SIXTH BOTTLE: 11th-14th September 2010. This bottle coincided with the 2010 Wagner weekend. This year it was Tristan and Isolde, which was stunningly good. I have never been quite so moved when playing music. Isolde's final song is desperately sad and beautiful. The first Music Club of the season returned me to more familiar, less exalted ground. We had the mezzo singing Brangäne staying with us – Magdalen Ashman – who is hugely talented and deserves to be lauded. She didn't want any wine though, pleading protection of her vocal chords.

SEVENTH BOTTLE: 1st October 2010. We shared this bottle at Graham and Liz's house in Napton-on-the-Hill, after a long, wet, and frustrating drive from the west coast of Wales. I spent five and a half hours driving and did not once turn off the windscreen wipers. In Wales there was always the hint of great scenery, but the cloud was too low to be certain. Liz, who has tried her hand at winemaking, said pleasing things about the wine. Her most recent flavour was 'Beetroot and Orange', which sounds lovely, but apparently is not.

EIGHTH BOTTLE: 29th October 2010. A bottle too far. My head is spinning and I dread tomorrow morning's headache. This is all because I am a show-off. Helen is visiting and I had already fed her Gooseberry and Spiced Beetroot, but we finished the second bottle before finishing our main course, so I opened the Elderflower. Somehow we managed to finish it. I could do without the dizziness that only sleep will cure.

NINTH BOTTLE: 19th November 2010. A Friday night bottle, drunk with 'vegetables-lurking-in-the-fridge au gratin' – which was surprisingly nice for something made of celery, artichokes and potatoes past their best.

TENTH BOTTLE: 13th February 2011. We have just come back from a lovely evening at Richard and Linda's where, as is obligatory, I ate too much. But what a feast! Stilton, potato and parsnip soup, followed by a mushroom and goat's cheese tart, with a huge carrot cake for pudding. Whilst there we finally made friends with one of their two new identikit cats. Either Dicken or Ollie.

ELEVENTH BOTTLE: 5th-8th March 2011. On Saturday night I had another Music Club performance. This time it was trios by Shostakovich and Ibert played with Theresa and Donald. We started and ended together, and in between were mostly okay. So, on the whole a success, and worth opening a bottle to celebrate. On Tuesday Claire came home giddy from playing Sibelius, which gave us an excuse – as if one was needed – to finish the bottle.

TWELFTH BOTTLE: 31st March 2011. This bottle has been drunk in commiseration. My shiny new job at Jarndyce & Snagsby has gone tits up and now appears not to exist. They have some 'internal issue' they need to 'resolve', but which has proved impossible to do. Consequently they had no right offering me the job in the first place, and I have spent the day in absolute misery. Life is pretty bleak at the moment. However, the elderflower wine has taken the edge off things, and I hope to sleep better tonight.

GOOSEBERRY

JULY 2007

Claire picked most of the gooseberries on 2nd July 2007 whilst I was picking strawberries. She was accompanied by Mendelssohn's Midsummer Night's Dream, and wore protective gloves. When I came to help I only got spiked the once. Gooseberries do look like little testicles. We needed six pounds, and probably picked seven. The remainder will be good for this year's Christmas Tutti Fruti.

I followed the recipe on page 160 of C. J. J. Berry, except I did not top and tail the gooseberries because I couldn't be arsed, and I crushed them with a masher rather than my bare hands. I added six pint of boiling water and will add the pectic enzyme once it has cooled a little.

The mixture was sieved (rather than poured through two layers of muslin, as suggested by C. J. J. Berry) on 5th July. This was far less faff than the Strawberry. I added 2½ lb of sugar, stirred, measured the specific gravity, and then put it all back into the freshly sterilised bucket. Once in the bucket I added the yeast, nutrient and 1 teaspoon of pectolase. Putting it into a demijohn at this stage (as instructed by CJJB) would guarantee detonation.

I put it into the demijohn on 9th July. It has clumps floating on the surface, which perhaps I should have sieved out.

By racking these clumps had sunk to the bottom. The sediment was far spongier than most, and some of the sponge got into the racked wine. I added a pint of water with 5oz of sugar dissolved into it. The wine is clear, but had that off-nutty smell that some homebrews have. Bah! However, see below for first impressions on bottling. It is entirely clear, and a pale yellow (rather than green).

Quantity:	6 bottles.
Region:	The 'Pick Your Own' Farm on the A61 before Harrogate.
Price:	£7.50 for the gooseberries, £1.20 for yeast, £1-ish for the sugar. My priciest yet?

Yeast Type:	'High Alcohol and Country Wines'.
Initial Gravity:	1.100.
End Gravity:	1.000.
Percentage:	16%.
Date Racked:	16th September 2007.
Date Bottled:	12th January 2008.

INITIAL TASTE:

The 'bouquet' is less than appealing, so it is with surprise and pleasure that I can report that it tastes really nice. The gooseberries are definitely detectable. As it is Claire's birthday I let her have most of the glass.

THE DRINKING EXPERIENCE

FIRST BOTTLE: 24th February 2008. Another self-opener. This time it popped its cork whilst I was in the bath. Claire, though, was downstairs and caught it quickly, so we only lost a glass. The appearance is close to perfect (at the top of the bottle at least). It is a clear, pale yellow, and has a slight fizz. The very first taste is of musty homebrew, which rapidly makes way for a sharp, tangy white wine flavour. If it was not for the mustiness this would be a contender for my best white. It is certainly one to repeat.

SECOND BOTTLE: 2nd March 2008. At this rate we will have finished the Gooseberry by April. As I was coming downstairs this morning I saw a cork fly with some force into a bowl of half-eaten cat food. I looked behind me to see who had thrown it and spotted Stan looking innocent. On closer inspection I saw a bottle of Gooseberry doing its best volcano impersonation. Good job it was upright. I bunged it into the fridge, and we drank it that night with a lentil and spinach curry, after Claire's Beethoven and Bruch concert, and my first 'King and I' rehearsal. There were several bits in the wine, which possibly explains its tendency to secondary fermentation. Still quite tasty though – better than last night's Tea wine.

THIRD BOTTLE: Feeling really quite woozy. Oh – 28th April 2008. This was another one that chose itself. It didn't quite open, but the cork was only just hanging on when I inspected the wine bottles late this afternoon. As it has been Claire's A' level performance exam today she insisted we drink the whole bottle before 7.30pm. In fact, Claire was effusive about this wine – wonderful colour, the nicest white I have ever made – all very satisfying.

FOURTH BOTTLE: 6th & 7th May 2008. Yet another bottle to pop its own cork. I'm pretty certain Gooseberry will not be making its appearance at this year's Wine Party. I put this in the fridge with a plastic cork, intending to save it for the weekend, but I kept on hearing explosions from inside the fridge, so had no alternative but to start drinking it. And once you start, you might as well finish.

FIFTH BOTTLE: 12th-14th May 2008. Oh dear, only one bottle of Gooseberry is now left. This opened itself in the usual manner, and we had to drink half a glass each before swimming on Monday night as the temporary cork kept blowing out in the fridge. My first taste was unadulterated gooseberry, and was delicious. We had more after swimming, but did not drink more than half a glass each because I had my final exam on Tuesday (which was fine), and then finished it over Tuesday and Wednesday. I only had a sip of Claire's on Tuesday as I had celebrated earlier with four pints of lager.

JULY 2008

Claire and I braved the weather on Saturday late afternoon 5th July 2008 to pick gooseberries with Julia at her allotment. It had been torrential rain interspersed with thunder and lightning for most of the day, but by 4.30 was merely threatening and dark, so we put on our waterproofs and old clothes and met Julia at the allotment gates. The rain stayed away and we quickly picked twice what was needed – hence the unplanned double batch. In fact we picked 13lb 5½ oz, so there will be some gooseberries in this year's Tutti Fruti. I barely got spiked, though the gardening gloves I was wearing were shredded by the end.

The fruit went into the bucket today – 6th July. This year I found it much, much harder to mash than last year, so I followed C.

J. J. Berry's advice and crushed several with my bare hands. As this was relatively inefficient and sticky, I then followed Claire's advice and tried slicing them in situ. Again inefficient, but not as sticky. Next year I will use a food processor.

I strained the liquid into two demijohns on 9th July, which took over an hour (well over, in fact!), during which I listened to the rain pound against the window. I poured it all back into the freshly sterilised bucket, added the sugar, measured the gravity, and put in the yeast and nutrient. It was all put into the demijohns late on 13th July, after a concert in Saltaire by the Skipton Building Society Camerata – Mozart's clarinet concerto being my highlight. I have never heard such quiet, exciting playing.

I racked this on 28th September. The sediment was considerable – about three fingers' worth – and uncompacted. It is an entirely clear wine, and the tiny taste was tart and recognisably gooseberry. Before I racked it, the initial gravity was 0.994. After I put in a pint and a quarter of water plus 6oz of sugar in each, it had increased to 1.010.

Quantity:	2 gallons.
Region:	Julia's allotment.
Price:	£2-ish for the sugar, £1.20 for the yeast.
Yeast Type:	Hock.
Initial Gravity:	1.100.
End Gravity:	1.010.
Percentage:	14%(ish).
Date Racked:	28th September 2008.
Date Bottled:	9 February 2009.

INITIAL TASTE:
I am slightly disappointed with the result. It is unbeatable in clarity and entirely flat, but it is too sweet. Claire loves it though, and declares it a superior dessert wine.

THE DRINKING EXPERIENCE

FIRST BOTTLE: 21st March 2009. Richard and Linda came over for a meal, and we independently both decided that Gooseberry would be worth opening. It was delicious – not as sweet as I had feared, with wonderful flavour and clarity. Claire's cooking was exemplary: poisonous-looking mushrooms in cream, a red pepper and tomato tart with asparagus and hasslebach potatoes, and ginger and Seville orange ice-cream in brandy snap baskets (which was the highlight), not forgetting the cheese.

SECOND BOTTLE: 18th April 2009. Delicious. Definitely to become a regular if I can get enough fruit. Renate, Thomas and Julia came over to play bassoon quartets (albeit Julia on cello as a bassoon substitute). We played both pieces Bob has written for me. The 'Variations on the Yorkshire National Anthem' was the more fun, but both could be great with practice. A wonderful evening. The poor neighbours.

THIRD BOTTLE: 25th April 2009. It has been a glorious April so far – certainly for the last fortnight. To accompany the good weather, and to celebrate Claire having finished the raised bed (even if the brickwork does go in a spiral), we opened another bottle of Gooseberry. In fact, I was in a cross mood on opening. I think it was for lack of food, but also we were getting in each other's way in the kitchen. Four mini chocolate eggs and a glass of this later, I was fine.

FIFTH BOTTLE: 20th June 2009. This was a post-concert bottle following Brahms' violin concerto (played by a Dutch troll) and Tchaikovsky's 5th Symphony. Both went well, though I could not get my F sharps in tune in the symphony, and (amazingly) my lip survived the experience. Chris came, and so this bottle was shared with him. We ate cheese, Parma ham, and olive bread while discussing the definition of 'Psychopathy'.

SEVENTH BOTTLE: 14th-15th August 2009. We needed more to drink on Friday than the fag ends of Prune and Parsnip, so I opened this. It was a quiet evening, during which we watched the first episode of a William Hartnell Doctor Who. It was rubbish, and there are still three more episodes to watch. Interesting from a historical view, but it was filmed only four years before we were born, which makes me feel ancient. It was a different world then.

EIGHTH BOTTLE: 27th September 2009. Home made pizza and a DVD on a Sunday night. Throw in a bottle of Gooseberry wine and you have the makings of a splendid evening. This is all on top of the news that Jaki is pregnant, so it looks as if I will be an uncle. The wine is really very good indeed – I think my best white. The movie was 'Slumdog Millionaire' and was excellent. Far darker than advertised, despite the surface Hollywood ending, and a film that I should have seen on the Big Screen, particularly for the early slum shots.

NINTH BOTTLE: 17th October 2009. The clear winner at this year's Wine Party. Of the five votes, four were for 'Favourite', and the other was in the 'Good' category. It got comments of "Complex taste – grows on you", "Very refreshing", "Wine, rather than clearly a 'country' wine" and "Fantastic!". Pop, again, has asked for a donation to some aging parents. He is shameless!

TENTH BOTTLE: 26th November 2009. This was the first of our Thanksgiving bottles, but was nearly empty by the time the turkey was on the table. I kept on entering the kitchen to ask if there was anything I could do, but this tactic in speeding the food along was unsuccessful. When it arrived it was wonderful – the full Thanksgiving spread of turkey, sweet potatoes, corn, mashed potatoes, cranberry sauce, gravy, cabbage, and a nut roast for Richard. Not forgetting pumpkin pie, of course.

TWELFTH BOTTLE: 20th March 2010. Our last bottle of Gooseberry was opened in very similar circumstances to the first, and almost exactly a year later. Richard and Linda came round for a meal, as did Leslie – an MA student in Medieval Studies who is pleasingly punk. The occasion was 'Our house is in desperate need of a tidy, so let's have people around', so guess how I spent the day whilst Claire cooked. This bottle served as an aperitif with a starter of mushrooms stuffed with breadcrumbs, and poisonous-looking mushrooms fried in butter. Wine and fungi were both fabulous, and now we are out of Gooseberry. I must bottle 2009's batch.

JUNE 2009

Julia and I picked gooseberries on Friday evening, 19th June 2009, whilst Claire was at home viola-ing. It was a pleasant evening, though needed two layers of clothing. This is earlier than I have made Gooseberry before, and much of the fruit I picked was hard and bullet-like. Accordingly, I am going to experiment by making one batch with under-ripe gooseberries, and then in about a month's time I will make a second batch with over-ripe fruit.

It took us about half an hour to pick 7lb 10oz (the excess is currently in the freezer), after which we wandered to a Tapas bar and had a beer outside, waiting for Claire. Because the bar was too full to get a table, we went instead to an empty Thai restaurant. The food was good and the 'Thai Dancing' was plain weird. On one side of us a middle-aged Thai woman in traditional costume performed elaborate and delicate Thai dancing to gong-like music. On the other side a speaker blared out Eric Clapton and Simon and Garfunkel. Dissonance was the order of the day.

I washed and (for once) topped and tailed the gooseberries on 21st June. This took about an hour, but it meant I could scrape the brown scabs off some of the berries. I picked one gooseberry from each of our bushes in the garden – which have been less nibbled by sawflies than in previous years – and then whizzed the berries through the food processor. I have added six pints of boiling water and will put in the pectic enzyme when it cools.

Because we are going to Wales for a week, leaving on Saturday, I have ignored the instructions about when to put in the yeast and when to filter out the fruit. Instead I put the sugar and yeast in on Monday morning (22nd June), and put it all into the demijohn on Friday night. I think it was a day too late though; the fruit had stopped floating on top. Judith, in an attempt to prepare strawberries and cream, kept on using sterilised equipment until I growled at her.

By the time of racking the wine is still a little cloudy, so I have put in half a teaspoon of pectolase. The sediment is two and a half fingers' width; enough to pour in a pint of water and 6oz of sugar. It needs the additional sweetness. Claire described the tiny taste as "dry and sweaty".

Quantity:	1 gallon.
Region:	Julia's allotment, near the apple trees.
Yeast Type:	Bordeaux.

Date Racked: 31st August 2009.

Date Bottled: 2nd April 2010

INITIAL TASTE:
The wine has remained fizzy, and now it is in bottles it will need to be stood upright. Despite the large amount of sugar it got on racking it is too dry, and the most disappointing Gooseberry I have made. It is still passable, but should be extraordinary.

THE DRINKING EXPERIENCE

FIRST BOTTLE: 2nd May 2010. This batch of Gooseberry definitely needs additional sugar. It is not as head-twitchingly tart as the Rosehip, but a spoonful of sugar concentrate per glass makes the drinking experience that much better. As I was on my second glass a Lib-Dem canvasser rang, wondering whether he could count on my vote. I decided to make him work and spent about twenty minutes discussing local politics – from the market to the bin strike, and the Liberal-Conservative coalition Council. Was he comfortable with this? He explained it well, but without answering the question. I'm sure Jeremy Paxman would have pressed harder, but I knew there was some asparagus waiting to be eaten, and that took priority.

SECOND BOTTLE: 9th-11th June 2010. We opened this bottle after a play-through of Beethoven's 7th at WYSO. It is a symphony with which I am not particularly familiar, except for the second movement, which I want played at my funeral. I insisted we have a glass on Thursday, 10th June, as this was the Feast of St Ithamar, about whom I am writing a 6,000 word 'Project'. And, it being an auspicious day, I used it to begin the writing. Our own feast consisted of a beanlash and home-grown leafy vegetables. The wine is far too dry, and needs several spoons of sugar solution, but once it gets that it is actually quite drinkable. This dryness may well be because the gooseberries were early, and therefore had not had time to develop their own natural sugar.

THIRD BOTTLE: 24th & 26th July 2010. Claire wanted a sharp white for our Saturday night meal, and you certainly don't get any sharper than this. We had mackerel with gooseberry sauce, freshly made bread, courgettes in lemon and dill, and some rather nasty samphire, which we shan't be trying again. The gooseberries, courgettes, and dill were home-grown. This was the last harvest of gooseberries, but only the beginning of the courgettes. I am busily collecting recipes for the latter, in anticipation of inundation. Claire has banned me from trying Courgette wine. I can't think why.

FIFTH BOTTLE: 18th December 2010. Gooseberry wine is a perfect accompaniment to oily fish. We drank this with a starter of soused herrings and sourdough bread, followed by a main course of grilled sardines and a spicy tomato sauce. The wine cut through the flavours perfectly. This rounded off a pleasant Saturday. I was going to describe it as 'lazy', but activities included two hours of clearing snow from my street armed only with a broom, beginning my 2010 Christmas Tutti Fruti, half an hour's bassoon practice, and a heavy session of sitting on the sofa reading the Saturday Guardian. The phrase 'working my fingers to the bone' sums all this up quite nicely. Now for the dishes.

SIXTH BOTTLE: 6th-8th February 2011. A summer salad, chicken breast grilled in Moroccan spices, and liberal helpings of toasted pitta bread, all washed down with a dry Gooseberry wine, were our attempt to pretend it was not a cold February evening. This not being altogether successful, we huddled up on the sofa and watched 'Muppets From Space' on DVD instead. This was actually all 'worry displacement' therapy. I am trying not to concentrate on either the fact I am facing redundancy at Emsleys or that I have a second interview for a job I really want at Jarndyce & Snagsby on Thursday. As 'therapy' the muppets are sufficiently silly. We finished the bottle on Tuesday night after a meeting at work where I discussed various options I had put forward so as not to lose my job. They were surprisingly receptive (ie. they did not dismiss the suggestions immediately) to the idea that I be retrained as a personal injury lawyer. That would be strange indeed.

JULY 2009

I had settled down for an evening of watching Torchwood on 11th July 2009, and had just finished watching the first episode when Julia rang. She reported that heavy rain was forecast, the gooseberries were very ripe, and that she was out most of Sunday. Did I want to pick the fruit now? Though it wasn't entirely within my plans for the evening that Claire was out being an emergency viola for Alwoodley Chamber Orchestra, it sounded like a sensible idea. I changed into my old clothes and headed out with plastic bags. Despite the darkening clouds and heavy atmosphere, the rain stayed away and I picked 6lb 6oz.

The experiment of an earlier batch and a later batch is not entirely valid as, whilst there is certainly a greater percentage of soft ripe gooseberries in this batch than the last, there are still many hard, unripe ones. Also, the yeast types will be different. I am going to follow the same timings and method as I did three weeks ago, as far as possible, except I could not be bothered topping and tailing six pounds of gooseberries this time. Scraping the scabby ones took long enough. As before I put in one gooseberry from each of our bushes, and then harvested the remainder.

I did the whizzing of gooseberries and the pouring of six pints of boiling water over them on Sunday 12th July. The pectolase, sugar, and yeast were all added on Monday evening, 13th July, so I am already twelve hours behind schedule. The yeast granules rather stuck to the packet, so took a good deal of scraping off with my (unsterilised) hands, though not my disgusting thumb. I put it all into the demijohn on 17th July while listening to Jeanette Winterson waxing lyrical about the Moon on Radio 4, celebrating the fortieth anniversary of the first lunar landing.

By racking, the differences between the two batches were evident. The first batch is murky, whereas this is the epitome of clarity. However, this wine had the largest amount of sediment ever encountered – nearly half the demijohn. I racked it into my smallest demijohn and added 3½ pints of water and 6oz of sugar, hoovering up some of the sediment in the process.

Quantity:	One gallon.
Bought at:	The yeast was bought at Abbey Brew, where I had a pleasant conversation with the owner of whom, in the past, I have been a little scared.
Yeast Type:	Hock.
Date Racked:	26th September 2009.

Date Bottled: 2nd April 2010.

INITIAL TASTE:
By bottling this batch is both clearer and sweeter than the June version. It is also fizzy, and a little nicer than the other. Still pretty average, though.

THE DRINKING EXPERIENCE

FIRST BOTTLE: 11th-12th April 2010. We had a fish feast on Sunday night. My mother was visiting, and last time she came she brought with her a set of fish cutlery retrieved from Great Uncle Gerry and Great Aunt Elsa's house clearance. This was an opportunity to bring some of it out for the first time. We had mussels to start, each of us very keen that we got our fair share, and then a marvellous fish stew stuffed with salmon, sea bass, and prawns, spiced with a touch of chilli. A white wine was required to go with this, and earlier I had asked Claire whether it should be Gooseberry or Elderflower. She chose the former, and in fact it is Not Bad. However, on her first sip Mom pulled a face and declared it far too sour. I admit it is sharp, but I like that in a wine. She donated the rest of the glass to Claire, I opened an Elderflower, and harmony was restored.

SECOND BOTTLE: 1st-6th July 2010. This has been one of those rare bottles that has been drunk slowly, generally as a late evening treat. Not that the wine is sufficiently nice to be classified a treat. Friday evening was interesting. We went to a 'Soirée' in Burley to listen to viola and piano music. The draw for Claire was a piece by Rebecca Clarke, an obscure Edwardian composer. When we arrived, though, it was clear there was gong to be a fair amount of solo piano music, which was fine. But the woman playing it was obviously created by Victoria Wood, and had an interesting approach to timing. Suitably, her last piece was called 'Fascinating Rhythm'. It felt like listening to someone practicing badly. A glass of Gooseberry proved welcome afterwards.

FIFTH BOTTLE: 23rd-25th January 2011. A bottle of Grape and Raisin was not quite enough for three people on a Sunday night, so I opened a bottle of Gooseberry to go with our cheese course. Chris was visiting in preparation for Monday's funeral, and as he is no fan of puddings Claire bought cheese instead. She also had a go at making oatcakes from first principles. These tasted far better than shop-bought, but had the consistency of wet sand. So, rather than spreading cheese on oatcakes, we had to cover the cheese in oatcake crumbs. The blackbirds in our garden are very enthusiastic about them, and that will be their fate.

SIXTH BOTTLE: 15th-16th February 2011. The cats chose this bottle. Whilst washing up on Sunday I heard a large crash and the sound of my bottles falling over in domino fashion. Two cats dashed through the kitchen and out the cat-flap in a guilty manner. I righted the bottles and, within a few hours, this one exploded. Tuesday's glasses were drunk after what had been a difficult day. I went to work convinced that the day would end with me receiving my formal notice of redundancy, and spent the entire day moping. In fact, Emsleys were rather marvellous. They actually listened to my suggestions and agreed to one. So I shall be put on an 'as-and-when' contract. It is not ideal, but I maintain my employment and things might get better. Yay Emsleys!

SLOE

SEPTEMBER 2007

I returned from the first day of my third year of term, the 25th of September 2007, exhausted and hungry. I was not sure whether to eat or sleep first, but knew that both were temptations to be avoided. Claire is currently in China at a conference, so she could neither feed me, nor tend my tired brow. Instead I inspected the sloe bushes – bought several years ago, under the impression they were a different plant – and saw that some sloes were being eaten or shrivelling. I grabbed a carrier bag and got to work, getting a little scratched in the process. Over three pounds of sloes have come off the bushes, and there are still many left for this year's Tutti Fruti.

I have followed the recipe on page 203 of C. J. J. Berry, except 8oz of raisins have become 4oz of sultanas and 4oz of currants. I hope that this will not matter. 3lb of sloes went into the bucket, followed by 6 pints of boiling water. It was odd mashing the fruit after the water has gone in, and not altogether successful. I then added the minced sultanas and currants.

I added the pectolase on the morning of the 26th, and then 2lb of sugar, the yeast, and nutrient on the morning of the 27th. I put it into a demijohn on 2nd October, halving the time C. J. J. Berry tells me to keep it in a bucket. I did not add quite another 1lb of sugar, but it was close. The mixture may have an enormous sediment. It is an attractive dark red colour at this stage, and will probably end up on the cusp of rosé and red. I have wrapped the demijohn in silver foil.

On racking it has cleared entirely and is about the same pinkness as Strawberry. The sediment was enormous. I have topped it up with 8oz of sugar and a pint and a half of water. The small taste was, shall we say, tart. I think the extra sugar can only be a Good Thing.

Quantity: Six bottles.

Region: The Front Garden.

Price: £1.20 for the yeast, £1-ish for the sugar, and whatever for 8oz dried fruit.

Yeast Type: 'High Alcohol and Country Wines'.

Initial Gravity: The method makes it difficult to measure, so I didn't.

Percentage: Unknown.

Date Racked: 23rd December 2007.

Date Bottled: 10th May 2008.

INITIAL TASTE:
This was bottled after a surprise concert in Guiseley. The tartness has been eliminated. It tastes a little bland, but in a pleasant way. Maybe I added too much sugar, but it is not overpoweringly sweet. On the whole I am pleased with this.

THE DRINKING EXPERIENCE

FIRST BOTTLE: 30th June and 1st July 2008. An unexpected explosion sounded in the hall on Monday evening. I rushed to catch what I could, and ended up losing a third of this bottle. I then found four other bottles and stood them upright. The sixth remains a time bomb. Much of the remaining bottle was drunk on Monday. Darren Stubbs, who was visiting to discuss residential leases, had a taste and declared it surprisingly good. I am pleased with the result: it is entirely clear, and a dark pink colour. The taste is sweet, though not at dessert wine level, and slightly medicinal in a thoroughly satisfactory way. We finished the bottle tonight after summer orchestra on our tenth wedding anniversary.

SECOND BOTTLE: 10th August 2008. I opened this before it opened itself. Prior to going on holiday I noticed the cork inching its way out, so I put it in the fridge. As it was our last night of holiday neither of us took much persuasion to open a bottle. This resembled either a fountain or firework when I pulled the cork out. My first solution (to put my mouth round the neck and suck) was more uncouth than it was successful, so I poured two glasses.

FOURTH BOTTLE: 1st January 2009. This was our second 'pre-meal' bottle, but as there were seven or eight of us sharing it, that is not quite as shocking as it sounds. The bottle was a good one – reminiscent of cough mixture, but in that comforting, tasty way. Our meal was the full turkey works, including sprouts (Claire had her annual one, and continues to declare them 'nasty'), forced meat balls, and Christmas pudding for dessert. I went to bed incredibly stuffed, and spent what felt like most of the night digesting.

FIFTH BOTTLE: 13th April 2009. I spent the day gardening and making an ambitious pudding. The gardening mostly consisted of turning compacted earth with a trowel and giving myself blisters. The pudding mostly consisted of pastry, chocolate, lemons and double cream. The wine was thin, yet a glorious colour.

SIXTH BOTTLE: 29th May 2009. It has been the warmest day of the year so far – the tomato plants spent the whole day outside. It being a Friday, a bottle was called for, particularly as there are suggestions, despite the poor economy, that my job may be made permanent. Whisper it quietly. When I opened this bottle the wine did its best volcano impression, fizzing over the top until I had poured sufficient out.

SEPTEMBER 2009

I have been picking sloes wherever I have found them since the end of August. Last year was such a poor year for sloes that this year I have been a man obsessed. The first lot of sloes were picked within spitting distance of the A1 near Wetherby, when Sooz was visiting. Then, on a walk with Rachel and Duncan, we found laden bushes by the River Wharfe. About a week later I stripped sloes from the bushes overhanging the car park at work. Last week, on the Hetchell Woods walk, Mom, Claire and I stopped at our usual supply, and were not disappointed. And then, today, I plucked ten sloes from the bush in our front garden. Other than these ten I am uncertain which sloes made it into the wine as they have all been kept in the freezer, and Claire has used a pound for sloe gin.

On 26th September 2009, whilst starting to cook the evening meal (a process that Claire took over, which was a Good Thing), I boiled up 3lb of sloes in three pints of water, and then poured this over 3lb of sugar and 8oz of minced raisins. I added a further 3 pints of boiling water, and spent some time trying to mash the fruit. After Music Club, at which Madeleine played Weber's Grand Duo wonderfully, and Fred and Belinda played a Beethoven piano trio dreadfully, I added a teaspoon of pectolase. The yeast went in just before lunch on 27th September. I filtered it all into the demijohn on 30th September, which was a day earlier than planned, but tomorrow evening is Ian's Ghastly Sextet, and I don't usually return from that until approaching eleven, and tonight I was back from orchestra before ten. There wasn't nearly enough water in the mix. I have added a pint and will need to add another when the yeast activity dies down. The colour is thickly purple, and I cannot imagine it will clear. The next and final (at least until it is racked) pint was added on 3rd October.

By racking there was a thick, dense deposit, but the wine has cleared. The sip I got was rather dry, so I added a pint and a quarter of water with 6oz of sugar dissolved in it.

Quantity:	One gallon.
Region:	Various – see above.
Yeast Type:	Champagne – which, frankly, is a weird choice, but all I had left.
Date Racked:	7th December 2009.
Date Bottled:	6th May 2010 – General Election Day.

INITIAL TASTE:
The colour is definitely the red side of Rosé, and it is clear and (mostly) flat. The taste is somewhat bland, which is not necessarily a bad thing. There is a dry texture to it, which sticks to the tongue, but strangely not a dry taste. Claire claims her first taste is 'bubblegum', but that is not one I detect. A qualified 'Hit'.

THE DRINKING EXPERIENCE

FIRST BOTTLE: 22nd & 23rd June 2010. We were lying in bed, and I was feeling all sleepy when there was a bang from downstairs. Claire leapt up and saved as much of the bottle as she could. This, for me, was the explosion that broke the camel's back.

I spent the next twenty minutes feeling more cross than sleepy, taking all the wine from the racks and storing them upright – mostly behind our sofa. The empty wine racks are now waiting to be banished to the attic, though I should probably first dispose of the desiccated mouse corpse which is stuck to one of them. Anyway, this wine is fizzy (obviously), and really cloudy. It has a dry but not unpleasant taste – which has the same acidic tang that is a feature of stewed rhubarb. And, though cloudy, the colour is an attractive purple. I drank my first glass with a lentil boll whilst Claire was at an International Melanoma Conference (handily held in Leeds), and we finished it tonight (another glass each) chatting merrily in the kitchen.

SECOND BOTTLE: 23rd-27th June 2010. Setting all my wine bottles upright proved to be the correct action to take. This bottle exploded within 24 hours of the last, and still managed to lose a glass. Though I did not find out till Friday, Bridget's daughter – Gemma – was born on Wednesday evening, and we must raise a glass to her. We have just finished the bottle on a warm summer's evening that has seen England knocked out of the World Cup. Claire is preparing a goat's cheese quiche, and the honeysuckle smells divine.

THIRD BOTTLE: 11th & 12th July 2010. Sitting on the sofa on Saturday I heard a squeak of cork moving against glass. I looked at my bottles intently, and put the Sloe I thought 'most likely to explode' into the fridge. A few hours later the cork from a different bottle instead flew into the air, so that went into the fridge as well. We drank most of the wine on Sunday, which was a lazy day. I registered at the International Medieval Congress, and bought a 1907 guide to Rochester Cathedral, but did little else.

FOURTH BOTTLE: 18th-23rd July 2010. On a matter entirely unrelated to this bottle, Claire has just stated that I say the words 'brilliant' and 'fifth' wrongly. I have no idea what she is talking about. Everyone knows the second 'f' in 'fifth' is silent, and 'brilliant' is impossible to mispronounce. This bottle exploded (quelle surprise!) on Sunday, and Sooz had half a glass to relieve the pressure. Then we drank it slowly throughout the week – sharing a couple of glasses on Thursday night in the kitchen, a little past our bedtime, catching up with each other. It has been one of those frantic weeks where we have been out separately, every night, so half an hour chatting was just lovely. The wine, though, was distinctly average.

FIFTH BOTTLE: 10th October 2010. I have been watching the cork on this bottle rising slowly from the neck over the last week. This afternoon it made its bid for freedom with a bang. So, rather than the anticipated bottle of Elderberry to go with our roast lamb, we had nasty Sloe instead. It was drinkable, but little more, and I predict that it will come near to last place in the votes at next week's Wine Party. Still, it did its job for a Sunday bottle of wine, closing a weekend that has seen Light Night, a posh meal out at Raymond Blanc's restaurant, two hours of being on hold to TalkTalk, and finishing reading 'Breakfast at Tiffany's', which was delightful.

SIXTH BOTTLE: 16th October 2010. This was the only bottle of this entire batch which I chose to open. I did so at the Wine Party as Sloe wine has not made an appearance before. After last night's general response it will probably not do so again. It came second-to-last in the voting charts, with only Nettle being less popular. Whilst a couple of generous souls (Sooz and Diana) gave it a '3', mostly it scored a '1'. Mom described it as both "scary" and "murky", whereas Angie's adjectives of choice were "undesirable" and "astringent". Julia christened it "Ratchet", and her pictorial representation of Sloe wine was a saw cutting through corrugated metal. I actually didn't think it was that bad. Okay, it was entirely cloudy and dried the tongue on contact, but there is an interesting base flavour. I have made it again this year, but it may drop off the list of regulars.

PUMPKIN

OCTOBER 2007

Pop's retirement do was held last night, 27th October 2007, near a graveyard. It being close to 31st October, there was a Halloween theme with about two thirds of the guests being in fancy dress. This was, of course, mostly witches and vampires, but there were several biochemists thrown in. One feature was a large number of Jack-o'-lanterns on the front steps, flickering their orange light into the graveyard. At the end of the night I pinched two large ones, though in fact one would have done.

I am following the recipe on page 126 of 'Winemaking Month by Month', which requires 5lb of pumpkin and 1lb of sultanas, and the method is similar to my first Rhubarb. I cut off the skin of the pumpkin, diced it into one centimetre cubes (approximately), and put these into the bucket. After pouring in 2lb 12oz of white sugar, I stirred it all around so each cube starts off with sugar on all sides. I do not know if this is correct.

For a few days the smell from the bucket was ghastly – like over-boiled cabbage. Then it began to ferment by itself (I'm not sure if this is a good thing), and the smell improved. On 3rd November I minced the sultanas, put them in a new bucket with 3oz of Demerara sugar (a detail missing from the recipe I am following), and covered it with a pint of boiling water. I then drained the liquid from the bucket containing the pumpkin into this, keeping the sticky/slimy pumpkin pieces in the mixing bowl. There was a lot of liquid, and it was thick, dripping like Alien blood. I then put the pumpkin back into the original bucket, covered it with four and a half pints of tap water (not boiled), and stirred it around. I drained it all again into the bucket with the sultanas, and it is now looking exactly like used washing up water. Bang go my dreams of a vibrant orange wine. I added yeast, nutrient and citric acid.

I put it all into the demijohn on 7th November, six days earlier than suggested, and it bubbled over the top immediately. I then poured some out into a bottle for topping up later.

By racking I added 1 teaspoon of pectolase because it had not cleared at all, and also 3oz of Demerara sugar and about three quarters of a pint of water. The small taste was abonimabal... abonimable... abominable... RUBBISH!

Quantity:	Six bottles.
Region:	A Halloween graveyard.
Price:	65p for the sultanas, £1-ish for the sugar, and £1.20 for the yeast.
Bought at:	Actually, stolen from – see above.
Yeast Type:	Champagne.
Initial Gravity:	I did not bother to measure.
Date Racked:	18th January 2008.
Date Bottled:	21st September 2008.

INITIAL TASTE:
The wine is the cloudiest I have made and tastes rank. Perhaps not as bad as the Potato, but close. Happily Pop was here for a meal, so he drove home with a bottle.

THE DRINKING EXPERIENCE

FIRST BOTTLE: Given to my father.

SECOND BOTTLE: 18th October 2008 at the Wine Party. In its defence this bottle was not quite as awful as I had feared. However, it either came last or second-to-last out of twelve bottles at the party. It all depends on whether Claire's score of '-7' for the Plum and Ginger is discounted, and how one interprets Catherine's scoring of 'Celery'. On the basis that Catherine considers celery the food of Satan, I suspect quite low. If you give that score a '-7', then the average was '0.43', and this wine comes last. If it is discounted, then it might still come last, with an average score of '1.43'. Four people gave it a '0'. Typical comments are "Very Bad", "Bleuugh" and "Slimy". Oddly, two people (Jon and Renate) liked it: "A riot of taste on the palate" and "A burst of taste". There is no accounting for it.

THIRD BOTTLE: 23rd-27th December 2008. I think I may have discovered the solution to this horrid wine, other than using it for clearing drains. Mull it. With half an orange, two dessert spoons of sugar, a handful of cloves, and some thinly sliced ginger, the taste is sufficiently disguised to make it nearly drinkable. I opened this as an example to Sooz and Andrew of quite how bad my wine could be. They each had about a sip, as did Marlo a day later, and all did that double take of initially thinking it was nearly okay, and then immediately pulling a face. Sooz reckons it might work as the basis of Miso soup.

FOURTH BOTTLE: Not drunk, but left at 3 The Alders as we made our escape on 3rd January 2009. I originally took this to Sooz's New Year party to force on people as a comedy forfeit. However, the only game we played was Jenga, and the bottle remained steadfastly unopened. Perhaps my comments of "This is ghastly" did not sell it. I tried my best to leave it with Sooz and Kirsty as we left for a chilly walk back, but they insisted I take it with me. Even Sam showed no interest. For the time being, it rests in a wine rack at Bob and Judith's awaiting an unfortunate victim.

FIFTH BOTTLE: 17th October 2009. I opened this at the 2009 Wine Party, partly as an example of 'When Homebrew Turns Evil', and partly because I don't know how else to get rid of it. While still foul, it has improved slightly, and most tasters claimed it was not as bad as I had proclaimed. Of the five ratings given, only one was in the 'Worst' category, three classified it as 'Poor', and one voted for 'Indifferent'. Somebody (I suspect Duncan) wrote "Slimy texture. Utterly disgusting", which captures my thoughts entirely. The party, though, was a success. I had worried that I had invited too many people, but twenty came and, whilst it was crowded, it was all rather jolly.

SIXTH BOTTLE: Gathering dust somewhere on my wine racks.

PINEAPPLE

JANUARY 2008

On my way home from Emmaus a couple of weeks ago, I noticed that the market was selling pineapples extraordinarily cheaply. I think I saw '3 for £1'. Last year I considered doing this wine, but discounted it when I saw that our greengrocer on Street Lane was selling pineapples for £2 each. As the recipe calls for four, this made it ridiculously expensive. As the market sells pineapples at the same price Paul sells lemons, I saw my opportunity. Earlier this week I failed to find the '3 for £1' stall, but did stumble across one selling two for 80p. This is only six and two-thirds pence more expensive per pineapple, so I can't complain.

I started this on 12th January 2008, and mostly followed the recipe on page 140 of C. J. J. Berry. Each of the four pineapples was sliced into between ten and thirteen slices, so less than a centimetre in width, and then each slice was quartered. I put them all in the big stainless steel pan and boiled them in approximately three pints of water for about half an hour. I poured the water onto 3lb 2oz of sugar (6oz less than suggested by Mr. Berry) in the bucket, assisted by Claire who used the pan lid as a filter. I then covered the pineapple (which had remained in the pan) with 4½ pints of tap water, and left it standing while we went to the Music Club party (mostly tedious and cold). Four hours later this was also poured into the bucket, and I stirred it all up, dissolving the sugar. There is a rather worrying foam already, and this was before the yeast was put in. As the liquid temperature was already cool enough, I added the acid, yeast and nutrient. I put it into the demijohn on 18th January, two days before C. J. J. Berry suggests, but fermentation had died down.

On racking I added not quite half a pint of water with 3oz of sugar dissolved in it. The wine is not quite clear but passable, and the small taste I got was rather good.

Quantity:	One gallon.
Region:	No idea – the Caribbean? Unlikely to be West Yorkshire.

Price:	£1.60 for the pineapples, £1-ish for the sugar, and £1.20 for the yeast.
Bought at:	A stall in the corner of Leeds Outdoor Market.
Yeast Type:	Bordeaux.
Initial Gravity:	1.120 (which is high).
End Gravity:	1.000.
Percentage:	More than 18% (surely not?).
Date Racked:	4th April 2008.
Date Bottled:	19th July 2008.

INITIAL TASTE:
It is flat (hurrah!), nearly clear, and syrupy. A bit 'full-on', and very alcoholic. Feeling quite woozy.

THE DRINKING EXPERIENCE

FIRST BOTTLE: 1st January 2009. A new year's bottle, opened at 3 The Alders and shared between eight of us. I was a little nervous, particularly after trying to force the Pumpkin wine onto people last night. However, this is actually rather good – full bodied, strong, and definitely pineapply. Andrew declares it 'Crofty', referring to the sherry. Kirsty's one word was 'Pineapply', but I had just written that. This was drunk in anticipation of a full turkey meal, and as an aperitif it has been particularly effective (though perhaps Sloe contributed).

SECOND BOTTLE: 9th-11th March 2009. Oily and syrupy. Far too thick for ordinary quaffing, and a strange flavour. Not my best, then. On Tuesday night, which is my night in alone, I only had a glass and a half. Much of the time drinking this was spent trying to bash my way through this month's Book Group Book – 'Gomorrah' by Robert Saviano about the Neapolitan (I almost wrote 'Nepalese') Mafia. The Nepalese Mafia would have been more interesting.

THIRD BOTTLE: 1st-2nd May 2009. After last Sunday's extravaganza it has been a virtually alcohol free week. Playing in 'Pirates of Penzance' in Bingley all week has helped. Whilst I have enjoyed this experience greatly, it has meant that I drive home half asleep and am too exhausted to do anything when I get back but go to bed. Anyway, I took Friday off work, spent much of the day slumbering, and so was very pleased when I got home to see Claire had opened this. A glass was sufficient – it is, after all, quite nasty. Sooz and Andrew helped finish it on Saturday before I inflicted Gilbert and Sullivan on them. "Pineapple Listerine" is how Sooz described it.

FOURTH BOTTLE: 6th June 2009. Maybe it is because this was the evening's second bottle, but I actually think it is rather good. Mom and Julia are both over, and we drank this to moussaka. I declared that I probably would not repeat Pineapple and got a disapproving look from Mom – so I might after all.

FIFTH BOTTLE: 17th-22nd October 2009 at the Wine Party. This was one of my controversial wines, though in fact this year many caused disagreement. Several people really liked Pineapple. I remember Tracey, in particular, cooing over it. But my mother thought it indifferent, writing "thick, disappointing" (however, see the bottle above), and Helen rated it as her worst – though she only tried this, Strawberry and Gooseberry.

SIXTH BOTTLE: 15th January 2010. Civilisation is hanging by a thread. We drank some of this whilst watching 'Hole in the Wall' – a remarkably silly programme where washed-up celebrities try to avoid being knocked into a swimming pool by a wall advancing towards them. A wall with a (mostly) human shaped hole. The problem is that it is engaging and entertaining in a purely slapstick way. I think that the Pineapple wine helped. We cleansed our palates afterwards with 'QI', which is far more intellectual, albeit mainstream. I think I will give Anna Karenina a miss tonight, though. Pineapple wine is certainly one of my more alcoholic brews.

CLOVE & GINGER

APRIL 2008

I wanted to try a new wine this month, looked through the books, and found this listed under 'November'. I was going to start it last night, 3rd April 2008, but Shirley reconvened the Quintet as her arm is feeling a little better. This afternoon has turned out to be an ideal afternoon for winemaking, as I have finished the first draft of my 'Heresy' essay, though it is currently unfocussed and 700 words too long. I also spent much of the afternoon making 'Black Millionaire's Shortbread' for Book Group tonight.

I have deviated from the recipe a little, in that I have used an ordinary orange because Seville oranges are a little thin on the ground at this time of year, and I peeled the citrus fruits thinly rather than grate them. Oh, rather than a muslin bag I have used a leg cut off a pair of Claire's tights. And I did not bruise the ginger – I have sliced it very thinly instead.

Weighing brown sugar is trickier than weighing white sugar – it comes out in clumps, and one pound has to be balanced carefully on the scales. The water, after having boiled for an hour with the ingredients in Claire's tights, is a dark brown. I added the yeast after Book Group, at which we discussed 'The Bell' by Iris Murdoch and ate lots of unhealthy nibbles.

DISASTER! This is not fermenting at all. I had my doubts before I went to London. I put it all in a demijohn anyway on 9th April, and posted a message up on a homebrewers' website to see if anyone has any ideas. On 13th April, after receiving advice from a somewhat irascible old man in the homebrew shop near Kirkstall Abbey (he was most unimpressed that I did not know the exact temperature of the liquid at every stage of the process), I added a restart yeast, after first ensuring it was fermenting in a mug with water at 27 degrees Celsius, and a teaspoon of sugar. The 'wine' is 23 degrees, so put that in your pipe and smoke it.

As of 16th April there is still very little activity. I have put it in the demijohn anyway (23 degrees), and the specific gravity is slightly lower, by about 0.04.

When I racked this the initial gravity had not changed at all. Bah! Either I am going to have to give up entirely or try the "If all else fails" method suggested by C. J. J. Berry.

Quantity:	One gallon.
Region:	I have no idea where cloves or ginger come from.
Price:	20p for the orange, 75p for the lemons, approximately 45p for the cloves, approximately £3 for the sugar, 12p for the ginger, £1.20 for the yeast, and another £1.20 for the next yeast.
Bought at:	A mixture of Street Lane, Harehills Road and Leeds Market.
Yeast Type:	Sauternes, initially, and then "NuStart" yeast.
Initial Gravity:	A little more than 1.100.
End Gravity:	A little less than 1.100.
Percentage:	Approximately 0% – which is not meant to happen.
Date Racked:	6th July 2008.
Date Bottled:	It has yet to be bottled.

INITIAL TASTE:
Not applicable.

THE DRINKING EXPERIENCE

Entirely inapplicable – I still have yet to decide what to do with this wine that has now been sitting in a demijohn next to my toilet bowl for nearly three years. By 6th September 2010 the initial gravity had gone down to 1.080 – which is a move in the right direction.

PEACH (& BANANA)

JULY 2008

When I last did Peach wine many years ago, it was absolutely disgusting. Possibly even worse than the Potato. We could only drink it with a liberal helping of tonic water in each glass. So why am I trying it again? Because Peach wine should be delicious. It just sounds right. Better than Strawberry even.

This time, on 19th July 2008, I have followed a different recipe; page 99 of Brian Leverett's book rather than relying on C. J. J. Berry; which may make a difference. Certainly, I do not remember 1lb of bananas from my first attempt. In fact I may have screwed up with the bananas. I balanced them precariously in a sieve over the bucket after simmering them in a pint of water for twenty minutes, hoping any remaining liquid might drop down into the peach mixture. Inevitably, when pouring the sugar in I knocked the bucket, the sieve fell in, and now the mixture has the boiled bananas swimming around with 3lb of chopped up peaches. And in fact (again) I am worried about the peaches. At least five of the twelve were less ripe than ideal, which is a euphemism for distinctly green. Watch this space.

Variations from the recipe include adding an extra pint of boiling water, so that I poured 5 pints of boiling water over the peaches, and weighing the bananas without their skins – there were no clear instructions on this point. The yeast, nutrient, and pectolase were added the same night, once everything was sufficiently cool. I put the drained solution into a demijohn on 23rd July and fear I may have made Banana wine by mistake. It is a peachy colour, but everything else suggests banana. Oops!

I racked it on the day I completed on the sale of Dreadful Mrs. Webster's fish and chip shop in Cleckheaton, and added just over a pint of water and 6oz of sugar. It is clear, and the taste I had was nondescript.

Quantity:	Six bottles.
Region:	Spain? Africa? The Americas? Not local.
Price:	£2 for the peaches, 70p for the bananas, £1.20 for the yeast, and more than £1 for the sugar.
Bought at:	Fruit: Leeds Outdoor Market. Sugar: Ex-Jacksons in a rainstorm.
Yeast Type:	Hock.
Date Racked:	10th October 2008.
Date Bottled:	Friday the Thirteenth, February 2009.

INITIAL TASTE:
Claire enjoyed the glass I poured whilst bottling. I thought it was only okay. There is a slight peach taste.

THE DRINKING EXPERIENCE

FIRST BOTTLE: 4th April 2009. Book Group on Friday was at our house, and we were discussing 'Rabbit, Run' by John Updike – brilliantly written, intense, and ultimately dislikeable. At the end of the evening Claire noticed that one of my bottles of Peach and Banana had popped its cork (no idea when), and shed half its contents over the carpet. Into the fridge it went, and we drank it on Saturday while I spent nearly two hours on the phone to TalkTalk and Norton, trying to get the computer fixed so it would connect to the Internet. The wine, despite inauspicious beginnings, was alright. Fruity and slightly bland, which is a success in my books. We also had the last bottle of Andrew's 'Malted Oat Stout', which was better than the wine.

SECOND BOTTLE: 3rd & 4th May 2009. Bang! Shriek! "Oh, that's just another of the wine bottles exploding." We had finished the 'Mutton Dressed as Raan' feast, and were playing cards as a cork flew through the air. Happily this bottle was upright, so I put a new cork in it quickly and shoved it into the fridge. Andrew had the first glass to relieve the pressure, and thought it impressive. Claire and

I finished it on Bank Holiday Monday with leftovers and spinach, and the wine was lovely. It is the right mix of peach and banana, is mostly clear (until the last glass), and the fizz is entirely beneficial. I am both pleased and smug.

THIRD BOTTLE: 17th May 2009. On Sunday morning, while tidying, I noticed this bottle has self-opened. The vacuum cleaner currently makes half-hearted attempts at sucking; it lacks a proper work ethic. We started the bottle at lunchtime, as Alison came over with her husband, Andy, and nine-year-old, George. Poor George. Though the meal was lovely, he was desperately bored and refused to eat much at all. Perhaps some emergency fish fingers would have been a good idea. I remember finding adults incomprehensible and dull at that age, but then I always had a handy sibling to annoy.

FOURTH BOTTLE: 24th & 25th May 2009. At this rate we will have finished Peach and Banana by my birthday. It just keeps on popping its corks. I noticed this one was open on Saturday, but for how long I am ignorant. After finishing a bottle of Christmas Tutti Fruti on Sunday night, and whilst watching yet another Doctor Who, we both decided that a further glass of wine would be disreputable and Just the Thing. By the time I went to bed my head was swimming. We finished it today after I had come back from visiting Shirley in hospital. She is worse again, and is losing both her mind and personality. Aging is a terrible thing, and I dread my own.

FIFTH BOTTLE: 4th & 5th June 2009. It was a rare hot weekend last weekend, and traditionally for weather of this type we spent much of it in the car. Before setting off this bottle had a cork; on our return it did not. Despite Claire's protestations I put it in the fridge, saving it for Thursday when Bob and Judith were visiting. I think the in-laws preferred the Elderflower, but this slipped down nicely.

SIXTH BOTTLE: 15th-19th August 2009. Whilst this bottle did not explode, it gave every impression of wanting to do so. The cork was slowly climbing out of the neck. I suggested that we keep this bottle in the fridge until the Wine Party, but the suggestion proved unpopular. When I did open it we lost about a glass as the wine fizzed over the kitchen floor, until I stopped dithering and poured some into Claire's glass. Our Saturday night meal involved black pudding, and putting all my squeamishness aside, I genuinely do not much like the taste of it. On Tuesday we each had a restorative glass after Summer Orchestra, which continues to sound dreadful. And so it is the end of another flavour: one which I have enjoyed and one that I shall revisit from time to time.

ROSEHIP

NOVEMBER 2008

On 2nd November 2008 we woke to grey skies and drizzle. Perfect weather for an autumnal Sunday walk. Though I could easily have been convinced to stay at home and continue reading about madness in medieval French literature, Claire encouraged me to find a relatively short local walk. I chose the six and a half mile circuit around Harewood, thinking it might have some rose bushes fruited with hips. Armed with small plastic bags we ventured out, and during the first half of the walk, found one significant bush laden. We picked about 2½ lb before getting bored and moving on. I was vaguely worried some Estate Manager would chase us away with a shotgun and large dogs, but we remained unchallenged.

The second half of the walk had many rosehips, virtually all the way (and lots of elder trees and sloe bushes too), and we picked the rest along a country lane running alongside the Harewood Arms.

I have (mostly) followed the recipe on page 136 of 'Winemaking Month by Month', which calls for 4lb of rosehips, 3lb of sugar, 2 teaspoons of citric acid, and 6 pints of boiling water, though I did not leave the hips soaking overnight, and I have minced them (not altogether successfully) in the food processor rather than leaving them whole. I added the yeast, nutrient, and citric acid on the morning of 3rd November. It all went into the demijohn on 8th November, and is a terracotta orange colour with huge amounts of clumps and swirls. I have added a pint and a half of water, and there is still plenty of space in the demijohn. A further ¾ pint of water was added on 9th November.

I never did top the liquid up to the neck of the demijohn. When racking this I made a shoddy job of it. My hand holding the tube slipped towards the end, disturbing the sediment, and then the tipped demijohn wobbled, and the tube came free. I stuck it in again to get the last remainder, but have ended up getting far more sediment than usual. It has hardly cleared, so I have added pectolase. A pint of syrup (ie. one pint of water and 6oz of sugar) has been added. I am not hopeful.

Quantity: One gallon.

Region: The Harewood Estate.

Price: £1.20 for the sugar, £1.20 for the yeast.

Yeast Type: Bordeaux.

Date Racked: 19th January 2009.

Date Bottled: 18th June 2009.

INITIAL TASTE:

The wine has cleared and is a golden colour. These are its positive attributes. I had worried that it would be excessively sweet, but I needn't have. More sugar would have helped. The taste is bland, but in a too-dry-and-unpleasant way.

THE DRINKING EXPERIENCE

FIRST BOTTLE: 17th-19th October 2009. This was the first bottle opened at the Wine Party, and the flavour I was most eager to try. I had expected something nastier than I got, but on the whole this wine is dry and unremarkable. Two people thought it 'Poor' and two 'Indifferent'. Julia, who describes things in terms of building materials, said "Steel with wobbles in it – a metallic tang", and on a similar theme someone wrote "Nice taste once got past initial hint of chewing on Bacofoil". I did not pick up metal as a flavour. It was also described as "horrible" and "only just passable". Hey ho.

SECOND BOTTLE: 18th-20th November 2009. Many of the wines I make are too sweet. This one, however, in best Mary Poppins fashion, needs a spoonful of sugar per glass to make it bearable. And even then, it is still moderately unpleasant. I was expecting Claire to open a Prune and Parsnip whilst I was at orchestra, struggling with Sibelius, but she went for Rosehip instead. And I have finished the bottle on Thursday and Friday, watching Torchwood Series One, whilst I should really have been reading 'Wolf Hall' for the Booker Party in a fortnight.

THIRD BOTTLE: 3rd-7th January 2010. We began this

wine as the last bottle of the Christmas holidays, safely back from Newcastle, watching the final episode of 'Life on Mars' whilst huddled under a blanket. This winter has been the snowiest and coldest I have ever experienced in England. There has been a snow covering since at least 20th December, and more is forecast. Both orchestras were cancelled this week, and schools are closed up and down the country. Anyway, Claire discovered that adding a sugar syrup to the wine helped. Her precise words were, "Yeah, with the addition of about two teaspoons per glass, this becomes merely nondescript".

FOURTH BOTTLE: 17th-19th February 2010. Claire and I fought over who should have the last glass from this bottle. Claire won, so the last glass was mine. It was drunk while cooking Friday night's meal and listening to Radio 4. In The Archers, Phil Archer has just died, and they are handling his death beautifully.

FIFTH BOTTLE: 22nd-24th April 2010. This bottle began life as a mid-week bottle; essentially something to drink on a Thursday. Our meal was entirely beige and consisted of 'things past their first flush of youth'. So baked cauliflower, mashed and spiced swede, and scalloped potatoes. All were actually rather nice. And we finished the bottle tonight after a WYSO concert in Wakefield. The music was all twentieth century and thrilling. Rhapsody in Blue was the highlight, with a fabulous soloist (Marc Corbett-Weaver), who played as if improvising the notes. And I am ashamed to admit that I absolutely loved 'The Phantom Menace Suite' by John Williams – particularly the last movement sung by an angry choir in an invented language.

SIXTH BOTTLE: 16th July 2010. Sooz is visiting, and I gave her a list of bottles that she was allowed to try. She chose Rosehip, and even though I gave her the opportunity to change her mind, this is what we had. In fact, it is a lovely colour – sunset orange. Sooz had one mouthful without the added syrup and declared it 'beer-like', but no further glasses went unadorned. We drank the bottle to compulsory salad from the garden, and then the best pizza that Claire has ever made. It had a sour-dough base, which I think was the deciding factor, as the toppings were pretty standard: goat's cheese, rocket, salami, and olive – that sort of thing. Anyway, this bottle of Rosehip was sufficiently nice that I may do it again one day. But not this year.

SPICED BEETROOT

FEBRUARY 2009

I started making this flavour on 9th February 2009. I have made Spiced Beetroot at least twice before, but it has been a while since the last batch. It is one of those wines that improves massively on keeping. Usually, because of the spices and the English growing season, this is done in December for the following Christmas. The current snow, though, brings a wintry feel, and Spiced Beetroot seems entirely appropriate.

After having spent the day translating both Old and New Testament Latin (David and Goliath and the Wedding at Cana, and note, if the first part of this sentence had been in Latin it would have been in the ablative absolute, and note too that that last bit was in the subjunctive), I have spent this evening washing, chopping, and weighing beetroot. I have put in just over 1oz of ginger (thinly sliced), and the 6 cloves dictated by the recipe. I have also added very small amounts of grated nutmeg, ground cinnamon, and allspice, none of which are in the instructions. I am hoping these won't impede fermentation. I have boiled the beetroot in six pints of water, and added a pint and a half of cold to the bucket.

I added the yeast and nutrient (no pectolase) on 10th February, and put it all into the brown glass demijohn on Friday 13th. It is all bubbling nicely. There was not quite enough liquid to fill the demijohn, but it is currently within half a pint. The recipe is very clear that this must be stored in a darkened container.

I have just racked this and it is an alarming colour – luminous purple. There was very little deposit, and the clarity is difficult to establish. It remains in a dark glass demijohn in an effort to maintain its hue. I added just over half a mixture of 3oz of sugar and half a pint of water. As the small taste I got was far too dry, I put in an additional two teaspoons of sugar for luck rather than for any practical benefit.

Quantity:	One gallon.
Region:	The beetroot is Spanish – I missed the English season.
Price:	£3 for the beetroot, 29p for the lemon, £1-ish for the sugar, low amounts for the ginger and other spices, £1.20 for the yeast.
Bought at:	Oakwood Fruit & Veg on Street Lane.
Yeast Type:	High Alcohol.
Date Racked:	15th April 2009.
Date Bottled:	20th September 2009.

INITIAL TASTE:

This wine has a slight mustiness, and is mostly unremarkable. The clarity is fine and the colour less exciting than hoped, though undeniably red. I can't detect a mouthful of spices, but perhaps it will mature. It is not as dry as I had feared.

THE DRINKING EXPERIENCE

FIRST BOTTLE: 7th February 2010. Gosh. The colour of this wine is splendid. It is the most purple wine I have ever made. Claire describes it as 'magenta', which pleases me. And the taste is actually rather good. Cloves are the dominant spice, but not in an overpowering way. There is a definite 'body' to this wine – so it is an overall 'Hit'. Today has been spent making Orange wine, buying boring things from Sainsbury's, and the dress rehearsal for 'Oliver!' which feels very much like a school play, because that is precisely what it is.

SECOND BOTTLE: 20th March 2010. I gave Leslie a free choice of which bottle to have as our second of the evening. Well, free-ish. She was intrigued by the Beetroot, and I managed to direct her away from Strawberry. This bottle was certainly not as lovely as the Gooseberry drunk earlier, but Leslie declared it Good. Richard, however, pulled a face. The wine has an odd, thoroughly beneficial

189

aftertaste, which warms the back of the throat in much the same way as whisky. Claire thinks this is probably the cloves. We drank the wine to an apple and gorgonzola strüdel, which was less bizarre than it sounds. Definitely not a pudding, and really rather tasty, and to a fabulous pecan pie that wobbled worryingly when it came out of the oven, but had set by eating. Now comes the ascent of the Washing Up Mountain.

THIRD BOTTLE: 1st August 2010. I took this bottle to the Lake District with me and shared it round many people on the Rydal Hall Orchestra course. Claire and I, with three others, had spent most of the day walking the Fairfield Horseshoe. Along the ridge the Lake District was spread out before us, each mountain a slumbering giant. After the evening's rehearsal – Beethoven's 5th Symphony and a dreadful piece called 'The Skaters' by Meyersbeer – I poured out the Beetroot. Leo, the conductor, asked pointedly "Do you ever make anything that tastes of wine?" and the Reverend Clack declared that it tastes of Christmas. In fact Robert was effusive, creating menus for this wine. Apparently it would go well with curry, or just a plateful of tomatoes and olive oil.

FOURTH BOTTLE: 16th October 2010. It was The Wine Party last night and, despite it being afternoon, I am still feeling delicate. The event was smaller than in previous years as many of the invitees couldn't make it, and some were ill – so it ended up that there were twelve of us. We still managed to get through most of ten bottles, of which this was one. It came sixth with an average score of nearly '3'. Sooz described it as "Christmassy", and Mom said it was "a winter wine". Duncan, however, drew a picture of a skull and crossbones, and awarded it a '1'. So not to everyone's taste then.

FIFTH BOTTLE: 29th October 2010. Helen, a PhD friend of Claire's, is visiting, and it has been at least eight years since we last saw her. I gave her an entirely free choice of wines to try and she chose this, on the shaky basis that she doesn't much like beetroot. Helen thought the wine tasted of spirits, agreed that it was a wonderful colour, and could not taste the beetroot. I think all those judgments are correct. One cup of proper tea and a mug of bush tea later, I now wish I had stopped at the Spiced Beetroot and not opened (and finished) the bottle of Elderflower.

SIXTH BOTTLE: 27th December 2010. And so another flavour comes to an end. It has to be admitted that its colour was somewhat better than its taste. There were exciting magenta hues unmatched by vaguely alcoholic flavours. I say 'vaguely alcoholic' but, in fact, the strength of this is not in question. If I were to ascribe an Olympic sport to my thought processes, it would be 'swimming'. We have returned from Newcastle today, after visiting Keith and family (including the adorable Ellis), to a desperately cold house and hungry cats. Both have been remedied, and only one with burning coals. Tonight's Christmas food has been a nut roast involving cranberries and chestnuts. My left thumbnail still hurts from divesting the latter of their shells. I have had enough alcohol to stun an ox, but my thumb continues to throb. Perhaps Spiced Beetroot wine is not quite as medicinal as it tastes.

NETTLE

APRIL 2009

This was supposed to be the wine that I made in May. I fancied trying something entirely new, and read the options to Claire. Pleasingly she picked 'nettle' – the archetypal homemade wine made in the 1970s by those trying the self-sufficient lifestyle. When I mentioned to Julia that I would be trying to make this wine in May, she said this would be too late. I needed to start it now, and she had plenty of nettles on her allotment that could do with being cleared. So, on 25th April 2009, after playing the Fasch bassoon concerto here with Claire, Julia, Laura and Barbara, and a meal of various cheeses and salad, Claire and I went to the allotment with plastic bags and rubber gloves.

Picking nettles in warm, late-afternoon April sun was delightful. Between us we picked at least four times too many nettles. Some have been transformed into a soup of verdant green, but most are destined for the compost heap.

I did not read the recipe closely before picking, and now see that I should have only used the nettle tops, but it is a little late for that. To compensate I have put in closer to six pints of nettles, rather than the four suggested by both Brian Leverett and C. J. J. Berry. I am mostly following the latter's recipe, though I have put in 2lb 12oz of sugar rather than the 3lb suggested. I am boiling up the nettles in six pints of water, and will pour this directly onto the sugar. I have yet to decide whether I will filter the nettles out at this stage. Berry says 'yes', Leverett says 'no'.

I went for the 'nettles in' option, and added the yeast on Sunday morning, 26th April. So far the liquid is less green than I had hoped. It all went into the demijohn on Thursday 30th April, in the afternoon of a busy day: work, Emmaus, Shirley, lamb-buying, and the fourth night of Pirates of Penzance. Worryingly, the colour strongly resembles that of phlegm.

By racking it has mostly cleared, and has a trace of green colouring, but nothing more dramatic. The sediment was relatively low, and I managed to pour in virtually all of a syrup made up of half a pint of water and 3oz of sugar. At this time the overriding taste is of lemons.

Quantity:	One gallon.
Region:	Julia's allotment.
Price:	58p for the lemons, 15p for the ginger, £1.20 for the yeast, £1.20-ish for the sugar.
Bought at:	The ginger and the lemons were bought from Paul's greengrocer's.
Yeast Type:	General Purpose (which is one I have not used before).
Date Racked:	8th July 2009.
Date Bottled:	8th November 2009.

INITIAL TASTE:
The wine is not absolutely clear, but it is close, and there is only the merest hint of green. The taste is unusual, but not in a bad way. It has a vague taste of beer, and you can taste the lemon, though not the ginger. Dry and odd.

THE DRINKING EXPERIENCE

FIRST BOTTLE:　　19th-20th January 2010. I came home from rehearsing a trio at David Wilks' to find newspaper on the hall floor, five bottles standing upright, and a pungent aroma in the air. The Nettle had exploded. Claire had, earlier in the evening, heard a noise and shouted at the cat to stop whatever it was doing. When the sound continued she went downstairs to investigate, and found two-thirds of a bottle forming a puddle. I have drunk the remainder over two nights; tonight's glass after a particularly ropey orchestra rehearsal, and the concert is on Saturday. Yikes. The wine has a strange, herby taste that just avoids being unpleasant. The lemon is obvious, but not overpowering. Until the last glass it has been clear with a slight fizz. For the moment I am reserving my judgment.

SECOND BOTTLE:　　2nd April 2010. Sooz is visiting for Easter, and I have spent the last month planning to force-feed this to her. Just for the comical reaction, you understand. In fact, Nettle wine is too strange to elicit much beyond a vaguely puzzled look. Claire and Sooz both claimed they detected 'meat' as a flavour – not an ideal taste for wine – and later Sooz changed this to 'cheese' and (I think) 'olives'. I picked up none of those flavours. For me, it tasted of a strong, herby, European lager, and not unpleasant. We drank it with wonderful lamb koftas, and then watched 'Strictly Ballroom' on DVD – a lovely, funny, corny film that just leaves you smiling.

THIRD BOTTLE: 31st May–2nd June 2010. Here is a wine on which Claire and I disagree. Whilst not conventionally lovely, I certainly think it has something going for it. Claire would prefer me not to make it again. Monday was a bank holiday, and we spent the morning helping Julia net her redcurrants. It looks like it will be a bumper year, and the more we can protect from the pigeons, the better. Between us we built a frame out of old tent poles, bamboo canes, and rope (though I did rather more 'holding' than 'building'), and threw a net over it. In the evening we drank Nettle wine with leftover roast pork, and I have finished the bottle over the following two nights – tonight whilst reading a Jeeves and Wooster, which is written with a tremendously light touch.

FOURTH BOTTLE: 21st July 2010. I do feel old. Tonight was my second night out in a row with the Medieval MA students. They are all in their twenties, and I am just not. Last night it was Leslie's 25th and we went to see 'Inception', which was excellent. This evening was JD's leaving party, so I took along a bottle of Nettle wine. Everyone who tried it was polite, though I suspect only Kerstin really enjoyed it. Matt, who has taken wine tasting exams, said there was a hint of Sauvignon – so he can come to this year's Wine Party. Anyway, I felt like an intruder at the party – lots of young people having young people's conversations. It was still good fun, but I recognise I need to have some quiet nights in shortly.

FIFTH BOTTLE: 16th October 2010. The clear loser at this year's Wine Party. It got an average score of '1.28' out of '5'. No-one awarded it with anything higher than a '2', and Duncan gave it a '0'. There was a theme running through the comments: "Worsens with experience – the reverse of an acquired taste", "OK at first – then stings", "Doesn't grow on me". Another theme was medicinal, with Diana comparing it to disinfectant, Sooz to Flash, and Angie to an 11th century purging cure. Mom claimed it plumbs new depths, but then remembered the Potato. Not a success.

SIXTH BOTTLE: This remains undrunk, and is liable to remain so for quite some time.

REDCURRANT

JULY 2009

I had not planned on making Redcurrant wine this year, but as I was picking gooseberries on 11th July 2009, Julia was busy picking redcurrants. She said that if she did not pick them now, some rather portly pigeons would take them instead. So, who was I to refuse? Redcurrants are such beautiful fruit. They are like clusters of jewels, hiding behind leaves. It was almost a shame to mash them up once they were in the bucket.

Today, 12th July, may not have been the best day to start a brand new flavour. This morning the thumb, which had become infected after an unfortunate incident involving pastry being rammed under the nail, burst. Happily, this was not during the winemaking process, but it meant that I have been leaking pus and blood gently for most of the day. My thumb looks much better (less colourful), and I think I avoided getting any into the wine.

I have followed C. J. Berry's recipe on page 163, except I reduced the water to 7 pints and the sugar to 2lb 12oz. Claire will want credit for stripping the berries from their stalks at about seven this morning whilst I was still asleep. I added the pectolase the same evening, and the yeast and nutrient the next morning. During its time in the bucket I removed one drowned beetle. The wine went into the demijohn on 17th July. It is a beautiful blood-red colour, and I have wrapped the demijohn in silver foil in an effort to preserve this. I could have added a pint less water.

By racking it has cleared, and is still a wonderful colour. The deposit was relatively large: I managed to fit in a pint and a half of water, and 6oz of sugar. It needs the additional sweetness – the taste was unpleasantly dry.

Quantity:	One gallon.
Region:	Julia's allotment.
Price:	£1-ish for the sugar, and £1.20 for the yeast.

Yeast Type: Burgundy.

Initial Gravity: 1.090.

End Gravity: 1.008.

Percentage: Around 14%.

Date Racked: 30th September 2009.

Date Bottled: 13th February 2010.

INITIAL TASTE:
I am pleased with this. It is Valentine red, absolutely clear, and has a sharp, fresh taste. The dryness is pleasing rather than overdone. Claire's first impression of the bouquet was 'cherry lips', and there is an element of that in the taste.

THE DRINKING EXPERIENCE

FIRST BOTTLE: 21st February 2010. Ordinarily I would wait a year between picking the fruit and drinking the first bottle. However, when I bottled this eight days ago, Claire thought it was ready for drinking. I suggested it would go nicely with tonight's roast ham, so the decision was made. The wine is wonderful – a gorgeous colour, perfect clarity, and a dry, sharp taste akin to cranberries. Today has been dominated by research for an essay on medieval attitudes to childbirth and children, mostly by reading Mystery Plays in Middle English, which takes some brain adjustment. But we also got excited by an early snowfall and four goldfinches flitting around the new bird feeder. It is surprising how engrossing this can be. Particularly when there is an essay to be done.

SECOND BOTTLE: 3rd April 2010. Apparently this wine is reminiscent of Norway, and would go well with reindeer... or at least according to Sooz. For what has been a lazy Easter Saturday, we have had a jolly day. As well as general sitting around, we planted potatoes in the new potato bed (formerly known as the 'lawn'), have eaten half a duck, and watched the first outing of Matt Smith's Doctor Who. The duck was fabulous, and Redcurrant wine went well with it – sharp enough to cut through the rich, meaty flavour. The new Doctor, on first appearance, is splendid. l I can now relax.

THIRD BOTTLE: 10th April 2010. This is a worrying development. Redcurrant has gone fizzy. I was sitting at the computer when I heard a pop. With my dizzyingly quick reaction times, only one glass was lost, and we took the remainder over to Julia's for a 'clear the freezer' feast. And what a banquet it was: roasted quail and partridge stuffed with redcurrants and various vegetables, including delicious prize-winning leeks.

FOURTH BOTTLE: 20th-22nd May 2010. It was late Thursday evening, and Claire and I were draining the last of a bottle of Crab Apple when there was a large bang. A cork had shot out of the Redcurrant, and pink liquid was foaming enthusiastically over the carpet. I grabbed it and ran to the kitchen, trailing wine as I went. Sucking at the bottle was inefficient, so I poured us each half a glass. We had planned to finish this on Friday, but came back from 'Death of a Salesman' thoroughly harrowed, and so were not in the mood. Instead we have brought this up to Newcastle as one of the four exploded bottles that could bear a car journey, and finished it with Sooz's homemade gnocchi.

FIFTH BOTTLE: 24th-26th May 2010. Yet another exploder during the hot May weekend. Claire drank most of this bottle, though I had a large glass on Wednesday night after a terrific evening of playing Beethoven's Sixth at WYSO. On Monday night I was still a little drunk from my lunch with Rodney, and on Tuesday I was out late watching 'Robin Hood' at the cinema with a load of medievalists. We sat in a row guffawing at inappropriate moments, muttering 'That never happened'. I was checking e-mails whilst drinking my glass from this bottle, and one popped up from Iona with comments on my 'medieval surgery' essay. It took an agonisingly long time to open, during which I tried to pretend the mark didn't really matter. Happily, though, I got a 'Low Distinction', with the criticism that I didn't discuss other historians' views enough. But I don't really care what other historians have concluded. I'm far more interested in how I interpret the evidence!

SIXTH BOTTLE: 16th October 2010. As this is a brand new flavour, I have been saving the final bottle for the Wine Party. I had remembered this as being rather better than it was and, before the party, would have predicted it to come second or third. In fact it came seventh, with an average score of '2.64'. Pop wrote "Don't like it much", Mom thought it was too dry, and Sooz wrote "Pretty,

but not keen – smells of burning plastic", and drew a picture of a
bimbo. Maybe I should use more sugar in the future as it does have
that sharp, pursed-lips taste which is prevalent in raw currants and
gooseberries.

CRAB APPLE & ELDERBERRY

OCTOBER 2009

Claire suggested this wine, partly, I think, in an effort to keep some usable space in the freezer. The elderberries are leftovers from those we picked on 20th September, and I picked 4lb of crab apples today, 3rd October 2009. Harvesting the crab apples was uneventful. It has been a sunny, windy afternoon (great for drying clothes), and I did most of the plucking from behind the tree where the apples seemed to be riper. This, however, had the disadvantage of thorny plants. My arse was attacked by a burberis (I think – whatever it was had sharp spikes), and my arms have been scratched by a pyrocantha. The apples were as plentiful as ever; I think I have taken about a third from the tree. Several plummeted into the undergrowth, which was frustrating. I rescued as many as I could.

I put 1lb of frozen elderberries into the bucket, made a half-hearted attempt to mash them, and then poured over a pint of boiling water, mostly as a defrosting agent. Mashing went so much better after this. I then sliced the crab apples using the food processor, and added those. 3lb of sugar was added next, and I stirred everything up. I then added five more pints of boiling water, and stirred thoroughly to dissolve the sugar. The yeast, together with 1 teaspoon each of nutrient, pectolase and citric acid, were put in about twelve hours later on Sunday morning. I put the liquid into the demijohn on 8th October, after an irritating sojourn to IKEA to pick up some shelves for my mother. IKEA, despite it being after six o'clock, was full of people walking slowly and getting in the way. This wine was quicker to strain than pure Crab Apple, and it must be for the lack of minced sultanas. I added about ¾ of a pint of water on 10th October.

The taste on racking was exceedingly dry, and because the sediment was relatively small I only managed to add about 4oz of sugar dissolved in half a pint of water. I fear this will be a failure.

Quantity:	One gallon.
Region:	The elderberries are from Hetchell Woods, and the crab apples from our tree.

> **Price:**   £1-ish for the sugar, and £1.20 for the yeast.
>
> **Yeast Type:**   Bordeaux.
>
> **Date Racked:**   20th December 2009.
>
> **Date Bottled:** 4th June 2010.

INITIAL TASTE:

Oh me of little faith. This has a definite taste of proper red wine. It is entirely clear and (thankfully, in this period of explosions) entirely flat. There is a faint hint of metal, but on the whole it is light, fruity, and rather good. A 'Hit'.

THE DRINKING EXPERIENCE

FIRST BOTTLE: 17th July 2010. Well, what an alcoholic evening it has been. This was the second bottle opened tonight, and the third one finished. Between four people – he said quickly in his defence. Sooz is staying, and Julia came for supper. The wine was really rather good. Sooz described it as a dark rosé, which is pretty accurate. It definitely has a taste of shop-bought wine; far more so than my single flavours. I'm not sure that this is a Good Thing – a certain distinctive quality is lost, even though a smoothness is gained.

SECOND BOTTLE: 15th-17th September 2010. I have had a rare week of working full time, and I don't recommend it. Too much having to be places and doing things in an organised manner. And I have been out virtually every evening, except tonight. Half of this bottle, therefore, has been drunk over a couple of nights as a nightcap, and I polished off the remainder whilst cooking and eating a fabulous cauliflower and lentil curry (if I do say so myself). The first reaction to this wine was 'thin' and 'tart'. However, with a bit of sugar and (oddly) over time, it has improved to really rather drinkable. Maybe it is just me getting less discerning towards the end of the bottle.

THIRD BOTTLE: 16th October 2010. This was the most controversial wine at the 2010 Wine Party. Whilst a couple of people gave it a '4', three thought it was horrid and awarded it a

'1'. Julia went so far as to describe it as the worst wine opened, and likened the experience of drinking it to "pins and needles on the tongue". It came eighth out of ten with an average score of '2½'.

FOURTH BOTTLE: 19th December 2010. This bottle has been excellent: sharp with a kick, admittedly, but really tasty. Today has been phenonemon-, er, phenemononen- phenomenally (that's better!) lazy. Apart from domestic tasks such as making bread, doing the first proper stage of Christmas Tutti Fruti wine, and washing dishes, I have basically sat on the sofa with a cat on my lap either doing a Sudoku puzzle, catching up with yesterday's newspaper, or reading 'A Company of Liars' by Karen Maitland, which continues to be gripping. Do I feel guilty? Well, yes, a little – but Sundays were made for idleness, and drinking half a bottle of Crab Apple and Elderberry just feels right.

FIFTH BOTTLE: 12th February 2011. Bob and Judith are visiting and using us as a stopover on their way to Leo's 60th birthday party tomorrow. To celebrate, I opened this bottle to go with a roast chicken dinner. It succeeded in sending Bob to sleep, snoring and open-mouthed on the sofa, whilst Claire and Judith discussed 'Hard Times'. Still, snoring is a better sound than his incessant dry cough that is likely to keep more than him awake tonight.

SIXTH BOTTLE: 6th March 2011. It has been an exhausting day, and a bottle of Crab Apple and Elderberry was a welcome reward. Today I was drafted into the Leeds College of Music Orchestra to play second bassoon in their concert. This is Claire's orchestra, and for the last few weeks she has come home from rehearsals complaining about tuning and timing and attendance. Despite this I enjoyed the play-through starting at 10.30am, and the concert was actually pretty good. We played Beethoven's maddest and loudest symphony, his Seventh, which I am also currently rehearsing with the Airedale, and will be doing later in the year with WYSO. Sometimes you can have too much of a good thing, but not Crab Apple and Elderberry wine, which is sharp, fruity, and well worth making. Yet again I shall ignore the market research tool which is the Wine Party.

GRAPE & RAISIN

OCTOBER 2009

This wine was entirely unplanned. On 10th October 2009 Mom and Pop visited to hear the Leeds Music Club concert where I was playing the Fasch bassoon concerto. They brought with them some clothes belonging to Great Uncle Gerry and a plastic bag stuffed with grapes grown at Chateau Hardy. I pulled them off their stalks on Sunday 11th October, which was a long and tedious task interrupted by a quick trip to Wakefield to play the bassoon part in a GCSE composition. These grapes are tightly bunched, making their removal awkward, and each ripe grape felt like it was about to explode in my hands, so I had to do this carefully. Many of the grapes were still green, but I put them in all the same.

Once all the grapes were plucked I had 4lb 9½ oz, which was not enough for a full gallon of wine by itself. I thought about adding crab apples, but the recipe books suggested 'Grape and Raisin' as a valid flavour, so this is what I have done.

I had planned on spending much of the day cleaning the house in preparation for next week's Wine Party, but this wine got in the way. I did not start crushing grapes and adding ingredients until after our return from a fantastic concert of a Brahms String Sextet and Mendelssohn's Octet (he wrote it aged 16 – now there is a quality GCSE composition) in Rawdon.

As well as the grapes I added 8oz of minced raisins, 2½ lb of sugar, and four pints of boiling water, which I suspect is too little. The yeast and nutrient went in on the morning of 12th October, and I put in a pint of cold water in the evening. I drained the liquid into its demijohn on 18th October, the morning after the Wine Party. It is a pale pink colour, but I was hoping for something darker. It is in a brown glass demijohn. I added another half pint of water to fill the container. It took a very long time for evidence of fermentation, but the air-trap is now bubbling away happily.

By racking it has become a ruby red colour, and is clear. The small taste I got was promising, and Claire was able to detect raisins. I added ¾ pint of water with 4oz of sugar dissolved in it, which was a perfect fit.

Quantity: One gallon.

Region: The grapes are from the back garden of Heworth Green. The raisins are Californian.

Price: £1-ish for the sugar, £1.20 for the yeast, and I didn't record how much 8oz of raisins set me back.

Yeast Type: Burgundy.

Date Racked: 10th January 2010.

Date Bottled: 20th June 2010.

INITIAL TASTE:

I am very pleased with this. It looks beautiful, and tastes good. Claire's first comment was "tomatoes", and then "raisins". There is a slight sweetness, but that will please my mother. This is definitely the way forward with grapes grown in York.

THE DRINKING EXPERIENCE

FIRST BOTTLE: 25th July 2010. The first bottle of Grape and Raisin was always going to be opened at Heworth Green, and tonight was a good opportunity as my Texan half-cousin, Lynne, was visiting with her family, Billy and Annie. The wine is a lovely pale red colour, and absolutely clear. This is usually the point where I talk about its foul taste, but in fact the taste was entirely acceptable. It was a rosé wine with a kick – Lynne said it sat at the back of the tongue. Mom pulled her "it's too dry" face, but then agreed it was not. I am genuinely pleased with this.

SECOND BOTTLE: 16th October 2010. Grape and Raisin was the surprise runner-up at this year's Wine Party. If I had made a list of predictions I would have put it around sixth or seventh, as I think it is pretty nondescript. However, it got an average score of '4', and was Pop's favourite. He described the wine as a "sweet rosé" and "delightful", which from him is huge praise. Mom commented on its attractive colour, and Richard drew a woman wearing a large hat covered in fruit.

THIRD BOTTLE: 13th November 2010. My maternal grandfather's wine glasses made a rare appearance for this bottle of wine. Because they are so fragile, we only ever use them for the most special of occasions, and today we bought a car, which is very scary indeed – particularly as it is Brand New. I had never imagined that I would buy anything other than second-hand. But it is small and red, and fits down the drive. After making the decision and paying the deposit, I had to have a quiet sit down with a stiff gin and tonic. This bottle also helped – it is a beautiful colour and tastes like a genuine rosé wine. We drank it with a chicken and prune casserole while having a long hard think about what we had done.

FOURTH BOTTLE: 31st December 2010. The runner-up for the Wine Party proved less popular at New Year's Eve. This might be because this was the last bottle from the demijohn, and therefore rougher in taste. We spent some of the evening discussing New Year's resolutions. Claire's is to do Grade 8 on the viola. Mine should be to lose the stone that I put on over 2010, but is instead to have a fabulous 2011. This was derided by all present as too vague. It is neither Specific nor objectively Measurable. So what I have is an ART target, rather than a SMART target (though I forget what the 'A' stands for), and I like that.

FIFTH BOTTLE: 23rd January 2011. This bottle was inexplicably better than the last. Chris is visiting so that the journey to cousin David's funeral tomorrow is more manageable for him. I gave him a choice of red, white, or pink, and unexpectedly he chose pink. We drank it with a casserole of rabbit in a creamy tarragon sauce, and twice the number of roast potatoes that Claire thought we could eat. The Hardy boys love a challenge, and we managed that one with ease.

SIXTH BOTTLE: 19th March 2011. I opened this bottle at an impromptu party back at our house following a WYSO concert. I say 'party', but it was more of a small social gathering. My parents, Fiona Crowther, Nigel, and Diana all came back and said nice things about how we had played. This was particularly pleasing from Nigel, who conducts Northern Ballet. I chose Grape and Raisin because my father was so enthusiastic about it in October. If anything I think this bottle has improved, and this is certainly what I will do with my mother's grapes in years of good harvest. It was a worthy celebration for the concert, which was an 'All

English' programme – the main work being Vaughn Williams' Fifth Symphony, a luscious and unjustly obscure piece. The interval was nearly a disaster, though. Many people brought cakes and biscuits, and the organisers did not put out the gingerbread violas that Claire had spent hours making on Friday. I retrieved the tin and marched round the room force-feeding the biscuits to hapless audience members who, on being pressed, agreed they were 'very nice, thank you'.

APPLE

NOVEMBER 2009

Oddly, Apple wine is not a flavour I have made before. There are a number of recipes in the books I have (well, three: but I maintain that is a number). Julia mentioned at Music Club that this year had been splendid for apples, to the extent that she was feeling oppressed by windfalls. I checked my three recipes, rejected the two that called for sensible numbers of apples, and asked whether Julia had a spare twenty four pounds of which she wanted rid. These were brought round in a laundry hamper on Sunday, and I have spent Tuesday evening, 10th November 2009, washing them and chopping them into bits. This took about two hours: there were 138 apples, which works out at 23 apples for each bottle, and I chopped each into about 18 bits. I can't be bothered to do the maths, but the brewing bucket is very nearly full.

There are three varieties of apple; I recognised russets, but not the other two. Many were wizened or bruised, but few contained livestock. I removed one woodlouse, but did not find any maggots.

I poured a gallon of boiling water into the bucket, and now I am instructed to stir several times daily, which will be quite a task. The yeast and nutrient were stirred into half a pint of water and poured into the bucket the next morning. Stirring has not been easy, and I keep on bashing my knuckle against the bucket, causing it to bleed.

Actually, the stirring process became easier as the apples rotted down. I filtered them out using a colander and my other, smaller bucket on 16th November, after an afternoon at York Minster with the Cathedral archaeologist, and added 3lb of sugar and a teaspoon of pectolase to the caramel brown liquid. This took far less time than I had feared. Putting it into the demijohn, however, took longer. I did this on 19th November, and there was a large amount of sludge to filter out. The liquid has not quite filled the demijohn, and it is a particularly unattractive brown colour.

This wine took an age to clear, and by racking it is still a little murky. The sediment lay in an odd way, at a steep angle, until it was moved by the cavity wall insulators. On racking I picked up some of the deposit, which was large, and added two and a quarter pints of water and 5oz of sugar. The taste was on the sweet side of 'medium'.

I had planned to bottle this on 25th June, but there was a relatively substantial sediment for this stage (about a quarter of an inch), so I racked it again instead, and added a quarter pint of water. It is a clear wine, and the taste was refreshing, slightly sweet, and rather good.

Quantity:	One gallon.
Region:	Julia's allotment.
Price:	£1-ish for the sugar, £1.20 for the yeast.
Yeast Type:	Champagne.
Date Racked:	6th February 2010 and again on 25th June 2010.
Date Bottled:	18th July 2010.

INITIAL TASTE:
This is fantastic – possibly my best white ever. I can't imagine sharing this with anyone.

THE DRINKING EXPERIENCE

FIRST BOTTLE: 30th August 2010. How utterly disappointing. This is an alright bottle of wine. I had expected it to be exquisite. Claire says there is a taste of damp dishcloth, though Bob has denied any taste of dead dog, for which I am grateful. There is a slight sparkle, and a taste of apple, and it is far from my worst, but 'quite good' is not good enough. Oh well. It has been an entertaining Bank Holiday Monday, despite the wine. We took Bob and Judith to Thwaite's Water Mills, which is a fascinating piece of industrial and social history. The noise produced by the two mills was glorious, percussive music, and our guide made the working conditions come alive. From here we went to Peter Ly's restaurant and ate Dim Sum of various textures and tastes. Thoroughly recommended.

SECOND BOTTLE: 16th October 2010. Apple wine came a very credible fourth (should that be 'creditable fourth'?) at the Wine Party, scoring an average of '3.28' out of '5'. It was far fizzier than the previous bottle, and Claire and I both thought this bottle better than the first. Angie commented on its summer flavours, and drew a picture of a badminton racquet and shuttlecock. Julia said it reminded her of daisies – pleasantly unmemorable – and Richard agreed with this, writing "Little bit nondescript but actually v. drinkable". So I am happier than I was when I opened the first bottle.

THIRD BOTTLE: 30th October 2010. Our central heating was fixed on Thursday. On the whole this is a Good Thing. However, it is unlikely to be a coincidence that on Friday night this bottle popped its cork, and spewed a third of its contents over our bedroom floor. Into the fridge it went, and out came the mop. We drank what was left tonight with a fabulous cheese and onion quiche – the onions coming from our garden. They tasted sweeter and more flavoursome than shop-bought ones. The wine was pleasant without being particularly interesting, and the somewhat-less-than-half-a-bottle has caused a certain amount of head-spinning, so it must be potent.

FOURTH BOTTLE: 25th November 2010. I took this bottle to Richard and Linda's for our annual Thanksgiving feast. It was a huge meal, and had all the traditional foodstuffs, but not all in the traditional way. Because Richard is a vegetarian, the vegetables were cooked with more imagination. The sweetcorn was in a vegetable bake with roast chestnuts and mushrooms, and the sweet potato had been marinated in spices. We had to have a short break before Claire's fabulous pumpkin pie.

FIFTH BOTTLE: 14th-15th December 2010. As I was wondering which bottle to open on Tuesday evening, Claire came into the kitchen with this bottle which had popped its cork at an unknown point within the past week or so. I started drinking it while learning how to make dumplings, and continued on the sofa whilst reading more of 'A Company of Liars' – a jolly Black Death romp. Apple wine slips down very nicely indeed – it has a crisp, sweet taste, and the fizz is entirely beneficial, apart from the unpredictable opening part.

SIXTH BOTTLE: 2nd-4th February 2011. This was not a happy bottle of wine. On Wednesday, when opened, I was worried about my job. Tonight, when finished, I had just received my 'Redundancy Consultation Letter'. Still, Thursday night's glass, drunk in a hot bath, was tasty. I have been quiet at work for several months, with a brief busy spell in October, so this hasn't come as a surprise. It still hurts, though. In the consultation meeting my employers made it quite clear that I should not take this personally. But how else should I take it? However they dress it up, it is still 'rejection', plain and simple. I can console myself that I have, at least, got a second interview at Jarndyce & Snagsby on Thursday. And I have to believe that I can get that job. But not to the extent that I will be distraught if not. Bugger everything.

EXOTIC TINNED FRUIT

MARCH 2010

I wanted to try a new flavour this month and suggested various root vegetables to Claire, none of which met with much enthusiasm. However, when I mentioned there was a recipe for Exotic Tinned Fruit wine, Claire suddenly seemed more excited. Within a week she came home from work brandishing tins of lychees, mangos, and guavas. So I have rewarded myself today, 7th March, for a heavy essay-writing session by starting this new wine. Today has been demanding. I started an essay about medieval childbirth and children at about seven this morning, and did not really stop until half past four. Then, suddenly, I realised my eyes had gone square. I felt dizzy, and the computer screen was making no sense at all. It was time to stop, even though I had yet to finish my first draft.

I have hardly followed the recipe in 'Winemaking Month by Month'. This recommends one tin of fruit, a tin of grape concentrate, and 8oz of sugar. Instead I have used three tins of fruit, no grape concentrate, and (so far) 2lb of sugar. Only the guavas were in a syrup: the other two fruits were in water. I chopped up the guavas, but they were so soft I probably did not need to, and I have poured 6 pints of boiling water over the whole lot. On Monday morning, 8th March, I checked the initial gravity, which was low at 1.080, so I have added a further 8oz of sugar. I also put in the yeast and a teaspoon each of pectolase, tannin and nutrient.

The fruit was sieved out and it all went into its demijohn on 14th March, after a day of essay-editing and going to Claire's Tchaikovsky concert. The amount of water used was perfect, and it is a greenish-beige colour, happily bubbling away to itself.

This wine took a little while to clear, and left a large deposit, so I have racked it into my smallest demijohn. It still needed over a pint and a quarter of water, with 5oz of sugar dissolved and added to it. The taste was (of course) too dry, but promising nonetheless.

Quantity:	One gallon.
Region:	Mangos from Thailand, guavas from South Africa, and lychees from China.

Price:	99p x 2 for mangos and guavas, £1.25 for lychees, £1.20 for yeast, and £1-ish for sugar.
Bought at:	Karim's on Harehills Road.
Yeast Type:	General Purpose.
Initial Gravity:	1.104.
End Gravity:	0.996.
Percentage:	16% – which must be wrong.
Date Racked:	27th May 2010.
Date Bottled:	23rd September 2010.

INITIAL TASTE:
It is entirely clear and pale yellow. As it is 10am I have only had two small sips. 'Bland' would be my description of choice, yet pleasantly so.

THE DRINKING EXPERIENCE

FIRST BOTTLE: 30th September 2010. I opened this bottle several months earlier than I might ordinarily have done on our last night staying with Sue in St Dogmaels, after a day of gentle ambling and looking around a ruined abbey. The wine is pale with perhaps the faintest tint of pink, and entirely clear. It is much like a German white which, for Claire at least, is no bad thing. The taste is pleasant, though the fruit is difficult to distinguish. I think the lychees are prominent, but that may be my imagination. Of the three bottles we have had over the last three nights, Sue said that she liked this one the least, as it has the least to it. I agree, but we liked it enough to polish the bottle off between us.

SECOND BOTTLE: 16th October 2010. Exotic Tinned Fruit and Apple wine were neck and neck in the voting stakes at the Wine Party. Apple won by a narrow margin, beating this into fifth place, and an average score of '3¼'. But virtually everyone liked it, even though Duncan described it as "bland", and Sooz as "not actively lovely", though she admitted it was definitely drinkable. Julia named it "Angel Fish" and drew an appropriate picture, describing it as "slightly frilly", which I think sums up this wine perfectly.

THIRD BOTTLE: 29th December 2010. We are in York at my parents, stretching out the Christmas celebrations. Tomorrow we have decided will be teetotal, but tonight involved blind whisky tasting, and a couple of bottles of wine. This was the first, and it has aged well. There is a real fruity taste, and it is a convincing semi-sweet white. Mom cooked a fabulous medieval meal – a sweet lamb stew and spiced greens. We could have had an authentic experience of ergotism, but Pop spotted the barley was eighteen months out of date, so threw it out. I think suffering from St Vitus's Dance would have been rather exciting, and could have brought the middle ages to life.

FOURTH BOTTLE: 26th & 27th January 2011. To decide which bottle to open after orchestra, Claire and I played 'Scissors Paper Stone'. Paper beat Stone, and therefore we had Exotic Tinned Fruit rather than Apple. Our first glass of this was drunk sitting in bed, feeling cold and cross. The remainder was drunk tonight during and after a meal of sea-bass and puy lentil salsa – which was part of my 'Something New And Possibly Exciting' (or SNAPE) Thursday cooking. I have about five dishes that I cook over and over again, so whilst I am unemployed on Thursdays, I do something new. Today's experiment was delicious, if a little stressful, and the wine went well.

FIFTH BOTTLE: 11th February 2011. Lambert came over for a meal. Within five minutes of entering the house he was bleeding profusely. Though Aggie is mostly to blame, there was a certain amount of contributory negligence. Anyway, he specifically asked for a wine where he could play 'guess the ingredient'. As we were having a Greek salad and aubergines stuffed with feta and pistachios, I thought white would be best. And this white had more ingredients than most. Lambert eventually reached 'mango' after travelling through pineapple, peach, and banana, but it took some dragging. It was a good evening, full of intense, quiet conversation, but as a less-than-perfect host I had to go to bed just after ten – it has been a stressful, tiring week – leaving Claire the entertainment responsibilities.

SIXTH BOTTLE: 5th April 2011. I think this is my only ever bottle of homebrew that has been decanted. It had an evil-looking coil of sediment which was probably best avoided. So there is still half a glass left in the bottle which I shall pour down the sink tomorrow. Today has been borderline-fabulous. I spent this morning trying to sort out my employment situation, following the Jarndyce & Snagsby debacle. Best (or worst?) case scenario is that I end up with five jobs, which would be greedy. Then, this afternoon, Claire and I went to the National Coal Mining Museum, which was excellent. The most interesting bit was going down t'pit – a claustrophobic, dusty place where we experienced a few seconds of utter blackness. Finally, this evening, I rehearsed Sibelius with Leeds College of Music Orchestra, and spent the time afterwards lounging on our chaise-longue, drinking wine and chatting pleasantly with Claire. Bliss.

HOW TO ACTUALLY MAKE THE STUFF

This section is for those of you curious enough who want to repeat my experiments. It only supplies the basics, and will be somewhat slapdash, but that describes my winemaking process too.

You will need to start with some equipment. All of this can be bought from any handy homebrew supply shop, and most of these will happily do mail order. Certainly the one I use, Abbey Brew in Leeds, will post things to you. The equipment will be your most expensive initial outlay, but as it has been a while since I have bought any, I cannot tell you what is and is not a fair price.

As a minimum, you will need:

- **a bucket with a sealable lid (preferably a 25 litre or 5 gallon bucket)**

- **two demijohns**

- **one rubber bung with a hole for the air trap**

- **an air trap**

- **a large wooden spoon**

- **a relatively long piece of thin, flexible plastic tubing**

- **a shorter piece of inflexible plastic tubing which has a 'bund' at the bottom (ask the wine shop – this bund is to stop the sediment being picked up when you 'rack' the wine)**

- **a nylon sieve**

- **a plastic funnel**

- **a measuring jug (mine holds a pint and a half of liquid)**

214

I know that sounds daunting, but in fact I have very little other equipment (other than another twenty demijohns, air traps, and rubber bungs which I have collected along the way), and once you have bought it all you have the off-putting part over with. Ask someone to buy you the bits for Christmas.

Step One – Select a Wine

Once you are kitted up, you need to decide which wine to make. I began with a pre-prepared wine from Boots (who have since stopped selling homebrew stuff). This is not a bad way to start – it is an opportunity to practice the techniques involved, and you will find these 'homebrew kits' in the supply shops. However, it does not produce an interesting wine, and for that I recommend picking your own fruit.

My best easy wines are Blackberry and Strawberry: Elderberry is just too fiddly, with all those tiny berries having to be stripped from their stalks. As a very approximate rule of thumb, get 4lb of the required fruit for a 1 gallon batch of wine. The advantage of blackberries is that they are free, and if you pick your autumn day well it is a pleasure to go for a walk at this time of year. I always find that I pick too much fruit, and a quantity ends up in the freezer, which you will see I tend to use at Christmas.

Step Two – Sterilisation

Now you have your fruit you need to do the really boring bit (sorry). This is the sterilisation process. Claire accuses me of not taking this seriously enough, in that I will ignore times that a non-sterilised piece of equipment comes into contact with one that has been sterilised. She is right, of course, but mostly my wine works out. Anyway, you need to get a container of Sodium Metabisulphite – which you can get from the homebrew shop (and all other things I will mention too). Take a teaspoon of this and dissolve it in a pint of water. Then cover all surfaces of the pieces of equipment which will come into contact with the fruit or liquid with this solution. You do not need to spend ages waiting for the sterilisation formula to have its effect: one slosh round should be enough. And do not throw out the solution when you think you have finished with it; instead, store it in a separate bowl. This is because you (well, I) will often forget to sterilise one bit of equipment needed later in the process, and it is handy not to have to make a whole new solution just for that. After this process I then do exactly the same thing again, but this time just with recently boiled water that does not have any chemicals in it. I have no idea if that makes a difference or not, it is just something I do. With every process I describe, whenever you use any new equipment you will need to repeat this sterilisation stage.

Step Three – Fruit Preparation

Now it starts getting interesting again. Choose whether or not you want to wash your fruit. Sometimes I do, and sometimes I don't: it depends on how the mood takes me. It also depends on the nature and appearance of the ingredients. Parsnips covered in mud? Wash. Elderflowers looking fragile? Do not wash. Blackberries tend to get washed, but you need to be a little careful that you do not crush them at this stage. Once you have washed the fruit (or not), put it into the bucket. You will need to decide whether you should cut it up before you do. The rule of thumb is that if it is easy to crush the fruit (any berries or some citrus), you do not need to cut it up, but if it is harder (apples, pears), then you should. Once the fruit is in the bucket, if it is crushable, mash it up with a potato masher until the contents of the bucket are more liquid than solid. Of course, if it is a fruit that does not mash, ignore that bit. Pour 3lb of white sugar over the fruit, and then 8 (English) pints of boiling water, and stir until the sugar has dissolved. The only time I never boil the water is for elderflower, as I think this would destroy the flavour. Then leave the mixture overnight to cool down with the bucket lid protecting it against fruit flies. The wooden spoon should stay in the bucket.

Step Four – Adding the Yeast and Chemicals

Next morning you will need to add the yeast, yeast nutrient and pectolase. A yeast packet will do anywhere up to 5 gallons, though I have never made more than 4 of any one flavour at one time. For 1 or 2 gallons I add just 1 teaspoon of each of the nutrient and pectolase: for 3 or 4 gallons I add 2 teaspoons of both. Stir it all around a bit, and then put the bucket in a warm room. Do not expect it to begin fermenting immediately – sometimes it takes two days. When it does start fermenting, you can get quite a buzz by sticking your head in the bucket and inhaling deeply. I have no idea how many brain cells this kills off, and you do it at your own risk. But it is fun. You should also stir the liquid once or twice a day. And the lid should remain on whenever possible.

Step Five – Transferring it to the Demijohn

After four or five days from putting in the yeast, you need to transfer the liquid to a demijohn. This time period gives enough time for the fermentation to die down a little, meaning that with any luck the wine will not fizz out of the glass container. To transfer the liquid I put the bucket on a stool, so as to avoid bending down further than necessary, and put the demijohn on the counter next to the stool. Usually there is newspaper covering the floor, as this bit can get sticky. You need to dip your (freshly sterilised) measuring jug into the liquid and then transfer the liquid through a nylon sieve into the demijohn with the help of a funnel. The fruit which you are sieving out just goes in the bin (unless the recipe says otherwise). I try to leave about an inch between the top of the liquid and the top of the demijohn, just to allow for unexpectedly vigorous fermentation. If there is any spare liquid I put this into a bottle for 'topping up' purposes for when I am absolutely certain the wine will not explode out of the demijohn (and it is usually apparent within a day or so if you are safe). Then put the rubber bung in the top of the demijohn and the air trap (with sufficient water in it) in the bung. Your first proper stage has now been completed. (Phew!).

Step Six – Leaving it to Ferment

Leave the demijohn for somewhere between two and three months. During this time it will start off with vigorous fermentation, but this will die down within about two weeks, and then you will notice the occasional 'bloop' of carbon dioxide being sent up through the air trap at irregular intervals. The wine will slowly clear (or that is the theory, at least), and send a deposit of sediment to the bottom. This sediment can be enormous – my record has been half the demijohn – or small. It depends on the ingredients.

Step Seven – Racking

When you think it is ready, which is almost always after six weeks, you need to 'rack' the wine. Get the two bits of plastic tubing and put them together. Put the demijohn with the wine in it at a higher level than your empty demijohn. Lower the end of the plastic tubing with the bund on it into the wine, and suck on the other end. This will send the liquid through the tubes and (provided you have put the sucked end into the other demijohn) into the empty container. You will need to try to avoid picking up any of the sediment, but if a little gets in, do not worry – it will be fine. The bund on the plastic tube is designed so that you can stick the bund into the sediment and still pick up as little of it as possible.

Once you have a clear liquid in the lower demijohn you will need to fill up the gap that has been created. I do this by putting in a syrup solution made to the ratio of 3oz of sugar to half an English pint of water. This does not always fill up the new demijohn, and so I often double that solution, but any more than 6oz of sugar may make the end product too sweet. So if it is still not full after a pint of water and 6oz of sugar, I just fill the remainder with water to the neck of the demijohn. Put the rubber bung with the air trap into the neck and leave the wine until six months or so from picking the fruit.

It is at this stage you need to be careful about the wine becoming fizzy. If you have followed the book thus far you will have read about my many explosions, where the cork shoots out of the bottle. Worst case scenario, though it has yet to happen to me, is for the bottle itself to explode, and all the damage that may cause. I am advised that the way to stop any fizziness is to add one crushed Campden tablet, and one gram of potassium sorbate to each gallon of wine on first racking. This should kill the remaining active yeast, and prevent much spilled wine once the weather gets hot.

Step Eight – Bottling

The penultimate stage, if you do not count drinking, is bottling the wine. One (English) demijohn provides six bottles, and the process is very much like racking the wine. The difference is that instead of transferring the wine into another demijohn, you are putting it into six bottles. There will inevitably be minor amounts of spillage while you swap the tubing from one bottle to another, and you should put down a layer of newspaper if you care about your floor. I choose which empty bottle will be last, and put this into the measuring jug, as there is usually an overspill into the last bottle, and the jug will catch it this way. I also have a wine glass to hand, and each time I swap the tubing to the next bottle, I let a little liquid pour into the wine glass for my first proper taste. At this stage be really careful not to knock over any of your full bottles, as this is absolutely tragic.

Step Nine – Corking

Once you have six full bottles you will need to put corks in them. I started off by using plastic corks that just slot in with a little pressing. These are fine, but if you use them you need to store the wine upright as they are not 'leak free'. What I now do is put proper corks in using a corking contraption. This is better, and means that I can store the bottles in wine racks, unless they have gone fizzy, in which case they pop their corks in hot weather and I have to mop up the floor. If you buy a corking machine, ask the vendor about how to use it – it does need a practical demonstration.

Ask the seller to also demonstrate the use of string in the process. It should be put into the bottle so that it dips into the wine, with the other end hanging out of the bottle (and long enough so that it is possible to give it a hard and effective tug once the cork goes in). You then put the cork in, effectively trapping the string. Often little bubbles will run up the string and fizz out at the end. You then give the string the aforementioned hard and effective tug, removing it from the bottle (unless the string breaks, in which case you have to take the cork out and start again. It is very irritating when this happens). And the reason for doing this? To remove the pressure you have created by compressing the air that was in the neck of the bottle as you inserted the cork, and the string, when removed, makes it less likely that the bottle will explode.

Do not, whatever you do, use screw-cap bottles. If the wine starts fermenting again in the bottle, you may have just made a time-bomb if there is no cork to pop out.

Step Ten – Drinking

From bottling, I will try to leave it for six months before drinking, but as you will have read, this is not always successful.

Feel free to get in touch via my blog, and I wish you the Best of British.

The Good Life Press Ltd.
Po Box 536,Preston
PR2 9ZY
01772 633444

The Good Life Press Ltd. is a family run business specialising in publishing a wide range of titles for the smallholder, 'goodlifer' and farmer. We also publish **Home Farmer,** the monthly magazine for anyone who wants to grab a slice of the good life - whether they live in the country or the city. Other Titles of interest:

20 Amazing Plants by Rachel Corby
A-Z of Companion Planting by Jayne Neville
A Guide to Traditional Pig Keeping by Carol Harris
Build It! by Joe Jacobs
Build It!.....With Pallets by Joe Jacobs
Building and Using Your Clay Oven by Mike Rutland
Craft Cider Making by Andrew Lea
Garden Projects for Ruffians by Phil Thane
Making Country Wines, Ales and Cordials by Brian Tucker
Making Jams and Preserves by Diana Sutton
Poultry Houses from Scratch by Mike Rutland
Precycle! by Paul Peacock
Raising Chickens by Mike Woolnough
Scenes from a Vegetable Plot by Chas Griffin
Sheep Book for Smallholders by Tim Tyne
Soap Craft by Diana Peacock
Talking Sheepdogs by Derek Scrimgeour
The Frugal Life by Piper Terrett
The Jammy Bodger by Mel Sellings
The Medicine Garden by Rachel Corby
The Polytunnel Companion by Jayne Neville
The Sausage Book by Paul Peacock
The Smoking and Curing Book by Paul Peacock
Woodburning by John Butterworth
Worms and Wormeries by Mike Woolnough

www.goodlifepress.co.uk
www.homefarmer.co.uk